INNER GLIMPSE

IDIL AHMED

INNER GLIMPSE

Accepting Your Divine Spark

Cover Art: Paola Tassetti @paolatassettiart www.paolatassetti.com

Printed in the United States of America

First Printing, 2020

ISBN Print 978-1-7323885-3-6

Instagram: Idillionaire

Twitter: Idillionaire

Facebook: Idillionaire

App: Idillionaire

Previous Book: Manifest Now

Idil Ahmed
San Diego, CA 92037
www.idillionaire.com

Dedicated to the reader of this book. Be prepared to discover your greatness, alter your state of mind, and ignite the memory of how powerful you truly are. Magical things will begin to happen for you after reading Inner Glimpse!

TABLE OF CONTENTS

INTRODUCTION

Welcome to a familiar space. Somewhere in the depths of your mind and spirit, you will remember your divine spark. This book is intended not only to bring you guidance, reassurance, and hope, but to also remind you how powerful and magnificent you are. *Inner Glimpse* will give you a feeling of greatness, the warmth of aliveness, and a surge of possibilities. You will not only feel like you can do anything, but you will also have a calm balance and peace of mind that radiates inner trust. You will start to feel empowered like never before. This is a major turning point for you, because you are now going to walk in a state of knowing that you are powerful, capable, and able to do anything...while at the same time overcoming everything. Your true strength will reveal itself, and you will start to recognize who you really are. There will be a sense of ease and a supernatural flow to all that you do. You will be living out your miracles and claiming your blessings daily.

We all have (or have had) an Inner Glimpse of who we truly are, what we are capable of, what we deserve, and how valuable we are. The Inner Glimpse has a superhuman effect: You feel like you can do anything, and that all is possible for you. You feel like you can overcome anything and survive any low point, only to come out renewed, reenergized, and filled with greater life. The Inner Glimpse is such an empowering feeling and reminder from your spirit when you need a gentle nudge that all is okay. That is what this book is all about: igniting the reminder within you to start claiming your natural gift. It is a reminder to acknowledge, to trust, and to allow yourself to live by your spirit—where there are no limitations to your dreams, no blocks standing in your way, and no end to your creative expression. You'll only go up from here, transcending anything that once stood in your way. You'll feel nourished and revived on a deeper level. Your outlook will be changed forever. You're going to walk this Earth with a new mindset and attitude. You're going to express your purpose and live out your dreams. Your Divine Spark is going to illuminate the world, and you'll be a reminder to others of what is possible for them.

I remember when I first experienced my Inner Glimpse; it was a moment when I discovered that life wasn't a coincidence, but rather a series of choices reflecting my state of being. Something within me was constantly nudging me in a gentle way to realize that there was so much more to who I was than what I'd known. This secret wisdom had been within me the whole time, and was finally making itself known through a Divine Spark. No matter what I was doing, there was always a sense that no single state was final for me. I could do anything I wanted. I could be anything I wanted. I was the one choosing what continued, remained, or changed. Knowing this shattered my fears, boundaries, limitations, and everything I thought was "real." I sat there for few hours, pondering, reflecting, and receiving. I wondered about my own thoughts, feelings, and energy. For a moment, I stepped outside of myself to reflect on my entire existence. It dawned on me with a sudden surge of energy and deep gratitude that this entire time, I had been creating my experience using my imagination, intuition, and thoughts. It suddenly occurred to me that I had never taken any form of action until I'd constructed the whole image and experience of each step in my mind first.

It was in my mind that I had to make a declaration, and it soon came out into the physical. I had to have faith first, and the vision to see it come to life. Mental energy is alive. It is a very active state for creating something tangible. It's a dance between the seen and the unseen. For me, everything felt like a movie, with segments that showed each one of my actions before it happened. So, I was the writer, actor, and director of my life? Something so simple, yet so profound. It was at that moment that I felt a weight being lifted off my mind and heart to accept my own inner truth. My outlook shifted from that point on. I packed my things and moved out of the imaginary "box" we put ourselves in.

There's nothing to fear. There are no limitations upon your imagination. There are no constructs or ideas holding you back but the ones you create and accept as truth. This understanding helped me recreate my life. It allowed me to stop trying to control every little detail, and surrender to receive a greater guidance. It also helped me love more, accept who I am, and share these insights with others so they, too, could remember their own greatness.

I knew I wasn't alone. We are never alone. We can ask for guidance, and we can stay open to receive. *Inner Glimpse* will change your life forever and ignite within you the awareness that you are already there. You have always been great. You are made from greatness. You are now going to start remembering, accepting, and owning it as your natural state. It's time to walk in your power! Enjoy the adventure!

1

INNER GLIMPSE

Inner Glimpse: The moment when you experience a spiritual revelation that reminds you of your potential, your power, and your ability to see in your imagination the multitude of possibilities that are within your grasp. The Inner Glimpse moment feels like a surge of energy on the mental, physical, emotional, and spiritual level. In that moment, you get an insight, an answer, or a divine intervention that changes everything in your life. Your possibilities are exposed to you in such a way that it feels so surreal and unexplainable. This is where you are lifted out of any darkness and into the light, from lack of motivation into productivity, from struggle to turning your dream into a reality, from sickness to health, from confusion to clarity, from desperation into freedom, from heartbreak to self-love. Everything in your life begins to illuminate when you follow the Inner Glimpse of your spirit.

Deep down, you want better for yourself. Your spirit keeps reminding you of all the potential you have. Sometimes, you might even get an Inner Glimpse of what's possible for you if you just applied yourself. It's time to break free from the repetitive habits that keep you stuck.

The moment when you experience an Inner Glimpse is a reminder from your spirit. It's almost like a realignment to get you back on track. It plants the seed of inspiration that you truly are capable of so much more. The Inner Glimpse feels like a nudge from the universe and a warm reassurance that all is okay. The Inner Glimpse can also come as a moment when you see how your thoughts have manifested. It's a blissful, overwhelmingly joyful feeling that you *are* powerful. This can also happen in situations where you think of someone and they call you, or you feel like something is about to happen, and it does. That moment when you pause and get into a state of awe is an Inner Glimpse. It is a view into your vast potential and a reminder of how interconnected we truly are. Most of the time, these moments leave traces in your mind and heart so you never forget your true identity. At the same time, you find yourself trying to explain it away or even wanting to share it, but you can't fully put it into words. Inner Glimpses are codes for you. They are reminders to accept your ability to go beyond the constructs you have created around yourself. Your spirit will never stop reminding you, even if it takes you years to finally accept it. Eternity is on your side. In the realm of the universe, a second is no different than 80 years. It's all taking place now, and as you exist within it, there's patience, support, and love coming your way. You can decide to claim it now or you can keep talking yourself out of it, but the glimpses, signs, and reminders never stop.

Accepting Your Divine Spark

You have such a special gift within you. There is something so unique about you. Every single moment, there is a Divine Spark firing off in your heart and mind, guiding you to remember your magnificence in this world. Your Divine

Spark is your natural gift, your undeniable talent, and your purpose to accept who you are without any labels or ideas or limitations. You are completely free to be who you want to be. You have to start seeing yourself as complete, whole, and already as blessed as possible. Your Divine Spark only requires you to accept yourself so you can begin to receive. This is where the magic begins: When you realize you don't have to fight against your inner calling, but can instead work with your inner guidance for better solutions, you'll start to see how powerful you are.

You have so much potential…and sometimes, that can scare you. Don't fear yourself or your abilities. Be bold. Be passionate. Be filled with so much life that you begin to start truly accepting your Divine Spark. Everything in your life will become miraculous when you accept your inner self and allow your inner voice to speak to you. You've been talking yourself out of your greatness for way too long. Enough is enough. Unleash the energy and begin now to claim who you truly are. Start right now by saying, "I ACCEPT MY DIVINE SPARK!"

From this moment on, all you'll see is expansion, growth, multiplication, abundance, and unlimited flow in your blessings, creativity, energy, and life. This is the turning point for you. This is your time to start receiving in such a divine way that it will all seem miraculous.

What Is This Powerful Natural State?

It is your spirit, your consciousness, your energy, and your natural essence. The power that lies within us is very present and subtle, but also very strong. You can feel your-self and your aliveness right now: your heartbeat, your next breath, your mind reading this and processing it all so quickly and so efficiently. There's a powerful force sup-porting you, sustaining you, loving you, guiding you, and providing for you effortlessly. You have to go from seeing only what's solid to feeling beyond what's physical. If you constantly remember this, you will start to naturally live magically, with a strong trust and deep connection that all is just and everything is working out for you.

Your natural state is a blessed state. It is a peaceful state. It is a trusting state. You go from seeing the world as dense and heavy to light and full of adventure. It is all a learning experience, and this book is meant to be a re-minder of what you already feel and understand so deeply. It supports your wildest dreams, and helps you remember that you are the miracle. You are the one who is beginning to see so clearly and follow your heart. Your imagination is firing up. Your heart is expanding. You are remembering your truth and accepting it. This is where it all begins: your inner self.

Feel that inner presence. It's not something you have to try to do; you just become aware of it and start to feel it in every area of your life. It is truly all a magical experience, and the more we go from "trying" to actually feeling and accepting, the more we can claim what's rightfully ours. This is where you can begin to see your Inner Glimpse as more than just some random thought. You begin to listen to it and follow it. You have had many experiences of not being able to put into words just how things have suddenly and miraculously worked out for you...but they did, and you were probably in awe. The point is to remember the feeling...that feeling of awe and knowing that you are supported. This is where you must remind yourself that you are connected.

Something magical happens when you're in a space where you're uncertain about what's next. There's a feeling of letting go that allows you to surrender to that moment. This brings in divine guidance for what doesn't make sense.

You have experienced thousands of miracles, some grand and some small. Every day, something happens to you that reminds you of this natural power. Don't explain it away as a coincidence or random anymore. Charge and accelerate the blessings when you recognize them. Your mind is very powerful, and the more you notice, celebrate, and give acknowledgement to these natural miracles, the more they start to show up in every area of your life. You were born with this gift. It is rightfully yours, and you have the ability to access it and tap into it right now by choosing to recognize its presence. This is the life force; the beaming energy that surrounds us and maintains order in the subtle aspects of life we sometimes forget.

It's time to start accessing your unlimited potential. There are untapped resources within you. Ideas are all in the mind. Motivation is all in the mind. The shift begins with you. It's time to make changes in your life, and above all, in your mind. If all of life is a just a thought constructed in the imagination through faith, divine will, and action, imagine what you are capable of doing. You can't be complacent anymore. You can't talk yourself out of your greatness. That inner voice won't allow you. Your spirit is ignited and ready to thrive. Only you can decide this for yourself. The inner declaration you make right now is so powerful. It is one of the greatest forces of the universe. Once you believe in yourself, you become unstoppable. Your energy thrives. Your relationships get better. Your outlook changes. You stop blaming the external, and harness the internal to guide yourself to the next level. You must focus on being you...the best way you can be. This is where your light starts to shine, and you become a contributor to the vast universe. You leave your mark in this world, but most of all, in all the lives you encounter. Discovering your unlimited potential is also a reminder to others that they, too, can access their inner wealth. There's so much more to life when we tune in and trust the Inner Glimpses we receive. We start to influence the world just by being who we are.

You're here to make a difference, in one life or one million. Your influence will be felt. Your light will shine even brighter. Your purpose is grand. Accept yourself, and step into your divine power.

How to Access Your Unlimited Potential

Start seeing yourself as a spirit. Start noticing the details of life. Start loving who you are. Start following your heart. When you remember that this is all a fleeting moment, you start to look at situations differently. You change what you give your energy to. This sudden realization taps into unlimited potential. Think of how focused you become when you find yourself in danger, or when you are put into a tough situation and have to think fast to get out of it. In that moment, you are concentrating completely. What is really going on? You cease mindless thoughts and overthinking. You forget the past and the future. You become fully immersed in the now. Your whole being is alive and present. This is who you are. Most of the time, you could be allowing your mind to wander all over the place, with no direction—but most of all, with no self-awareness of who you are. This really plays tricks on you. You forget that you are a spirit. You can easily give in to the emotions of everyday life. Situations might be pulling you left and right, but this ends now. This is a new start for you. Right now, there's so much life in you. You are a magical being and a special gift. There's an unlimited flow to you. Where are you directing it? How are you treating your inner self? How are you empowering yourself?

Tap into your unlimited potential and switch things up.

The Inner Glimpse is also showing you your unlimited potential. How are you responding to your inner guidance? Are you hiding away from your creative ideas? Are you still talking yourself out of your greatness? This is where all of that has to change. You can't waste any more time in fear, so just go for it. Ideas come to your mind for a reason. You are receiving so much right now. Open yourself up to it. Welcome it. Each time you listen and follow your heart, you receive so much more energy to create, to express, to make a difference. You are the receiver, and when you are ready and allow it, you then become the giver. You share only when you have accepted the flow. This is how you start to pour into other people's lives. The point is to recognize who you are first, so you can come from a place of strength, wisdom, and unconditional love. Begin today to notice the small things about your life that seem mysterious and unexplainable. When you start to notice the miracles that surround you, you awaken to your truth.

You choose what you see. You can see disaster, or you can see beauty. You can see chaos, or you can see order. It all depends on how you feel at any given moment. When you feel happy, your mind doesn't dare show you what's wrong. When you feel sad, you look for all that's wrong with the world. Your choice is to stand firm and strong in your spirit, no matter what's happening in your life. You can choose right now to see the bigger picture in all situations, and tell yourself, "This is a moment in time!" Stand up for what you believe in, but don't let what you believe create fear, outrage, or anger in you. Your inner world must be constantly balanced until it becomes a habit for you to not personalize what's happening. The more you become refined in your growth, the better you can handle any situation. The point is to never forget that you are a spirit who has access to things beyond what is imaginable. Don't be distracted from your potential. Real solutions arise when you step into your power and claim your truth.

It's time for something new. Your spirit is calling for you to step into your purpose and own your truth. All the transformations and great changes you're experiencing mentally, physically, emotionally, and spiritually are unveiling your potential. You are here to do great things.

You Already Know What You're Capable of

You already know your potential. You forget sometimes, but you really, truly know. There isn't one person alive who can say they haven't experienced some kind of profound miracle they can't explain. Sometimes, people don't share it, because they don't even know how to put it into words; and most of the time, it isn't meant to be explained or shared at all. It's a special moment for you to remember who you truly are and what you're capable of. You might've gotten the perfect idea at the right time. You might have healed through the most traumatic experience. You might have turned your vision into a reality, or you might have manifested exactly what you wanted at the right time. You did all of this. You have to remember your abilities. Your strength can't even be put into words. No matter what tested you, challenged you, or tried to push you to your limit, you still came out on top. You still showed your resilience in your own natural way. This is who you are: unstoppable, unbreakable, and unlimited. You can't forget this.

Your greatest discovery begins when you accept how powerful you really are.

Reminders from Your Spirit

Every day, there is some kind of reminder given to you. This can be a sign that all is okay, or that you are on the right path. Reminders can come to you right when you need them, in unexpected ways. Someone can come into your life to give you a message that lifts you further into your purpose. You might even find the right book at the right time that changes the direction of your life. Things are placed in your path in order for you to be guided along the way. This is very obvious, and something we have all experienced. If you are aware of it, you smile and know how much you're being supported. If you're unaware of the signs, you might feel the Inner Glimpse for a moment, but you might think it is random and a big coincidence. Either way, there is a Divine Spark taking place. The meaning of these signs is a very personal thing. Only you know what they mean for you. You just have to listen, trust, and follow through. Everything always seems to make sense, looking back. You notice how things always happened perfectly in order for you to arrive where you are today. Even if something seemed like a bad thing or an ending in the past, you can now consistently see that you are in a better place, and that the situation had to happen the way it did. So look at it like that right now. Everything is all good in this moment. All is well, because it is taking you to your higher purpose.

You're getting so many signs. Trust them.

Daily Spiritual Rebirth

Every day is another chance. Every moment is another opportunity. You are shedding the past and everything that once confined you. You are in an awakened state. You are more aware. You are following your Inner Glimpse, and things are all happening so fast for you. Your body is integrating all of this new information, and there are times when you have this surge of energy and feel you can conquer the world and create nonstop. At other times, you just need to rest and rejuvenate. Both are part of the spiritual rebirth. All changes produce a state, and sometimes, this can be a clearing process where you release so much of what has held you back. At other times, it is a newfound hope in life to do more. Ultimately, both help you to accept your natural inner gift.

This is why you have to be patient with yourself and accept your timing, which is so specific to you. Don't look left or right; look within. You are you, and your process, your experience, and your results are just for you. This is a time to listen to yourself and your needs. There's no competing or wondering why something seems to happen more quickly for someone else. You have no idea the amount of inner work going on for others. We can't judge by external results the amount of cultivation, fertilization, and nurturing it took for ideas to flourish. This is one place where you take your power back. Stop comparing yourself with others. It's quite a paradox to think that all we see is all that's going on. There's so much more to everyone and every situation. You can't understand things just from an image, a word, or how you want to see them. Things become so much more complex when you try to analyze others externally. Take that energy back, and give it to your growth and evolution. Refine yourself. Alter your reality to be the way you want it, step by step.

Each moment, you are reborn. Each moment, you are brand new. Are you going to repeat the same thoughts? Or will today be a new day for you? The universe is vast. Don't be confined to a few thoughts and perspectives. Allow yourself a new vision. While all this is happening, give yourself time to reconnect. Ask for divine guidance. Ask for direction. Ask for a breakthrough. You have the ability to ask. Let things be shown to you. Each revelation will renew you, and give you stronger faith to trust yourself. Your source of guidance will flow from within. You'll begin to master yourself and accept your own personal spiritual rebirth on a daily basis. Yesterday is gone. The past is gone. That one situation is gone. Don't let things live on within you. Your imagination belongs to you. Your emotions belong to you. It is all done now, and today is a new beginning for you. You are renewed right now, restored to your natural state.

Things will begin to get very clear for you. Give yourself as much love as you can right now. You're entering a new state. It feels like a rebirth. The past is shedding away, and you're starting to emerge with more aware-ness, more power, and more purpose. It's your time now.

Key Points

- *The Inner Glimpse is a state in which you receive an inner revelation of empowerment that awakens you to your purpose, passion, and divine truth.*
- *Your Divine Spark is your natural gift, your undeniable talent, and your purpose to accept who you are without any labels or ideas or limitations. You are completely free to be who you want to be.*
- *Your natural state is a blessed state. It is a peaceful state. It is a trusting state. You go from seeing the world as dense and heavy to light and full of adventure.*
- *Every day, something happens to you that reminds you of this natural power. Don't explain it away as coincidence or random anymore.*
- *Start seeing yourself as a spirit. Start noticing the details of life. Start loving who you are. Start following your heart.*
- *Stand up for what you believe in, but don't let what you believe create fear, outrage, or anger in you.*
- *You already know your potential. You forget sometimes, but you really, truly know. There isn't one person alive who can say they haven't experienced some kind of profound miracle they can't explain.*
- *Every day, there is some kind of reminder given to you. This can be a sign that all is okay, or that you are on the right path. Reminders can come to you right when you need them, and in unexpected ways.*

- *Every day is another chance. Each moment is another opportunity. You are shedding the past and anything that once confined you. You are in an awakened state. You are more aware. You are following your Inner Glimpse, and things are happening so fast for you.*
- *Each moment, you are reborn. Each moment, you are brand new.*

2

SELF-LIBERATION – RECLAIMING YOURSELF

Self-liberation is the ultimate freedom. It is the start of releasing yourself from ideas, concepts, and beliefs that you've attached to your identity. You are unbounded, limitless, and free to be whatever you want to be. You can begin to start reclaiming yourself today. You don't have to live by ideas, constructs, and thoughts that no longer serve you. You don't even have to keep yourself stuck by following rules you created. There's no end to who you can be, what you can do, and how you can live your life. There's so much life force in you waiting for expression. The life force within you is unstoppable, powerful, and full of potential. Decide right now that you will no longer limit yourself. Anything that makes you feel like you can't do this is a lie. It can be a lie you tell yourself, or a lie someone else tells you. You are the one who can start to step back right now and look at what keeps you from being your greatest self. You have to allow introspection, self-reflection, and listening. You have all the answers within you. The point is to start trusting yourself.

Listen to your inner voice. Ask for guidance. Things will be revealed to you, and you will receive signs at the right time.

The best way to begin reclaiming yourself is to listen to your inner voice. We can get so caught up in what's happening all around us that our natural intuitive voice becomes a whisper. You know deep down that your inner voice has guided you in many ways. At times, you might've said, "I knew that was going to happen," or "I had a feeling about that," or "I should have listened to my gut." You are constantly being guided. This is something that's hard to put into words, but it is an innate feeling and understanding we all have. Listening to your inner self helps you realize so much. You gain clarity, trust, understanding, and strong faith. Listening also means letting go. You don't have to overthink any situation. You don't have to worry yourself to the point where your body feels tight. Breathe. Let yourself surrender and listen. For far too long, external things and situations have distracted you; too many people have told you about yourself, how to think, how to feel, and how to live your life. The real truth is that you are the master of your life. You have all the answers. Start liberating yourself and reclaiming your inner truth now. I am just here to remind you of this so you can expand further and know what's best for you.

The external aspect of life is a reflection and projection of your inner state. The outside can be used to design, create, and receive signs from your inner world. This is not something new or shocking. It might be something you're becoming more aware of every day, but this is the point of life. All things are energy that we produce from our minds and form into matter. Things we project become our reality. Things we give our attention to become our reality. What we focus our emotions upon with strong feelings becomes our reality. Every single moment, you are deciding your next vision. The universe wants to provide for you just as it does the entire planetary system. You have to stop being so afraid of your own power, your own greatness, and who you truly are. You can no longer talk yourself out of what is brewing inside of you. The signs are getting more obvious. The push is getting stronger. Your awareness is expanding, and this is your time to finally receive. This is the time to start allowing. You can't hide from your Inner Glimpse.

The power of your mind can build worlds, turn thoughts into tangible form, and manifest your wildest dreams into reality.

What's true is what you accept. There are a trillion+ things happening at any given moment: so many different thoughts, livelihoods, ideas, and existences beaming with life, all occurring at once. Why is what you're aware of the truth? Why is it so important? Because it is to you, and you have decided through repetition in awareness to accept it. Nothing defines your spirit. What we choose are momentary experiences that teach us something or help us evolve. The point is to start seeing what it is that you are allowing to construct your reality for you. You could be a totally different person if you decided right now that you want to live a new way: the way you want. Let's use health and wellness as an example. Just by making a new choice about your fitness, what you consume, and how you take care of your body, you get different results. The probability of that reality has always existed. It was just waiting for you to choose it. This goes for many things in life: your mental health, your business ideas, your relationships, and your visions. There are so many things and so many probabilities that can manifest and be created through the choices you make right now. It can all be so different for you. The point I am making here is that nothing is final. Nothing is over. Every moment, there is a chance to recreate yourself. Literally recreate a completely revived, renewed, and empowered you. You never have to accept any situation as final. When you accept a situation by being emotionally controlled by it, you enter a hypnotic state that makes that reality seem real. By hypnotic, I mean something we repeatedly do that forms into a habit. We use these states to stay "comfortable," but mostly to keep our habit safe, because at some point, you will have to get out of the trance and say, "I am actually not any of this!" This is when you start to step back from your situation and see the bigger picture. This is when your self-liberation begins.

Freedom from Your Own Perceived Limitations

You're one mindset shift away from living the life you want. Shift your thoughts from lack and limitation to freedom and abundance, and watch how quickly the blessings start to pour in.

What do you think is stopping you right now from being your greatest? What did you even tell yourself when you read that? Any thought that did not say "nothing" is firmly operating from a perceived limitation, not a real limitation. There's nothing in your way. There is nothing stopping you. The point is to get used to doing things that scare you or make you uncomfortable initially. New habits that work in your favor need to be formed today.

Introspection helps me take some time to actually look at what I am projecting into the world. The kinds of thoughts I am repeatedly saying or silently affirming to myself determine a lot. Introspection allows you to look at what you are saying that's keeping you in the same cycle.

Some people use perceived limitations they have been creating for years, and say, "That's just who I am!" Who you are is free from all constructs that limit you. Who you are is a dreamer, a believer, and a spirit that is unlimited. You are free from any ideas that keep you small. You are so grand, so full of life, so full of potential, and so filled with blessings. You can't deny this any longer. You are imagining daily. Imagine the best-case scenario: a better life, a better world, and things actually happening for you. Why use your most powerful faculties to imagine the worst? This must end today. Play with the concept of training yourself to imagine all the best for yourself and others. Have fun with it. You don't have to be hard on yourself or try to say, "What am I even doing?" You're doing what is naturally your gift. You are imagining what you want.

Is there even one thing that exists that wasn't once a thought? Human creation stems from the imagination. This is something that feels so liberating. This is you reclaiming yourself, when you begin to actually imagine what you want on purpose. Anything that tells you otherwise is a perceived limitation, and not real. Go right ahead, right now, and get into your imagination and see things you want. This is the beginning of you getting comfortable with what you think and expect to happen. You are very powerful. Starting today, you must end perceived limitations and enter your world of possibilities. It's time to move forward in what you want to do. Create a new life. Revamp the one you have already created. Do something you never dared to do. Follow your heart. Move, express, and be the best you. This is literally a world of possibilities. Release out of your mental space anything that says otherwise. It is all a lie trying to stop you. Today is a new day for you.

Freedom from Your Own Thought Forms

You are entering a whole new mindset, and you can feel everything in your life shifting, transforming, and changing for the better.

Let's get the mental realm in check. You might have heard you are not your thoughts, but also that your thoughts create your reality. I am sure this might seem confusing, but truly, the thoughts you decide to think are the ones you want, and the ones you have consciously chosen to entertain are key. Sometimes, thoughts come in through conversations or situations, and they linger on. You can go into a cycle of talking to yourself about that one situation over and over again. It can be very draining to be stuck in that cycle. Let's begin to understand that you can choose what stays in your mind. You can be free from thought forms that don't serve you by not taking them seriously or even giving them attention. Switch up your thoughts. Replace what doesn't add value to your vision. How are doubt, worry, or even over-thinking serving you? A lot of energy gets wasted there. I know this is very direct, but I want you to be patient with yourself, because all of this is a step-by-step guide to help you remember your inner freedom to choose, to decide, and to be anything you want. No thought can stop you. You have to remind yourself of this each time one thought tries to get in the way of another. Thought forms are energy. Each thought you consistently entertain forms into a structure. It seems real, but it is not. You can break it down and recreate new thoughts—ones that are healthy, vibrant, and supportive to your existence. Day by day, it gets easier and easier. You are the master of your thought forms. You are designing what you want in your mental world, and eliminating what doesn't serve you. At the end of the day, you know nothing defines you, so why not have fun with your creations? Keep things light, and trust yourself.

Freedom from Other People's Thought Forms

Your greatest power is believing in yourself. Nothing and nobody can stop a person with purpose, a vision, and strong faith.

Your mental world belongs to you. Nothing and nobody can influence you unless you are careless and unsure about what you want. This is why your mindset has to be strong, certain, and direct with your plans, visions, and what you choose to allow. Sometimes, what other people say lasts way too long in your mind because you are determining your value based upon what they think, not who you are. Nobody can tell you what you are worth. You determine your self-esteem. You determine your success. Your faith and power come from deep within, not from what anyone says. So many dreams and visions are tarnished because people give away their power. Who cares if they don't believe in you? Why allow the thoughts of others to grow roots in your fertile soil that's precious to you? If something happened yesterday with someone else and you're overthinking it today, then it's automatically wasting your precious life force. Don't give thoughts power over you that you have not agreed to allow in your mental world. The past is done. What that one person said is done. What that one person thought is done. They have no power over you. You are the master of your mind, and the one who decides what lasts in there. Snap out of it each time a thought tries to creep up on you. Your mental world is very valuable. You have standards for what comes in and stays.

Freedom from Other People's Validation and Approval

God has already validated you by giving you life. You don't need to do anything extra. Just accept yourself and feel love from the source. Your heart will expand, and your aura will naturally be magnetic just by being you.

Reclaiming yourself and becoming self-liberated begins with deciding that you are valuable already, you are powerful already, you are a spirit, and you are beyond all the little games and nonsense that try to steal your life force. You must claim your divine power first, before you can ever be free from caring what others think. If you haven't even spoken power over your existence, how can you expect to be liberated? The key word is SELF-LIBERATED! You have to decide to be free from all limitations, including the small words and thoughts of others. You are whole, complete, filled, and absolutely incredible. No amount of praise can tell you about you. No amount of negativity can stop you. No amount of validation and approval can make you who you are. You have to personally and boldly decide to unapologetically be yourself and stand up for what you believe in. There's way too much life force to give your worth away freely. Is the life energy you have right now even worth being worried about approval? No way! There's not enough time in the day for any of that. You are a creative genius and a beaming light that came here to do so much more. Accept yourself. Shine your light, and laugh at anything or anyone that tries to even think they have access to your mental and emotional world. The standards are way too high in your mental and emotional world for any nonsense. Starting today, the only validation you need is what comes pouring in from the inside. You are approved by the Source that created you and brought you here. Look how incredibly you are designed. You are the magic.

Freedom from Fears and Doubts

Don't let doubt make you forget your greatness. Speak power over your life. Reaffirm your vision. Remember why you even started on this path. One challenge shouldn't make you forget the bigger picture. Stay inspired and hopeful. Be positive in all situations. You have a great purpose here.

There's absolutely nothing to be afraid of. If you do something and win at it, great. If you don't, then it leads you to another path so you can succeed in ways that you can only imagine right now. You are always great. You have so much creative energy in you. Self-liberation and reclaiming yourself start with ending the illusion that something is hard or difficult. Think about this thing we call life; it is so vast, and so filled with possibility. It is already a miracle just being here. We can't explain how weird it all is, but we can wake up and trust. Get into that wave and flow. If you fear living, then you put nonexistent boundaries around yourself and stay hidden away from the show. Everything you dream of can happen for you. You have to accept that just because doubt or fear enters your mind, it doesn't mean it is real, or that it even has to stay. Push through those moments, and watch what happens to your self-belief and self-trust. You will experience things that will make you a believer that life isn't meant to be feared. It is always all good. The point is to just keep going and see what happens. You will never know unless you enter the unknown.

Freedom from Self-Judgment

Power your self-talk with more self-love. Catch any self-judgment and replace it with words of encouragement. Refine your inner state to lift you above thoughts that try to make you forget your greatness. Be actively positive with yourself.

Don't be hard on yourself. You can be doing your best and still find ways to look for what's wrong. Thinking you're not good enough is an illusion. This must come to an end now. You have overcome so much, you have shown how strong you are, and you have grown in ways that were once unimaginable. The point is to start celebrating yourself on a daily basis. Give yourself credit. If you are busy saying positive things about yourself and encouraging yourself, then you will grow stronger. The more you busy yourself with that, the less time you'll have to judge yourself. You can speak self-improvement over your life and take action on it, but also recognize how special, powerful, and gifted you already are.

Reclaiming Yourself

You're going to be telling a different story very soon: a story of how miracles have found you. A success story filled with so much inspiration. You will give so much hope to so many people when they see how much you have overcome and still come out on top. Your life is the movie that's unfolding right now.

Once you have liberated yourself from all these things and claimed your Divine Spark, your spirit comes alive within you. Your life will seem like a complete miracle from the outside looking in. You'll start to see things happening for you, because you have started to trust yourself and love who you are unapologetically. Everything about you will seem supernatural. You will feel a sense of renewed energy—mentally, physically, and spiritually. Your life will begin to have more meaning and purpose because you've started to live from within. The path of self-liberation is worth every moment. You'll return to your true nature and remove all the noise that once kept you stuck. There within you, your heart opens, your awareness expands, and you begin to find a new drive that can only be obtained from within. Your Inner Glimpse is activated, and you are now fully reclaiming yourself, your truth, and your natural state. This is the beginning of great miracles.

Key Points

- *Self-liberation is the ultimate freedom. It is the start of releasing yourself from the ideas, concepts, and beliefs you attach to your identity. You are unbounded, limitless, and free to be whatever you want to be. You can begin reclaiming yourself today.*
- *The best way to begin reclaiming yourself is to listen to your inner voice.*
- *Starting today, you must end perceived limitation and enter your world of possibility. It's time to move forward in what you want to do.*

- *Switch up your thoughts. Replace what doesn't add value to your vision.*
- *Your mental world belongs to you. Nothing and nobody can influence you unless you are careless or unsure about what you want.*
- *Reclaiming yourself and being self-liberated begins with you deciding that you are valuable already, and you are powerful already. You are a spirit, and you are beyond all of the little games and nonsense that try to steal your life force.*
- *Everything you dream of can happen for you. You have to accept that just because doubt or fear enter your mind, it doesn't mean they are real, or that they even have to stay.*
- *If you are busy saying positive things about yourself and encouraging yourself, you will grow stronger.*
- *The path to self-liberation is worth every moment. Return to your true nature and remove all the noise that once kept you stuck.*

3

SELF-MASTERY — TAPPING INTO YOUR POTENTIAL

Self-mastery is the ultimate freedom. Getting to know yourself, but also directing your life consciously, purposely, and actively, is what will truly get you great results. After you have liberated yourself from all that I mentioned in the previous chapter, your next step will be to start the self-mastery program. This is meant to help you gain control of what you think, feel, and experience in this life. Mastering yourself is becoming free from external control, but also learning to trust your inner self. There is this beautiful balance of directing and allowing that helps you be completely connected to yourself. Mastery has an element of grace to it. It is a higher trust in the Divine. It is no longer being swayed left or right emotionally, mentally, and spiritually. It is a firm place where you stand as life flows. You observe, but you are also actively designing. This is your gift.

You're going places. New worlds. New creations. New ideas. New experiences. All is coming together for you. You're the master of your reality. Own your truth, and be more confident. The universe responds to how you feel about yourself. Feel good, be great, and attract the best.

Self-mastery is learning to accept your divine power to alter anything and everything about yourself right now. You can be your greatest self today. The start is the declaration that you truly can make it happen. It starts with you knowing this and believing in yourself. Self-mastery frees you from the past and gets you into a mindset of recreation and reimagining better. You don't have to accept what is happening right now. You can be at peace with it, but you cannot accept it. All change begins with a feeling of wanting better for yourself. There's this deep push toward greatness. All situations, challenges, and experiences are a reminder from your spirit to move forward boldly. No more wasting your time living mentally where you are no longer physically. It is a new day to be a new you.

It's a new day to speak something greater into existence.

Self-mastery also frees you from procrastination, laziness, and wasting time. You'll learn a lot in this chapter. The most important thing you will gain is learning how to train yourself so you can be optimal in many ways. Remember, the possibilities do exist. It is all just waiting for you to decide to shift something in your life. You must be the one who plays it all out. Self-mastery will begin to help you be more present, more connected, and more conscious of everything you're doing. You'll start to see and notice how much of what is happening in your life is connected to your energy and what you are here to do. This is the beginning of your highest expression, at one with yourself and living purposefully.

Goals, Focus, and Concentration

Self-mastery begins with having a vision. This vision can be something you receive through an Inner Glimpse, or it can be something you want to create in this life. It can be small or grand. It can be personal or impersonal. The whole point is that you have a vision of yourself, of something, a desire to manifest. We all have visions, dreams, and goals. The point is how to make the things we want to experience come to life. It's not a matter of what is possible; it's a matter of what you want and how much you believe in yourself. The start is to have a vision, then enter the training of your mind to make this real and tangible.

Goal:

There is something right now that you want to manifest or bring to life. You might even want to change a habit of yours to create a more productive, self-aware, active you. The start of your self-mastery is to train yourself to be able to make your goals a reality. This is not something that could "possibly" work; this is something that will work right away. You must know what you want right now, and give yourself some time to think about the bigger picture of your overall vision. Who do you want to be? How do you see yourself living your life? What do you want to change right now? What are your dreams? Think of all of this from a place of complete freedom, a complete feeling of it being possible for you. This area is where you really get clear about what you want. The self-mastery begins with you. It all starts with a goal and a choice. If you really think about it, if you followed a consistent plan for a week on a new habit or thought pattern, you would see the change no matter what. This is a must, and the results come from change and consistency. There is no denying this. The goal is now to get clear and honest with yourself about where you are and where you want to be.

Focus and Concentration

The most important step in self-mastery is focusing and concentrating on your vision, goal, and new lifestyle. There are way too many things trying to distract you or looking for your attention. If you have not mastered yourself and learned how to hone your energy, you'll be giving it away daily for free while realizing that time keeps passing by. Where are your attention and energy constantly going? How is that serving your ultimate goal? You must accept that your attention and time are valuable. You have standards. You are the master of your world. When you have practiced self-mastery, distractions can no longer affect you. You do the things you want when you want to do them. You have decided to stop giving away your life force.

Give your attention to what you love and what you want to experience. Your focus is your power.

On a daily basis, practice focusing on a goal until you complete it. Initially, when you start to concentrate your mental energy, you will notice a tendency to want to do something else. There's an urge to move around or check your phone. The goal here is to train yourself to be able to learn how to complete a task fully. The best thing to do is to make a daily list for yourself in areas you feel need more focus. Do something toward the creation of healthier habits, and take time to practice mental visualization. I'll be going into more detail on this later in the 15-Day Self-Mastery Program. For now, get familiar with focusing on purpose and getting things done. The more items you check off your goals list, the more you free up your mental energy for something new. The most uncomfortable feeling is knowing you're wasting so much time doing things that have no purpose, when you actually have a list of goals that can produce tangible results in such a short amount of time. One of the best feelings is when you're just relaxing and enjoying yourself, knowing that you have completed a lot from your list. It feels good to do whatever you want after that. We are all familiar with these feelings. It is liberating to know the bliss your inner strength and focus produce when you are done concentrating for the day. You also know that what you have accomplished is now building momentum for your creations and ideas to manifest.

High-Value Individual

Feel worthy. Feel valuable. Feel special. How you feel about yourself is a powerful force that is magnified and felt all over the universe. Your inner self-worth sets the tone for how everything responds to you. Get yourself in order. Invest in self-improvement and self-love.

You are very valuable. I must keep reminding you of this so you don't think anything less of yourself. Your time is valuable. Your mind is valuable. Your attention is valuable. Everything about you is very valuable. You have to start living your life that way. As a person of high value, what should you be doing with your time and your attention? A part of your self-mastery is already claiming the fact that you are here for a great purpose, and you are busy allowing this to reflect in your life. How you take care of yourself is a form of self-mastery. When you treat yourself with the utmost respect and stay true to your visions, goals, and word, you become unstoppable. Take care of your body, mind, and energy. Take care of your spirit, ideas, and heart. Being the best you can be makes you a great light and a contributor to society. Your aura and energy will radiate because you take care of yourself. Feel this energy now. Claim this state now. Be surrounded by the feeling that right at this moment, you are a high-value individual. Respecting access to you, your thoughts, and your energy means you are making an impact. You don't allow just anything to enter your world. You are a master of your reality, and what does present itself has to go through your approval to stay. This automatically shifts what you attract, what you allow, and who enters your world. Nothing is random. Be firm and bold. Be daring and direct.

High-Functioning Individual

You're receiving more energy to be productive, active, and creative. You're thinking greater thoughts. You're starting to move differently. You're visualizing and manifesting actively. You're speaking power over your life. You've shifted. This is your new beginning.

Starting today, you will begin to gain momentum and energy to complete anything and everything you start. You are a high-functioning individual because you have energy. You have creative life force energy supporting you. You add to your momentum by producing, taking action, and seeing results. You no longer complain, dwell, or stay stagnant. You have no idea how you tapped into this unlimited source, but you did. This was always available to you. You are now out of any dull thoughts that try to take the color away from your life. You are not accepting anything but greatness, because you are the master of your life. Being a high-functioning individual doesn't mean you have to live life overworked or burned out. High-functioning individuals learn to tap into their inner resources for more life energy to do what they came here to do. You follow your heart's passion and calling. When you are living your purpose, there is a fire energy within you that pushes you forward. You can get through anything and everything. I am sure you've met some people who do 101 things a day, and you probably wonder how they do it or where they get that kind of energy. The point is, when you step up into a new reality of doing the things you want, the energy is provided. You are filled with a reservoir of life force waiting to be tapped into. We are supported and loved. Instead of thinking you don't have enough energy, ask for more energy. Be passionate about your life. The more passion you have, the more energy you access. Make every day a new day filled with unknown blessings. Look forward to your life, and be active in your movements. If you have an idea right now that came to you through an Inner Glimpse, follow through. Listen to your inner voice. Listen to your heart. Your light is ignited when you follow your spirit's guidance. This is why you appear mystical and magical in everything that you do. How is it even possible that you do all that you do so effortlessly? It is possible because you have discovered the energy of passion, and your life looks and feels miraculous now!

Ultimate Self-Mastery: Following Your Inner Guidance

The ultimate self-mastery is accepting that you are a spirit. Feel the life force flowing through you. Feel the warmth of your body. Feel how alive you are. You exist right now on this Earth. You are a part of this era. It's so magical, and so special. It is all filled with so much life. There's a guiding light within you that brings warm reminders. There's an inner guidance that holds you together even in the darkest moments. You are still standing today. You are still here, full of life, and the world is ready to feel and experience your expression.

Trust your inner guidance. Your spirit is giving you signs and helping you redirect your focus. Tune in and trust yourself. Great things are coming your way.

Following your inner guidance is what will help you the most in life. You will begin to receive ideas, energy, and guidance to do things you once could only imagine. This is the love that is being given to you. You have to master getting out of ideas that prevent you from really feeling and experiencing your complete truth. You are divine. You are blessed. You are okay. Start listening to your heart, and master trusting yourself. You no longer have to force anything to happen; you know that it will happen naturally because you trust. You believe you are being guided. This makes you feel safe and helps you maneuver through life with a plan that no matter what happens, there is a higher purpose for everything. You will no longer be drained by fear of life. You are stronger today for discovering this. You are more at ease knowing that nothing is as bad or as hard as it seems.

Trusting your gut feeling is connecting with your intuition. Your body has the natural ability to detect and read energy. Trust the signs.

Start trusting your intuition more. That feeling that keeps tugging at you—and the recurring thought to follow your gut—are actually inner guidance. There's something very special about our body and consciousness. We already have inner knowing, but because of the need to try to do everything ourselves, we may have forgotten how to trust it and follow it. Start mastering your inner world by paying attention to your gut feelings. Follow through with them, and believe in yourself. Every day, you'll increase your ability to know things in advance. You'll get really good at detecting energy and what certain signs mean. Nobody can guide you like your inner self. Tune in and enjoy your experience.

Boldness: in Action, in Uncertainty, in All Situations

You can't fear uncertainty. You must chart the unknown and the unseen with faith. You must believe, even in the darkest hour, that somehow, this time will give birth to brighter days. You must stay strong, positive, and hopeful through all the unpredictability of life. Trust your spirit.

Mastering yourself also means being bold in uncertain situations. What could go wrong? Absolutely nothing. Uncertainty is going into the unknown and not using your past awareness to create your next step. These moments of uncertainty require boldness in action. Move forward into the unknown. You are the master of your life. There's nothing to fear. It can only get better, and you can only learn from it. Take that chance with every step. Everything you do must be taken on directly, without fear of the outcome. You already know your change and transformation require a choice in the right direction. Make that choice today, and trust yourself.

Build Your Mental Architecture

Design your mental world. Part of your self-mastery is understanding how to build the thoughts you want within your mind. Let's start by discussing the moment when you first begin trying to think more positive thoughts. Initially, it seems like hard work to constantly change your mind from any kind of negativity to actually just being in your natural state. Day by day, you continue on, starting to build a new mental architecture that you have personally designed. It starts to become normal for you to remain optimistic and positive, even in trying situations. There's something about thoughts that are energetic and consistent in repetition: The more you think about it, the more it becomes real. You start to create an inner world in which you establish your identity according to what you have designed in the past. This is why people easily say, "That's just who I am" to describe behavior patterns. It can be something they (or even you) have repeated over and over, to the point where it has become an established belief.

Imagine yourself as a healthy, positive, vibrant, energetic, magnetic, loving being. Let your mind be filled with strong, positive visions of yourself. You are greatness. You are strong. You are whole and complete already. Accept it, and allow yourself to have this mindset as your truth.

At any moment, you can revamp your mental world. This naturally happens when you start to follow the Inner Glimpse your spirit has been giving you. I am sure you have grown and changed so much that you might say to yourself, "I can't believe I use to think like that." This is just another sign of hope that what we think and believe now isn't final. We can change anytime we choose, even when we are pushed into a corner. At the end of the day, you end up evolving. This is just a reminder that if you are experiencing repetitive thoughts that aren't helping you, you can begin to master yourself by building your new mental architecture exactly the way you want it. Think new thoughts, and repeatedly entertain them. Give life to what you want to grow. Water what helps you thrive, so you can flourish. It's a new day and a new life for you. You can and will come out on top. Believe in yourself.

Habits and Willpower

Don't be distracted from your vision. Your spirit is pulling you upward and forward for a reason. Your habits and daily choices are being tested to redirect you to a greater place. Listen to the signs. You have so much potential.

There's something you're doing right now that is a habit you've repeated so many times, it seems natural to you. Anything new can be learned through repetition and creating a new habit. A part of your self-mastery is forming new habits that will help you live as optimally as possible. You know that there's something you are doing right now that you would just love to change. You can. You have to stop living life drained by things that don't help you become your best self. Is there a habit that's making your life feel heavy or drained? Is it controlling you? This can come to an end. It can change, because you have decided today to create new habits. You have such strong willpower that can be activated when you decide to make that transformation. Initially, it seems so hard, because you are literally breaking down past mental structures, rebuilding your cellular habits, and rewiring your brain. A lot goes into changing a habit. It starts with a mental declaration and the will to follow through. The minute you decide is the minute the entire universe begins to support your transformation. It all starts with you making that choice today. Remind yourself of why you started. Remember what made you want to change in the first place. You want better for yourself, and you actually can have it. This is not something far-fetched. This is all about daily declarations, a strong mindset, and activated willpower to follow through. You never have to look back again. You have what it takes to be renewed.

Consistency

Everything is all about consistency. Your self-mastery journey must be a daily dedication that becomes so normal for you. The more you invest in your own personal change, the greater the benefits you will receive. Don't let the initial adjustments scare you away from moving forward. You are transforming—not only physically, but also mentally, emotionally, and spiritually. You are being completely renewed. Stay on course, and stay focused. You'll look back soon and smile at the moment you began this journey. You'll feel empowered, encouraged, and unstoppable. You'll be a believer, and by then, you'll be creating so much more for yourself and the world. Shine brighter!

Key Points

- *Mastering yourself is becoming free from external control, but also learning to trust your inner self.*
- *Self-mastery is learning to accept your divine power. You can alter anything and everything about yourself right now.*

- *The start of your self-mastery is training yourself to be able to make your goals a reality.*
- *Self-mastery frees you from procrastination, laziness, and wasted time.*
- *The most important step in self-mastery is focusing and concentrating upon your vision, goals, and new lifestyle.*
- *The more items you check off your goals list, the more you free up your mental energy for something new.*
- *Your aura and energy will radiate because you are taking care of yourself. Feel this energy now. Claim this state now. Be surrounded by the feeling that right in this moment, you are a high-value individual.*
- *You are high-functioning individual because you have energy. You have creative life-force energy supporting you.*
- *The ultimate self-mastery is accepting that you are a spirit. Feel the life force flowing through you. Feel the warmth of your body. Feel how alive you are.*
- *Following your inner guidance is what will help you the most in life. You will begin to receive ideas, energy, and guidance to do things you once could only imagine.*
- *Mastering yourself also means being bold in uncertain situations.*
- *Design your mental world. Part of your self-mastery is understanding how to build the thoughts you want within your mind.*
- *Everything is all about consistency. Your self-mastery journey must be a daily dedication that becomes so normal for you.*

4

YOUR 15-DAY SELF-MASTERY PROGRAM

This self-mastery program is meant to assist you on your journey to becoming your best and greatest self. Every aspect of it focuses on tapping into your inner potential and magnifying it a hundred times over. As I discussed in the previous chapter, mastering yourself begins with training your mind to focus on what you want while at the same time being present enough to receive the signs and guidance to navigate your path. There must be a healthy balance between the physical and spiritual. Being the master of your life allows you to connect to your higher power, which makes you completely strong, trusting that every situation is working in your favor. You will begin to go from uncertainty to trust in the unknown. You'll also discover how to maintain power over your emotions so you aren't constantly drained by every little situation that presents itself. You'll learn how to open your heart to trust your divine nature naturally. Mastery also means expressing your natural talents and gifts. In the self-mastery program, you'll learn how to trust yourself, follow your intuition, and live purposefully so you can make an impact in your lifetime. It's time for you to tap into your own personal resources. Deep within you, you have the most powerful abilities at your fingertips. You have the imagination to invent, recreate, design, and alter anything and everything. You are full of life force, energy, and vast capabilities that can now begin to be expressed. Starting this program is the beginning of the most powerful, life-changing adventure you will ever take. It is not only going to guide you to face your mind; it will also allow you to start to accept your mystical, supernatural nature. Mastering yourself is awakening to your natural truth that you are a spirit: unbound, unstoppable, and unlimited. You hold immense power, and this is the start of remembering, recognizing, and celebrating your truth.

Within this Self-Mastery Program, you will spend 15 days working on one step daily for self-optimization. The goal is for you to commit to each step totally and completely before moving on to the next. I know for myself that I have repeated a step for week at a time to make myself sharper and better at that section. You can do this, too, but I also recommend making each step a daily habit, as you are building your self-mastery step by step. Before beginning this program, I want you to feel very committed to yourself. I want you to be committed to your transformation, your mastery, and your vision. This isn't something you start and give up on. This is something you set an intention to utilize and receive so much from. Self-mastery isn't for someone who doesn't want to take charge of his or her life. It was you who decided to get this book. Your first step is complete. Now, you must tell your mind that for the next 15 days, you will stay determined, focused, and purposeful so you can reap the greatest possible benefits. Your commitment to your self-mastery is truly just stepping out of any routine, habits, and thoughts that have kept you small and away from your greatness. You will no longer deny yourself what you deserve. You will now begin by spending one full day setting your intention for the next 15 days. You will get your mind into a space where you will not abandon your own self-mastery. This is the pre-game. Before starting anything, you have to make the mental declaration that you will see it through no matter what. This is how you become refined. Once you have prepared yourself mentally, you can begin the 15-Day Self-Mastery Program.

The first five days of the Self-Mastery Program will focus upon mastering your mental state. The goal is to get you into the right mindset in terms of determination, concentration, willpower, and thought force. This will involve how you talk to yourself, the state from which you create, and how much you know about your own potential.

The second five days of the Self-Mastery Program will focus upon mastering your physical state. The goal in this section is for you to know and trust your body's potential as well as your environment and how it responds to your energy. This section will be all about newness. You don't need to hold onto a past identity. It is all about boldly recreating yourself and transcending anything that tries to limit you.

The last five days of the Self-Mastery Program will focus upon mastering your own connection to the Divine Source and the ways you can begin to trust the Inner Glimpses you continuously receive. This section will tie everything together, as you have learned how to work on yourself on different levels.

Mastering Your Mental State

Day 1 – Clear Vision/Visualizing/Imagination

Visualize and imagine your greatest self first, then live, breathe, think, and feel that into existence. You are what you believe about yourself. Recreate and upgrade as often as possible. The past should look so unfamiliar that it shocks you. Tap into your unlimited potential right now and switch things up.

Begin Day 1 by paying attention to your thoughts. How many of your thoughts are random? Do you have a vision for something in your life? How are you using your mental energy? The goal here is to go from random, unwanted thoughts to precise focus and learning to completely harness your mind's power to direct your thoughts where you want. You feed what you want with mental energy, so let's practice being precise. On this day, it's all about seeing which thoughts actually run your mind. In order to make changes, you must first identify repetitive thoughts so you can completely get rid of them. Or, if your thoughts do support you, how can you amplify them even further? One thing that has helped me toward self-mastery is learning how to use introspection to my advantage. It is all about being honest with yourself, and confronting areas that might seem uncomfortable to face. The more you get rid of any masks or layers that scare you or make you feel insecure, the more you can accept yourself. This is when things begin to lighten up and you start to free up space in your mind to focus on what you want. Go through a mental check within your mind to remove what doesn't belong.

This is your first step before you get into a clear vision. It's all about getting rid of anything that tries to steal your mental energy. This is where that ends, and you begin to redirect, retrain, and refocus your mind.

Lesson for Day 1

Clear Vision/Visualizing/Imagination:

We spend all day imagining. We see scenarios, story-lines, and what-ifs in our mind. We dream, and sometimes we even think of worst-case scenarios. We love to ponder situations. This is our natural ability to go beyond what is in front of us. In this Self-Mastery Program, you'll learn how to visualize what-if situations that support your goals. You'll start to imagine great creations and actually believe that they are already your reality. You'll start to create a mental world that supports the health and wellness of your physical world. You'll build everything in your mind, and you will consciously do it. This is where your self-mastery reaches a powerful turning point.

Let's create your own mental virtual reality. Remember one thing before we move forward: Your mental virtual reality is real. All thoughts you imagine, support with mental energy, and focus upon must manifest into physical reality. The key words here are *it must* and *it will*. The point is to start getting comfortable creating how you want to see your physical world in your mental virtual reality first. Begin today by seeing yourself in your mind in a state you desire. This can be in your healthiest state, ultimate business success, your relationship thriving, your energy field expanding. It can be anything. It is up to you to decide. You can even create multiple outcomes in one visual experience. It's like you are watching your own movie that's a true depiction of what is about to happen. Use this setting as a predictive tool. Start by seeing yourself

49

in your most optimized state. See yourself thriving, moving, and beaming with so much life. Spend some time doing that. Create a setting in your mind where you walk through a desired state in a complete manner. How would things look in your world right now if you could imagine them into existence? Take a break from this book for a moment, and just create a mental virtual reality. Start with one setting. Example: Let's say you want to feel and look healthy. Go into an imagined state and see yourself in that new look. An imagined state is closing your eyes and putting images and experiences together in your mind that you want to see happening in the physical. Focus more on creating a feeling with this. You are so healthy, so optimal, and so focused on being the best you can be in this image. Create sensory experiences in the image, as well...like feeling a breeze against your skin or even touching an item you're wearing in the image. The point is to engage all your senses within your imagination so you can feel this new reality as your truth. Take some time to set up a scene you like, and make sure it is one that has a desired outcome.

All of life is imagined. Every thought you hold consistently will produce a physical, emotional, and environmental change that represents what you see in your mind. You are always influencing the outcome.

The more you get the hang of building up yourself and your reality in your mind first, the more you start to master yourself and how you create. Most people want things to happen for them, but they haven't built or strengthened their mindset to believe in themselves. The point of mastering your mental state is to build yourself up from the inside out. When you are strong on the inside, you have indescribable self-determination. It will magnify your aura, and anyone who comes into contact with you will know and also feel that there is something incredibly supernatural about you. You will go out into the world stronger, wiser, and surer of yourself. You will have the attitude of "it is done already," because you have already mastered building your world within first. This will make you unstoppable, because a vision you have imagined as complete is already coming together in the physical world. Now you know that it is all showing up for you.

Bonus:

I wanted to add this bonus insight on building yourself up in your mental world. I know so many people experience self-image uncertainty because of how they see themselves in their minds. This can all change right now. You can be more confident, more radiant, more certain, and more loving to yourself by completely declaring today that you accept yourself fully and wholly in your mind. Anything you feel unsure or insecure about, put it to an end in your mental world. Redesign yourself to be all that you can be. See a vision of yourself in your best state. Build confidence in your mind. Your future is comprised of your most consistent thoughts about yourself. Every day is your day to love yourself.

Mastering yourself in this section also means knowing that you are a spirit. This is something you must not only know, but also understand. Nothing defines you. What anyone else thinks can't be not real if you don't accept it in your mental world. People can say anything, but it is the mind of the person that decides how they want to perceive or feel about it. This is a secret that can help you take your power back. In your magically designed mental world, opinions that don't resonate with you can no longer enter.

This is how you become stronger emotionally, as well. You never take anything personally. So with creating your own mental virtual reality, you can also add mental images that help you create a healthier self-image. This will help you be successful in every area of your life. Thrive from within first, and watch everything around you shift in your favor.

Key Points for Day 1:

- *Observe if your thoughts are random, or focused and precisely connected to your vision.*
- *Set aside time for introspection daily. Check in that all is aligned with your greater vision.*
- *Spend 30 minutes to one hour building the mental virtual reality of your choice. Your ability to spend time in your mental world will get stronger.*
- *Add images, experiences, and scenarios that you want to experience.*
- *Create a healthier self-image using your mental virtual reality.*

Day 2 – Concentration

Concentrated energy is power. Pull the forces within you and all around you into one goal and vision until you manifest it. This is what makes you unstoppable. Hone in!

Day 2 is all about creating momentum for your mental virtual reality, but this time, I would like to add the importance of concentrating on what you're working on, as well. One of the most powerful things I have discovered about self-mastery through my experience is the wonderful results that concentration can produce. Each detail of your vision is energy. Never look at your thoughts as random. Your thoughts are vital energy beaming with so much life. The more you concentrate that thought, the more it builds exactly what you want. The goal here is for you to learn how to hone in on your mental powers. In self-mastery, distraction is something that keeps you from your ability to execute a particular vision or thought. Lack of concentration turns into procrastination. This is why months and years can go by without fully bringing your vision to life. This must end now. The world needs what you have to offer. You have a great purpose here. You can no longer scatter your energy. The more you accomplish, the more you'll enjoy a sense of leisure. However, there's always the ability you'll learn here to concentrate your mental energy to produce the results you want. I believe in the balance of full commitment/accomplishment of vision, but at the same time, daydreaming and pondering. The imagination is sharpened when you just allow yourself some time to take things in. Self-mastery is all about balancing the physical and spiritual. Activity and rest. One thing I have noticed is that when I just go for a walk or do something that involves play, I often get answers to something I am working on. To be a master of concentration, you also have to know how to allow yourself to receive answers and guidance in unexpected ways.

"I woke up early one morning and sat in the park. It was a beautiful day, and the flowers were blooming." In 1951, Charles Townes sat on a park bench and came up with the Nobel Prize-winning theory that would lead to the invention of the laser.

"The idea came like a flash of lightning, and in an instant, the truth was revealed. I drew with a stick in the sand the diagram shown six years later in my address before the American Institute of Electrical Engineers." – Nikola Tesla on inventing the alternating current (AC) induction motor.

Inner Glimpse to Physical Results

Your ability to concentrate and allow yourself to receive guidance will completely alter how you think, create, and receive in this world. You must always believe that anything you imagine can be a physical manifestation. The Inner Glimpse is your spirit communicating with you through powerful visions. You can no longer deny yourself or even the world the talents you have. Bring them to life. Procrastination must end. You must respect yourself and your own life force. You always feel like your potential is at your fingertips. This feeling is a real state of being. It is a push from your spirit to take what is yours. If you have been having ideas constantly repeated to you, this is your sign. Concentrate, and get this done. The repetition of signs and feelings—and the sense of a calling—are all indications of something wanting to be birthed through you so you can reach the next level of your evolution. You are here to experience abundance, health, happiness, love, and bliss. You can have it all. You can be your greatest. This is your natural state. We are all learning and being reminded so we can ignite the energy of passion for life. How many success stories have inspired you to be great? This is what all humans do—they inspire each other by showing that they have overcome hardship to finally take back what is theirs: their natural divine powers. It's time for you to do the same.

Lesson for Day 2:

Concentrating

The lesson for Day 2 is to completely dedicate yourself to a particular task without losing focus. This is your test phase to see how long you can hold your attention on something you want to accomplish. Start by making a list at the beginning of the day of some tasks you have been procrastinating on, and completely focus your mind and energy on accomplishing them. This can be anything you feel like you've been avoiding doing. Step by step, you'll see the full vision come to life. This will be the start of your momentum and power over tasks instead of feeling like there is so much to do to the point where you just avoid it all completely. Time will start to feel different when you live like this. You'll stop feeling regret about wasting time, and you'll feel the power of maximizing your time so you can do what you want, whenever you want. It's interesting how much free time you'll have mentally and physically when you actually start making things happen. Concentration is overcoming distractions and a short attention span. This also applies to learning something new, or even reading. How many books have you actually sat through and fully read without bouncing around? This is a great way to teach yourself how to concentrate. Focus on reading a book without picking up your phone or doing something else for twenty minutes straight. The more you can expand your ability to concentrate, the more you will build the power of your mind to master yourself and everything around you.

Don't be distracted from your vision. Too many things are calling upon your attention, but you must stay determined, positive, and focused on your greater purpose.

This will also increase your self-esteem and confidence, because you'll no longer be letting your dreams slip away. You'll no longer have mental battles or regrets about your goals and successes. You'll start to feel this new surge of energy that allows you to do anything. This is where you open yourself up further to receive from the universe. A mind that is active, open, and ready always gets the best ideas. It is a stream of consciousness. Solutions come, guidance arrives, and instant results are produced.

Key Points for Day 2:

- *The more you concentrate upon a thought, the more it builds exactly what you want. The goal here is for you to learn how to hone your mental powers.*
- *Your thoughts are vital energy beaming with so much life.*
- *Self-mastery is all about balancing the physical and the spiritual. Activity and rest.*
- *Your ability to concentrate and allow yourself to receive guidance will completely alter how you think, create, and receive in this world. You must always believe that anything you imagine can become a physical manifestation.*
- *You can no longer deny yourself or even the world the talents you have. Bring them to life. Procrastination must end.*
- *You are here to experience abundance, health, happiness, love, and bliss. You can have it all. You can be your greatest. This is your natural state.*

- *A mind that is active, open, and ready always gets the best ideas. It is a stream of consciousness. Solutions come, guidance arrives, and instant results are produced.*

Day 3 – Your Willpower

Don't be intimidated by challenges. Remember who you really are. Your true self dissolves obstacles with a single thought and strong faith. You have this willpower. Activate it!

Your willpower is the fire passionately burning inside of you that awakens and says, "This is it." When your willpower is ignited, nothing can turn it off or stop it. You can will anything into existence, because you stop being so afraid of life and start fully living. You have no idea how much willpower you have. Your self-mastery will reach a whole new level when you start really activating and using your untapped reservoir of will and accomplish your life goals. The difference between where you are now and where you want to be is how much of your willpower you're willing to activate right now to make it happen. This is not some distant future or dream. This is now.

Lesson for Day 3:

Willpower

Begin the lesson for Day 3 by taking a state of discomfort or uncertainty and exerting your willpower over it. This is a quick start to maximize some energy to show yourself how your awakened, conscious state can impact your everyday life. One of my favorite ways of using my willpower is to do something I know will produce great results, even if it is initially uncomfortable. I know if I show up to my fitness class every morning, in a few weeks, I'll start seeing the mental and physical benefits of exerting my will. You, too, can do this in any area of your life you feel like you want to transform or step up. The more you do what seems impossible, the more energy you will receive. This is a great life secret I discovered through my daily habits. Don't wonder about how you'll be able to do something; just do it, and see the gates, the dimensions, and the universe completely open up to support you. You are not alone. There's so much power within you and all around you, just waiting for you to utilize it. It is free energy.

You are now in a vortex of blessings. You'll begin to receive in ways you have never imagined before. Feel it!

Always remember that you have so much energy. You just have to get out of the drained, tired mindset and push yourself just an extra bit. This isn't for the rest and rejuvenation aspect of life. There's always a place for that. This is in the space where you feel like you need to get something done, but aren't fully activating your will to accomplish it. Willpower comes from the spirit. This is available to you at all times. Try it out in areas you feel need more willpower, like sticking to a goal or doing something you know is beneficial, even when you want to avoid it. This self-mastery tip will help you discover your true potential and expose you to how much you can actually accomplish when you move forward boldly into your dreams.

Key Points for Day 3:

- *Your willpower is the fire passionately burning inside of you that awakens and says, "This is it."*
- *Your self-mastery will reach a whole new level when you start really activating and using your untapped reservoir of willpower and accomplish your life goals.*
- *The difference between where you are now and where you want to be is how much of your willpower you're willing to activate right now to make it happen. This is not some distant future or dream. This is now.*
- *Always remember that you have so much energy. You just have to get out of the drained, tired mindset and push yourself an extra bit.*
- *Willpower comes from the spirit.*

Day 4 – Redirecting Your Thoughts

You're gaining momentum. You're moving forward from the past. Your thoughts are becoming more positive. You're starting to see the power of believing in yourself. You feel connected, and your inner light is starting to shine brightly.

Let's start Day 4 with a very important lesson on thoughts. Starting today, you will no longer allow yourself to be drained or brought down by a thought you can replace. You are the master of your mind. Get yourself out of the repetition of a habitual thought that takes so much of your energy. Don't even think about telling yourself it is hard. That is a thought that keeps you in the loop and cycle of staying stuck. Never say that something is hard. This is a sign of giving in to lack and un-activated potential. You must make some bold declarations in your mental world. Whatever has been on repeat must be redirected to a new thought of your choice. Unwanted thoughts are not welcome, and if they do show up, you will not entertain them. Your mastery in redirecting your thoughts and attention to what feeds you is the start of your mental and emotional healing. You do not need to revisit thoughts or overthink anything. You don't need to get carried away with what could have or should have been. This is a new day for new thoughts. Your mental world belongs to you. Remind yourself of that every time you feel overwhelmed by a situation. Take your power back. You have a bigger purpose here.

Lesson for Day 4:

Redirecting Your Thoughts

The goal of this lesson is to not stress over every single thought. The main focus is on which thoughts are repetitive, and also which thoughts have strong emotion connected to them. Unhealthy habitual thoughts make you doubt and judge yourself while limiting your true light. These thoughts also carry strong emotion. You can start to redirect and change them right away. Mastering your thought realm has a lot to do with how you manage repetitive thoughts and turn them into healthy, vibrant, and supportive ones. This will initially seem impossible, but that is a mental lie. You can, and you will. Day by day, you will get stronger and better at this. Today, begin to notice any negative habitual thoughts, and start redirecting them toward the desired ones you prefer. Do this throughout the day, and build the momentum to make it a lifestyle. You have to be patient. You are training yourself, and that means you're building from the inside out. The better you become at mastering your thoughts, the healthier and more vibrant you'll feel.

Key Points for Day 4:

- *Starting today, you will no longer allow yourself to be drained or brought down by a thought you can replace.*
- *Get yourself out of the repetition of a habitual thought that could be taking so much of your energy.*
- *Your mastery at redirecting your thoughts and attention toward what feeds you is the start of your mental and emotional healing.*
- *This is a new day for new thoughts.*
- *Your mental world belongs to you. Remind yourself of that every time you feel overwhelmed by a situation. Take your power back.*
- *The better you become at mastering your thoughts, the healthier and more vibrant you'll feel.*

Day 5 – Boldly Think It and Affirm It

Ask for it. Ask for healing, clarity, peace, wisdom, and guidance. Ask for abundance, creativity, light, and love. Don't be timid in your prayers or requests. Be bold. Be passionate. Be positive. Be so grateful about everything you're asking for, as if it has already happened. It is done!

Think it, feel it, and speak it into existence. If you are busy thinking and speaking what you want, you will not have a single second to feed what doesn't deserve your life force. Being a master is being bold in your self-declarations and attitude. Day 5 is all about being bold with the words you speak to yourself and into the world. You will be paying attention to your own self-talk and what you say to others. This will help you see how much you say on autopilot, and how many of your words carry a positive force that penetrates the ethers with direct intention. One thing I have started doing is listening to how other people talk about themselves. I am sure you've had the experience of paying someone a compliment, and they started downplaying what you had admired about them. This is something that can be on autopilot. The person assumes they are not worthy of the compliment, or they feel like they need to be humble about it. The reality is that you can just receive gracefully, and own your state graciously. You never have to downplay your success, accomplishments, beauty, or what you're good at. If you feel the need to, then switch it up. Be confident about your accomplishments. You have worked masterfully to be who you are.

Lesson for Day 5:

Boldly Think It and Affirm It

You are an inspiration when you believe in yourself. You show others through your action and radiance all that is possible. This day will be all about paying attention to how you speak to yourself and what you speak into existence. All your conversations should be intentionally positive or encouraging of greater potential in others or yourself. Never gossip about others. People pick up on subtle energy, and they also start to appear in life as they do in your thoughts about them. Remember, each time you are speaking to others, they are co-creating with you based upon the information you share with each other. The mind of another reacts powerfully as you draw an image into it; the other person will begin to see you in that light. You don't want to be complaining or sharing bad news. Share what you want to expand. Anything you need to release can easily be let go of, but know that all you share becomes associated with you in the other person's mind. Becoming a master of boldly affirming and thinking what you want into existence has a lot to do with being consciously present with what you project into the world. It is not necessarily about being calculating. Follow these tips closely, and you'll notice your life becoming much greater and more peaceful as you speak positivity into the world while at the same time speaking positivity to yourself.

Key Points for Day 5:

- *If you are busy thinking and speaking what you want, you will not have a single second to feed what doesn't deserve your life force.*
- *You never have to downplay your successes, accomplishments, beauty, or what you're good at.*
- *Be confident about your accomplishments. You have worked masterfully to be who you are.*
- *You are an inspiration when you believe in yourself. You show others through your actions and radiance all that is possible.*
- *All of your conversations should be intentionally positive or encouraging of greater potential in others or yourself.*
- *Becoming a master of boldly affirming and thinking what you want into existence has a lot to do with being consciously present with what you project into the world. It is not necessarily about being calculating.*

Mastering Your Physical State

Day 6 – Follow the Signs – Integrating the Inner Glimpse Daily

You're starting to see more clearly and feel more deeply. You're starting to trust yourself more and listen to your inner guidance. You can feel yourself awakening, emerging, and reclaiming what has always been yours. You are becoming more powerful within and accepting yourself unconditionally.

Mastering yourself also means becoming great at listening to your own inner guidance. You are constantly receiving signs every single day. Are you truly listening? Are you present enough to receive? Day 6 is all about trusting your gut and looking out for signs connected to your vision. The Inner Glimpse is about tuning in and trusting your own intuition. Becoming a master at listening to your spirit starts by completely surrendering to the fact that you might not have all the answers. This creates a space where you grow away from trying to control every aspect of your life, and toward allowing divine intervention in situations and circumstances you don't currently understand. You are a spirit. You are beyond what you can see in the physical alone. This is something you might need a moment to fully digest so you can further ignite the light you are already carrying. It is one thing to say *I am a spirit*, but it is another thing to fully understand, accept, and trust. This allows you to proceed from mere words and sayings to mastery.

Knowing that you are a spirit enriches your life in ways you can never fully explain or comprehend. This is what makes your life seem so unexplainable. There is a fascinating mystery to life. We all experience the concepts of life and death. We might not see it, but we can all accept the energy and spiritual nature of life that is beyond the physical. Think about how everything is perfectly orchestrated; how your body works day in and day out without you seeing, feeling, or hearing anything going on inside. Think of the trillions of molecules that hold you together, and the unfathomable chemical reactions all taking place right now. This is just your own body. Now imagine other people, the Earth, the galaxy, and the cosmos. Think of the perfection of this design. This is what you are connected to. Free yourself right now from any feeling of loneliness, uncertainty, self-judgment, overthinking, or worrying. Release your stress. Let yourself surrender to your spirit anything you are holding within you right now. You do not have to research 101 papers, books, and websites to find what is already within you. Be still for a moment. This is meant to bring you back to yourself so you can hear again. Nobody knows better than yourself what is best for you. The Inner Glimpse is just the return of trusting your spirit and allowing your Divine Spark to light up the world.

I wrote all of the above just to say that you can begin right now to be present. All that weighs heavily on your mind and heart is just you trying to control why something happened the way it did, or why you think something should happen a certain way. Between these two states, worry develops, and anxiety takes over. This is an indication of a lack of trust. Get out of your own way. Step to the side. Let go of the obsession of having it all figured out right now, and enter the mastery of knowing that it is all working out. You will go from why, how, and when to yes, done, and complete. Your inner vocabulary will change. The way you speak will change. You are the master of this realm. You have power in this reality. You must claim your divinity and take what is already yours. Be firm about where you stand. This is where you'll begin to receive your ultimate inner guidance. You have finally decided to re-lease control and allow yourself to speak power, hope, and trust over any situation. You have now decided to start let-ting the past go and begin to receive emotional healing in this moment, not tomorrow or years from now. This is the day you will receive it. This is part of being present in the moment. Time diminishes because you go from the one-day mindset to accepting your state in this moment and living it. This empowers you, providing the possibility of rebirth and a new outlook on life.

Lesson for Day 6

Follow the Signs – Integrating the Inner Glimpse Daily

Now that you feel energized and more connected to your spiritual nature, let us move forward to the lesson about how to integrate the Inner Glimpse on a daily basis. What you'll start doing on this day, and every day that fol-lows, is to begin trusting that gut feeling you keep getting. Pay attention to something that's nudging at you to make some kind of change, or a choice about area of your life you need answers for. Also, start looking at all the signs around you that keep coming into your reality. Repeated signs are a form of guidance. You must be present daily in order to be open to see. There's so much happening around you that when you are busy in your mind, you miss what is there. However, your spirit is very intelligent, and will keep giving you signs over and over again until you finally acknowledge them and follow through on them. The better you become at listening to your own inner self, the clearer things will become. Your core focus here is to live according to faith in the unseen and the unknown. You'll start to trust yourself even more. You'll have a calm nature, because you'll acknowledge your divine inner connection instead of overwhelming yourself by trying to force things. There will be something smooth, easygoing, and gentle about you. It will just seem like everything is always magically happening for you. However, you know that your faith has brought you to this point. You are living by your spirit. This can only be understood from the inside, and can only be seen as external success, peace, and an undeniable sense of confidence. You are showing clear signs of self-mastery because you are now in a state of full trust.

Key Points for Day 6:

- *Mastering yourself means becoming great at listening to your own inner guidance.*
- *Becoming a master at listening to your spirit starts by completely surrendering to what you might not have all the answers to.*
- *You are a spirit. You are beyond what you can see in the physical alone.*
- *The Inner Glimpse is just the return of trusting your spirit and allowing your Divine Spark to light up the world.*
- *Let go of the obsession of having it all figured out right now, and enter the mastery of knowing that it is all working out.*
- *You are the master of this realm. You have power in this reality. You must claim your divinity and take what is already yours. Be firm about where you stand. This is where you'll begin to receive the ultimate inner guidance.*

- *Repeated signs are a form of guidance. You must be present daily to be open to see.*
- *Your core focus here is to live by faith in the unseen and the unknown. You'll start to trust yourself even more. You'll have a calm nature, because you'll acknowledge your divine inner connection instead of overwhelming yourself by trying to force things.*
- *You are living by your spirit. This can only be understood from the inside, and can only be seen as external success, peace, and a sense of confidence that's undeniable.*

Day 7 – Do Something New – Embracing Spontaneity

New energy is entering your life: new opportunities, new paths. You are being renewed on a deep cellular level. You are shifting energetically and spiritually. Things are clearing up for you. Be ready to receive, and be open to changes. This is your time to truly shine!

Day 7 will be all about newness and changing things up. One thing I have learned during my own self-mastery journey is to do something completely different every single day. I have noticed that there is an immense presence within your mind and energy when you change your normal routine. It is like you are completely alive and engaged. Your senses go through a different experience than usual when you don't repeat the same cycles every day. For Day 7 of your self-mastery, dedicate yourself to a new way of living life. The experience of this day is meant to help you see how, on a subtle level, you will begin to enrich your life in ways you could only imagine previously. Remember, the universe is vast, the Earth is full of life, and there's so much to learn, see, do, and try. Why remain in the same habitual routine? You can start today by switching things up. Do something new every single day. Try new foods. Meet new people. Have different conversations. Learn something you normally don't find yourself delving into. You have immense potential and so much life force. When you decide to stay the same, you allow your body, mind, and spirit to play it safe. This makes you rigid and confines you to what has always been.

Life is so much more. You do not have to identify with one thing and do that same thing over and over again. Yes, you might have some healthy routines. That is wonderful; but have you thought about what else you can explore? You are literally here to be all you can be. You can see new places, look at art, see beauty, expand your tastes, and open yourself up. Self-mastery in terms of newness is learning how to open your heart to all the wonderful, enriching experiences the universe offers. Don't be afraid of newness. You never have to stay in the familiar out of comfort. Let your spirit live this life fully. Find out what makes your heart sing, and what truly makes you come alive...then do it. You're not chasing anything; you're simply playing, learning, and expanding yourself. What memories do you want to ingrain? Imagine watching a movie of your own life right now, and each day you get to see what you are doing. How do you want to remember your life?

Self-mastery of embracing newness also shows that you are not afraid of change. This will teach you to let go, because each day won't be about how you can repeat the same experience. The point of this day is to help you embrace the feeling of spontaneous occurrences. The more you allow yourself to be open in this way, the more the universe can put unexpected gifts in your path. You have no idea how many doors and opportunities will begin to open when you decide to live the self-mastery of newness in life. Newness will teach you to not tie yourself to things and situations you have outgrown. This can be relationships, jobs, and/or environments that no longer enrich your soul. You already know what needs to change. This is the sign you have been waiting for. This is the sign to let go and trust the unknown. Walk boldly, and you will encounter the assurance of the source, which you have trusted through faith. We believe first, and experience second. Trust yourself, now more than ever. A new path and a new beginning await you.

Lesson for Day 7:

Do Something New – Embracing Spontaneity

Day 7 is all about new energy and new experiences. On this day, I want you to do something you have never done. I also want you to carry out your day-to-day routines completely differently. Add a little twist to them. Make yourself feel more present instead of going through your day as if it is a chore. Newness is meant to help you feel more alive. Can you do something completely new for the entire day? Start somewhere, and build it up. Soon, you will experience a thrill to explore and live life in ways that used to seem like something only seen in movies or other people's lives. No. Your life is your own movie. If you really want to make magical things happen, you can. Don't tell yourself to be realistic, either. That is the biggest trap. Faith alone shatters anything that stands in your way. All thoughts of fear are now banished from your mind. These were just a form of comfort to talk yourself out of truly living. If you really want something, it will happen. The *how* is not your business. What is your business is the driving force behind your energy to bring to life your passion, faith, and deep desire to fully live. The Source will provide. It is a must, and it is natural.

Key Points for Day 7:

- *Life is so much more. You do not have to identify with one thing and do that same thing over and over again.*
- *Self-mastery in terms of newness is learning how to open your heart to all the wonderful, enriching experiences the universe offers.*
- *Find out what makes your heart sing and what truly makes you come alive, and do it.*
- *The self-mastery of embracing newness shows that you are not afraid of change. This will teach you to let go, because each day won't be about repeating the same experience.*
- *Newness will teach you to not tie yourself to things and situations you have outgrown.*
- *Faith alone shatters anything that stands in your way. All thoughts of fear are now banished from your mind.*
- *The Source will provide. It is a must, and it is natural.*

Day 8 – Reach Your Full Potential – Break Free from Habits

You're no longer settling. Self-awareness is bringing you to a whole new level of understanding your true potential and your undeniable self-worth. You're starting to value yourself, your energy, your mindset, and your time. The changes you're making are going to shift your life in a positive way, starting right now.

Every single one of us has the ability to optimize ourselves. You are great now, but deep within you is a ball of energy that's filled with so much potential. You can love who you are, but you can always evolve and transform as you embrace yourself every step of the way. One part of self-mastery is learning to identify what stands in the way of your vision so you can break free from habits that keep you stuck in a cycle. Your full potential wants to reveal itself to you in so many ways. It keeps tugging at you, silently whispering that you are better than this. It's reminding you of who you have always been. Your true self is unlimited, full of life, unconditionally filled with love, and a daring creator. Imagine this: You can see a vision today and work toward it coming to life right now. You know this to be the truth. Anything you want is possible. You must decide, move forward, and release yourself from the habits that are keeping you trapped. You can break free, and that is your power. It will be uncomfortable, but it will be worth it. You can't fear getting out of the usual routine. You have to see a greater vision for yourself, and feel it as your true reality. This is your spiritual ability—to imagine and bring to life. This is a message to remind you that you can be free right now. You can start today. You can reclaim yourself.

Life offers chances because we are always learning. Nothing is ever final, and you are not a victim of your past. You are brand new every single moment. On the cellular level and in your whole physical state, you are always being renewed. Now, it is your mind's turn to accept the renewal and prepare for the transformation. We are now going to get into ways you can reach your full potential so you can break free from habits that are keeping you stuck.

Lesson for Day 8

Reach Your Full Potential – Break Free from Habits

Start by identifying a vision for yourself. What is it? Write it down. Now put yourself mentally, physically, and emotionally in that physical state through your imagination. What does that person look like? What are you doing? What surrounds you? How do you feel? Write down the answers to these questions. This step will help you identify what is actually standing in your way. Now that you have a clear vision of your goal and where you see your life heading, ask yourself: What habits do you have right now that are standing in the way of you getting there? How can you change these habits so you can master yourself and reach your full potential? Once you are clear about this, we can start working on ways to stay empowered day by day.

You are literally one habit, one energy shift, and one mindset change away from a completely new life. You have to accept this as your truth before you move forward. These aren't just words; they are powerful reminders of who you truly are. It is all within you right now. I am just here to guide you to accept it, acknowledge it, and take action upon liberating yourself from the illusion that your dream is hard to obtain. You can be, do, and have anything. You came into this reality out of thin air from another human's body. Isn't that alone just magical and special? Think about the trillions of miracles taking place every moment that you can't even explain. The life force and energy state of the universe is so obvious. There is a subtle world that is powerful within you and all around you. Don't be distracted by the thoughts we humans have created in physical form. These are all just thoughts. Surrounding you are the ideas that came to life from other people's minds. The external results of multiple minds constantly co-creating to produce tangible forms should not make you forget that you are also in the field of creation. Don't depend on the external to dictate what is possible for you. You have to declare that for yourself. You have to claim it, speak it, believe it, imagine it, and feel it into existence.

May my full potential be revealed to me.

In this lesson on reaching your full potential, you have to start by optimizing yourself in every way. How do you feel physically? Do you take care of your body? Do you say kind and encouraging things to yourself? To be optimal, you must first honor your body and break free from any habits that make you tired, sick, and weak. Habits can be physical (in what you consume) but also mental (in what you think, feel, and give your attention to). Right now, decide that you will remove any habit that isn't helping you be optimal, and be bold about it. Habits have been created through repetition, and that cycle has to be broken. It is like learning something new and writing a completely different program. The moments you feel tired from change are good news that you are progressing. You're removing anything deep-rooted and coming out on top. You are literally awakening out of your slumber and reclaiming yourself. Nothing can stop you after this.

Confront your daily habits, and be very honest with yourself. Do your current habits match the vision you have for yourself? Do they support any of your goals? If not, break free today. Your true potential will come alive day by day as you move toward shedding past energy and allowing yourself complete renewal. It will begin to happen instantly, and you will notice newfound energy, focus, and direction. From this day on, you will not allow yourself to remain stuck. Your potential is calling you. You have a great purpose here.

As you are breaking free from past habits, practice patience, self-love, self-care, and daily affirmations. These will also be great tools for you as you master yourself and reach your full potential. Do things that lift you higher. Entertain what expands your heart. Experience things that enrich your life and add value to you. Your renewal is happening right now, so be gentle and kind to yourself. Every day, you are becoming stronger, wiser, and more energized. You are liberating yourself from the false illusions and habits that held you back from your dreams and goals. You are now officially stepping into it and walking in your authentic state. This is truly the beginning of something special for you. Take action now, and never look back.

Key Points for Day 8:

- *You are literally one habit, one energy shift, and one mindset change away from a completely new life.*
- *Don't depend on the external to dictate what is possible for you. You have to declare that for yourself. You have to claim it, speak it, believe it, imagine it, and feel it into existence.*
- *Life offers chances because we are always learning. Nothing is ever final, and you are not a victim of your past. You are brand new every single moment.*

- *Confront your daily habits, and be very honest with yourself. Do your current habits match the vision you have for yourself?*
- *Do things that lift you higher. Entertain what expands your heart. Experience things that enrich your life and add value to you.*
- *You are liberating yourself from the false illusions and habits that have held you back from your dreams and goals. You are now officially stepping into your light and walking into your authentic state.*

Day 9 – Emotional Health – Inner Wellness

Prioritize your mental health, emotional wellness, and inner peace right now. You need to take care of yourself so that you can be optimal in all areas of your life.

Emotional health is a staple for mental health and self-mastery. This is a crucial lesson for attaining inner balance and knowing how to use emotional intelligence in everyday situations. In life, we experience many things that test us and trigger us to react. There's nothing wrong with experiencing these emotions and becoming aware of them. The point is to learn how to evolve from things that cause you to respond and react in ways you end up regretting. Self-mastery of your emotions is actually a learning process. You'll see how much you actually have evolved when you look back after applying these powerful tips. One thing you must know is that things happen in life. There's always something coming up that can be unexpected. This is meant to refine you, so you can build emotional intelligence and awareness while consciously observing all that is taking place within you. One thing I have learned is that every moment and situation eventually passes. The only thing that lingers is how we decide to respond. In moments of anger, we feel the aftereffects longer, and sometimes even regret the way we responded. The point is to be clear-minded in all situations so you can respond effectively to anything that happens. You will have greater solutions for a lot of the unwanted, unexpected circumstances that actually end up making you stronger and wiser.

There is nothing to fear. Don't be afraid of your own emotions. What comes up is meant to surface, so you can face it and clear it out. Work through your emotions so you can be more empowered instead of controlled by them. Don't play the hiding game. Don't play the *why am I feeling like this?* game with yourself. Avoiding your own emotions makes them linger longer and causes unnecessary overthinking and worrying. Face what comes up, and always work through it directly. Ask yourself: *What is this teaching me? How can I evolve from this situation?* Every single thing in life is about learning and getting better. It is so liberating when you begin to get to know yourself. You realize that you no longer need to live your life avoiding heartbreak, sudden unexpected circumstances, and/or loss. You'll be better-equipped to respond in a way that expands your heart and mind to greater heights. You'll find yourself being understanding in every moment instead of judging yourself or even living in regret.

Emotional intelligence is knowing that your inner world belongs to you. How you feel, respond, and think when challenging situations occur is up to you. You can instantly empower yourself by stepping back and asking yourself, *what is the best way to handle this?* You literally have all the answers within you. Start asking yourself questions, and give yourself some time to receive. Your spirit already knows that you are a very intelligent being. Mastering your emotions isn't avoiding feelings, but learning how not to be controlled by emotions to the point where they affect your overall wellness. Never suppress emotions. Be strong enough to know it's not as painful as it seems to just let go and reclaim your natural state of being. You deserve your peace of mind. Your heart can be at ease. These are all states available to you right now. You can decide today that others will no longer control you emotionally. You won't be controlled by the past. You won't live in fear of the future. You are free right now to own your inner world. What has happened has passed. You are mastering yourself, and you have no time to sit around wasting your emotions pondering regret. Get yourself together, and get right within.

Releasing grudges frees you. It helps you stop overthinking past situations and frees your mental and emotional energy to create something new. Forgive yourself for not knowing better, and redirect your focus to a more healed, more loving, and more self-aware you. Move upward!

All things in life are momentary. Each emotion is fleeting, and what remains over time are the lessons that help us get better and better. Think of how much you grew when you were at your lowest emotionally. Imagine how resilient and strong you have become. The results are in your growth, not really in what happened in those past moments. What you took from those past experiences in awareness is still with you as a guiding compass. This is what I mean by self-mastery of your emotions. It is all about propelling forward and allowing yourself to be clear-minded. Emotions carry a powerful force. When they are unchecked and allowed to run on their own, you might experience a loop in overthinking when all you really had to do was check in with yourself and see what brought that feeling up. Sometimes, an emotion can come up, which triggers a thought, which goes back to triggering more emotions. Stop yourself. Take a deep breath and say, "I release all unwanted emotions, and I choose my peace instead of overthinking and worrying. I welcome a greater solution right now." This will automatically increase your emotional intelligence because you'll no longer just be reacting to everything that surfaces.

Lesson for Day 9

Emotional Health – Inner Wellness

For Day 9, you'll be paying attention to how you feel. This day is all about seeing what's running within you that causes overthinking, worry, and stress. These emotions can be subtle or obvious. You'll take this day to look at yourself from the inside as a silent observer. You'll reflect upon what comes up without any kind of judgment. This is meant to show you that what you are feeling can be transformed into greater harmony instead of reactions to your own emotions and getting carried away. Get out of the mindset of creating scenarios you fear. This only triggers more emotions. We love to imagine. Instead of imagining worst-case scenarios, why not entertain best-case scenarios? Why not give thought and emotion to outcomes you'd love to see? This is also a great time for you to check what you are imagining that's creating an emotional reaction or anxiety. You don't have to fear what's not real. It's all just thoughts and feelings. Boldly command greater. Boldly speak power over your life. Don't be timid of your inner world. Once you observe yourself, you'll find that you have the ability to alter any state instead of being reactive to it. The more you continue to do this, the more it becomes a natural state for you to cultivate a healthier attitude.

May your heart be at ease, and may a rush of calm surround you as you try to figure everything out. Pray for mental, emotional, and spiritual peace so all that weighs heavy on your heart and mind can be lifted off you right now. May you receive the wisdom and guidance to grow through it all.

Another thing I want you to do is free yourself from other people's thoughts: what they think of you, how they feel about you, what they are saying, and even how you want them to see you. Self-mastery of your emotions is about inner strength. People outside of you have no say, control, or access when it comes to what you feel. You decide what stays within you. Things always come up, but you as a master your emotions, you'll know how to quickly and easily clear them out. Don't waste your lifetime trying to impress or seek approval. Don't let your creativity or light be dimmed by words. You are a powerhouse and a source that's unstoppable. Only you can decide to stop yourself. Only you can decide what stays on repeat within you. Reading *Inner Glimpse* is meant to bring you back to your true power, so you can be emotionally free and healthy from the inside out. You'll find yourself with more life force and energy because you have stopped depleting yourself. Check with yourself. Clear everything. Take note of what triggers you, and put an end to that connection. Once you sever triggers, you become free. You are doing your best, and you are growing in so many ways. This newfound freedom to live consciously is going to empower you spiritually, mentally, emotionally, and physically. You are returning to your natural state: a healthy, balanced, and more vibrant you. This is the beginning of great blessings. Things will begin to be revealed to you now because you are open and emotionally unoccupied. Your intuition and inner guidance will start to become clearer.

Key Points for Day 9

- *Emotional health is a staple for mental health and self-mastery.*
- *There is nothing to fear. Don't be afraid of your own emotions. What comes up is meant to surface so you can face it and clear it out.*
- *Avoiding your own emotions makes them linger longer and causes unnecessary overthinking and worry. Face what comes up, and always work through it directly.*
- *Emotional intelligence is knowing that your inner world belongs to you. How you feel, respond, and think is up to you when challenging things happen.*
- *Never suppress emotions. Be strong enough to know it's not as painful as it seems. Just let go and reclaim your natural state of being. You deserve your peace of mind. Your heart can be at ease.*
- *You are free right now to own your inner world. What happened has passed. You are mastering yourself, and you have no time to sit around wasting your emotions pondering regret. Get yourself together, and get right within.*
- *Boldly speak power over your life. Don't be timid of your inner world. Once you observe yourself, you'll find that you have the ability to alter any state instead of being reactive to it.*

- *Self-mastery of your emotions is about inner strength. People outside of you have no say, control, or access when it comes to what you should feel.*
- *Don't waste your lifetime trying to impress or seek approval. Don't let your creativity or light be dimmed by words. You are a powerhouse and a source that's unstoppable.*
- *Things will begin to be revealed to you now because you are open and emotionally unoccupied. Your intuition and inner guidance will start to become clearer.*

Day 10 – Treat Yourself Well – You Are Valuable

You are so valuable. You are worth so much more. You deserve the best. Start believing in your own greatness, and be patient; things will start aligning for you right now.

You are the most important person in your life. The more you feel alive, vibrant, and filled with love, the more you can do and be for the world. Self-mastery and self-care go hand in hand. The more you treat yourself well, the more you'll feel confident and energized. Remember, the world only knows about you what you radiate. Everyone around you feels your energy on a subtle level. Don't think you have to try to convince anyone to see you in any specific way. You don't have to wait for external approval to validate yourself. The most important thing you'll learn in this book is that you are the center of how the outside world responds to you. People only know about you based upon what you project. You attract what you allow and tolerate. There's so much going on at all times on the energetic level. Too many people think life is only what we see, and they work on the external while feeling insecure on the inside. External images come from the inside. Long-lasting happiness starts within you. When you decide to accept who you are, you begin to project that energy outward. The world is literally responding to you. So if you stop doubting yourself and start feeling confident, the outer reality starts to show you a new world. You'll meet people who understand your standards and how you move. It won't be a coincidence. Everything around you right now came from within you first. I am sure you have had friends or relationships during certain seasons in your life that you have decided to evolve and grow past. Once you did this, a new experience showed up. The reality of the new experience was always there. It was just waiting for you to finally decide to have a better experience.

Release any energy that doesn't deserve your attention. Your thoughts are way too valuable to waste.

Life is not random, and nothing is a coincidence. You are projecting your inner thoughts and feelings energetically, which creates an aura around you that's like a signal to the outside world. We all feel energy. There's so much happening all around us that we might not see or hear. This is what makes life magical and full of possibility. Start today to feel empowered, full of hope, and deeply trusting that you are a valuable person. The goal for Day 10 is to reclaim your value on all levels. You don't have to prove a point. You don't have to try to force anything. You honestly don't even have to try so hard. You actually just step into the state. You own yourself. You set within yourself how you want the world to respond to you. If you're waiting for words to validate you or approval to free you from your own inner insecurities, you'll remain needy and controlled by everything but yourself. You are a powerful spirit. You are a valuable being. You have to stop denying yourself this truth. Walk boldly, and firmly claim your new state of thinking. Live your life from this place. The outer world will adjust, even if it has to remove a lot out of your life to create a whole new world of experiences for you. Remember, everyone is living the reality they are tuned into. When you switch things up, everything around you alters in the direction of the new thoughts and feelings you are having.

Elevate, and never look back. There's a whole world waiting for you to discover it. Don't let one situation hold you back from seeing all the miracles, blessings, and opportunities that surround you.

If you continue to allow the past to label who you are, you'll continue to create energy that makes that reality seem real. The universe does not disappoint when it wants to show you what you want to see. You will be presented with what you want to experience in order to validate your reality. The complaining must end. The self-judgment and talking to yourself or about yourself in any unhealthy manner must also stop. Start treating yourself well from the inside first. Cultivate healthier thoughts by feeling worthy of the best. This is such a liberating feeling that you'll no longer have to depend on outside approval. Your strength will start to radiate to the world the minute you actually make these changes. Everything up to this point has been just. It is all okay. You have been brought here now to finally realize that your identity and value aren't determined by the outside world. You have to keep remembering that you are a spirit, and so alive. You can shape-shift or change anything. You can renew yourself at any time. Nothing keeps you attached to the past but your own thoughts and feelings. Imagine if you were busy creating what you wanted all day long. Everything else would seem like a distant memory.

Feel how valuable you are right now—just completely valuable being you. Not valuable because of this or that. You are already complete. Everything else is just an experience that enriches your soul to learn and thrive. You are not your past, and you are not defined by it. Everything has happened to bring you to this moment, where you stand strong. You can be grateful for the lessons and the growth you have received, but never, ever feel trapped by the past. Now that you understand the power of treating yourself well and feeling valuable, let's get into the steps you can take.

Lesson for Day 10

Treat Yourself Well – You Are Valuable

Day 10 will be all about creating a strong, powerful inner you, so you never again have to depend on the fleeting energies of external validation and approval. You will begin to set standards in your life for what you truly want and plan to experience. You can start by declaring that your inner world belongs to you.

You can start by claiming what you want to feel and see, on the inside and the outside. Your self-worth is beyond what is tangible. It is an energy state—the chemistry of your thoughts and feeling about yourself. To alter these states, check with yourself and remove all forms of neediness. Be cool, calm, and at ease. Nothing is getting away from you. You are okay. You are whole. When you remove any thoughts of neediness and stop seeking validation to gain worth, you start to take your power back. You'll experience something so special, you might not be able to put it into words. There's a level of freedom you will obtain by approving of yourself. Self-acceptance begins with knowing that nothing can add to you or take away from you. You are already complete. Feel this feeling of completeness all day long on Day 10. With each thought or feeling that comes up, say, "I am complete!" If that's your main thought, you will not be feeling needy. You will just be, and that is just a beautiful state to be in.

Loving yourself will heal you. You are perfect no matter what your past was, or what you're currently experiencing. You can't be broken. You are whole, complete, and divine. Let it all go. Feel light in your heart and mind. Claim your peace. It is a new day to celebrate yourself.

Spend this day saying positive, encouraging words to yourself. Take note of how each thought makes you feel, and how it changes the way the world responds to you. You'll begin to notice a shift in others because they can feel your confidence. You'll start to be treated better, and even receive so much love. Everyone wants to be their best self. When they see someone else's light shining, they feel inspired. Your aura, actions, and results do all the talking for you. You become strong day by day, and you become a walking impact, just by being you. During this time, allow any changes that need to take place. You are growing so fast, and sometimes the world around you has to shift to the point where you might find yourself living a completely different life. Be okay with any and all changes, even if this means that the people and environment that once surrounded you completely alter. What are you allowing in your life? What are you tolerating? Are you a reflection of what you want to attract? Are you just being you and enjoying your life? Take some time to think about these questions. You can start setting the standards in your world. Believe that the universe must deliver. Never settle or accept what doesn't make your heart sing and your mind expand. Don't go through life barely getting what you want, or tolerating just anything to feel one small ounce of validation. You can have way more. You are so much more than you actually see. You are literally awakening and remembering yourself as you read every single one of these words. It is liberating. It is true freedom to reclaim yourself.

Key Points for Day 10

- *You are the most important person in your life. The more you feel alive, vibrant, and filled with love, the more you can do and be for the world.*
- *The more you treat yourself well, the more you'll feel confident and energized. Remember, the world only knows about you what you radiate.*
- *Long-lasting happiness starts within you. When you decide to accept who you are, you begin to project that energy outward.*
- *Life is not random, and nothing is a coincidence. You are projecting your inner thoughts and feelings energetically, which creates an aura around you that acts as a signal to the outside world.*
- *Start today to feel empowered, full of hope, and deeply trusting that you are a valuable person.*
- *Nothing keeps you attached to the past but your own thoughts and feelings.*
- *You have to start treating yourself well from the inside first. Cultivate healthier thoughts by feeling worthy of the best.*
- *Everything happened to bring you to this moment, where you are now standing strong. You can be grateful for the lessons and growth you received, but never, ever feel trapped by the past.*

- *Don't go through life barely getting what you want, tolerating just anything to feel one small ounce of validation.*

Mastering the Inner Glimpse

Day 11 – Make Ideas Come to Life – The Habit of Action-Taking

Make sure your actions are aligned with what you are praying for.

The last five days of the self-mastery program are going to be all about how you can make your Inner Glimpse come to life. I am sure you have received tons of creative ideas, inner guidance, and subtle hints about things you can do. These insights might have been grand and filled with life energy. You might have looked at it as just a dream before, but not anymore. Day 11 will be about learning how to make your Inner Glimpse manifest into tangible physical results. Mastering yourself is knowing how to listen to your inner guidance while taking the necessary action to make something go from a dream to reality. A lot of people have big dreams. A lot of people receive even greater ideas. The only difference between those who make ideas come to life and others is their trust in their vision. You have to start trusting yourself and the visions you are receiving. You are a visionary. Stop doubting your greatness. Stop waiting for someone else to solve something. You have been chosen for the vision you have been given. Step into your authority and claim your divine position. You came here with a mission, and you are being reminded right now through these words (and this book) that you can make your ideas and thoughts come to life. Nothing is random about what comes to mind now. When you feel a surge of energy and find yourself pondering a wonderful glimpse you've received, act on it. Don't wait around in awe of it. You've received this insight for a reason. Apply it. Integrate it into your life. Move forward.

Lesson for Day 11

Make Ideas Come to Life – The Habit of Action-Taking

You'll spend this day writing down ideas you have received for a project or some other important thing in your life. Let this idea be the biggest dream you have ever had...or something as small as a change you need to make. It makes no difference what it is. The goal here is for you to completely believe that your idea is 100 percent possible. There is no question about it. You have spent way too long talking yourself out of these wonderful, grand ideas, thinking they were too big or not even possible. It completely goes against your spiritual nature as a powerful being to think for one second that you don't have access to the field of abundant resources and unlimited supply. You were created out of thin air, and emerged into this physical reality. If that's not miraculous enough already, I don't know what else to tell you. You literally have to start feeling a new sense of empowerment: not just a quick high from some inspiration you read, but a deep-rooted declaration and strong stance that you are a powerful spirit capable of making great things happen. You are already divinely connected. Now that you understand this, stop taking your ideas and potential lightly. You are constantly receiving for a reason. It is up to you, through your own free will, to take the action needed. You can wait one month or three years and finally do it, or you can start today and look back as you celebrate your success.

Do something in the direction of your dreams. Movement creates momentum. You will start to take action and show the universe that you are determined to receive.

Once you get into the habit of taking action on all your ideas, you become unstoppable. You'll naturally start to be deeply connected to your spirit, which will then provide inner guidance through your intuition and a strong feeling to make something happen. You'll start to operate on another level. Spend Day 11 creating a plan of action for your vision. What is one step you could take right now that would propel you forward? What is one thing you could finish right now that would change your life? What ideas have you been sitting on that the world needs to see? So many people are literally waiting on what you have to offer. You will do it differently, and in such a unique way that your touch will be felt. Understand that no one is you, and no two people are alike. We are all uniquely designed and magnificently created. You have been given a vision that only you can express. This is why you came here. This is why you are needed. You have something special to offer. If there is something a million and one people are doing, and you come in and do it in your own unique way, you automatically make an impact. There's nothing more special than your energy expressed. It is your own unique signature.

Begin now by using this surge of energy to catalyze your vision forward. Don't let any more of your creative ideas go to waste. This is your time. and the world is waiting to experience your energy signature. The entire universe and cosmos support you. You have a great purpose here. and you will express it in this lifetime. You will live abundantly and make an impact. Live every day from this moment forward making all your ideas and insights come to life. Once you believe and start moving into your truth, you will make all your dreams come true. The universe is waiting for your expression to be felt, seen, and heard. We are ready to applaud and cheer for you as you change many lives—yours and those all around you.

Key Points for Day 11:

- *Start trusting yourself and the visions you are receiving.*
- *You are a visionary. Stop doubting your greatness.*
- *You have been chosen for the vision you have been given. Step into your authority and claim your divine position.*
- *You must literally start feeling a new sense of empowerment. Not just a quick high from some inspiration you have read, but a deep-rooted declaration and strong stance that you are a powerful spirit capable of making great things happen.*
- *You are already divinely connected.*
- *You have a great purpose here, and you will express it in this lifetime.*
- *You will live abundantly and make an impact.*

Day 12 – Follow The Signs – Trust Yourself

You have officially entered a state in which you win at everything you do. Things just start happening in your favor. You notice signs, symbols, and synchronicities that remind you of how powerful you are. You accept it. You accept yourself. You are completely unstoppable!

One of the great ways to start mastering the Inner Glimpse you are receiving is to begin to follow the signs you are getting from your spirit. Understand that everything around you carries a message. The only way to start receiving is to be present enough to recognize the patterns, signs, and synchronicities that connect you to your own hidden messages. Things will go from appearing solid and firm to fluid and changeable. You'll start to realize that nothing is as it seems. At the beginning, it will seem surreal how many of your own thoughts and feelings come up in your outer reality. When you're not fully present, you miss the magic happening all around you. What takes you away from seeing the signs and receiving them is being mentally and emotionally caught up in the past and the future, which removes you from your aliveness now. There's so much taking place in this moment. The most powerful thing about mastering the Inner Glimpse is that you allow yourself to be guided. This is another means of beginning to trust yourself. When you know you are connected, you never worry. You walk through life with faith and remain hopeful. These are inner states you can begin to accept right now.

You will now start to see through the illusions that keep you emotionally attached to what you think is happening, and break free from any overthinking that doesn't provide solutions. You will begin to see beyond the challenges and cultivate your vision. It will almost feel like you have a new set of eyes. Things will seem so clear.

Your mind has shifted. You are now consciously living in spirit. You are now walking with so much power in you, because you understand that you are truly present and deeply connected to your highest truth. You feel a sense of trust in what you can't understand. The mystery of how things work no longer makes you question if something is even possible for you. You just know that it is. All of this awakens within you when you begin to follow the signs and trust yourself. The unknown and what comes next are nothing to fear. There is so much potential in the ethers. You must put your thoughts out, then allow yourself to watch the signs show up. Miracles will fill your life because you have discovered your divine truth as a spirit who encompasses the greatest life has to offer. The more you believe in yourself, the more obvious and prominent the signs become.

Lesson for Day 12:

Follow The Signs – Trust Yourself

You'll spend Day 12 recognizing the patterns and signs all around you. What sign has been constantly coming up in your life? Do the signs you've been getting have strong emotion attached to them? Do you feel urgency to act on your signs? The more you begin to trust a sign, the more you will start to receive guidance. The important thing to learn about how to interpret what comes up is to pay attention to how you feel. Don't talk yourself out of the obvious just because you prefer to avoid change. You can't hide from the inner shift taking place. You are realizing so much, and now, the universe is showing you just how powerful you are by sending you gentle nudges to help you reflect, integrate, and upgrade yourself.

I am connected to the most powerful force in the universe.

Another important message I have received about signs is that they are incredibly personal. If you receive one, ask yourself what it means, and connect with the way you are receiving guidance. So many people ask others to interpret for them *why* they keep seeing certain numbers or signs. Nobody knows better than you. Nobody can give you a clearer answer than your own self. People can guess, or give you a generic review of what they might think, but you are far too complex for anyone to try to read you. You know yourself best. You know the layers, the depth, and the grandness of your life. When you are receiving signs and trusting yourself, you will also learn how to depend on your own inner self to review and understand your divine guidance. Begin now to look all around you, and notice repeating patterns. When you see these patterns and signs, write down what you have seen in your personal journal. If you have further questions, ask to receive greater clarity. Always ask yourself what you want to know. I have noticed that when I need a solution, I just ask the question and send it out into the universe. The guidance and answers always come. Just release and trust yourself. The Inner Glimpse will begin to shed more light on your life as you begin to discover the meaning of all the wonderful signs you are receiving from the universe.

Key Points for Day 12:

- *Understand that everything around you carries a message.*
- *The only way to start receiving is to be present enough to recognize the patterns, signs, and synchronicities that connect you to your own hidden messages.*
- *What takes you away from seeing and receiving signs is being caught up mentally and emotionally in the past and the future, which removes you from your aliveness in the present.*
- *The most powerful thing about mastering the Inner Glimpse is to allow yourself to be guided.*

- *You mind has shifted. You are now consciously living in spirit. You are now walking with so much power, because you understand that you are truly present and deeply connected to your highest truth.*

Day 13 – Spend Time Listening – You Have the Answers

Don't give up! Answers, blessings, solutions, and unexpected miracles are on the way. The most challenging times are only preparing you to receive something bigger and greater. You might not know how or when, but trust in your own spirit and what is possible for you are what is going to get you through.

It's time to start taking your inner guidance more seriously. You literally have the answers you need within you. Mastering yourself is learning how to hone in and trust your own inner guidance. You can spend years searching outside yourself for that which has always been inside of you. The most powerful thing I've discovered has been following my heart and my inner self to guide me. You, too, can begin today to start tapping in and letting all the confusion go. There is no search. Mastering the Inner Glimpse is all about trusting yourself. You'll gain so much clarity and peace...and a deep inner connection you'll have access to for the rest of your life.

When is your spirit communicating with you? When are you being guided? When you get a strong gut feeling. When you know that this is the right time to take that one action you've been meaning to take. When you feel and sense an inner voice cheering you on and telling you to keep going. It is all a positive aspect. You will know when your spirit has stepped in. Most people feel this when they are in dire situations, because they get into the energy of surrendering. They pray passionately. They ask for guidance. They let go of the need to control everything, and completely allow their true inner power to awaken so they can be moved, guided, and redirected back to their purpose.

Listening and trusting your inner voice has a lot to do with letting yourself relax and letting the need to control everything go. When you want to figure things out, your mind starts to race. You find yourself overthinking and getting overwhelmed. This is when you have to go from searching to asking. Get into the habit of asking yourself questions and waiting for the inner answer to provide the way. Get into the habit of trusting the strong urges that provide you with solutions. You have been receiving your entire life. Now, you're consciously aware of it, and things will begin to take a turn in your favor. You'll stop living in uncertainty, and begin to cultivate a deep faith that all is well. Nothing is a mistake. You may have been through some hurdles, but each moment has made you a better listener to your own inner self and allowed you to trust yourself more and more. You might still sometimes refer back to the way you overcame something and use it as inspiration to move through current circumstances. You already know you can make it. You experience a natural inner knowing that you can and will survive any situation. You're built for it, and you know this.

Lesson for Day 13:

Spend Time Listening – You Have the Answers

You'll spend this day doing two things. The first is learning how to ask yourself questions you need answers to and surrendering so you can receive. The second is starting to listen to the inner voice that is constantly trying to guide you. One thing I love doing—and it works incredibly well—is speaking passionately about what I need answers to. This is a way to release control and allow yourself to gain greater perspective. Asking takes the burden off of your shoulders in terms of the small slice of reality you're currently aware of. When we do this, we tap into the part of our memory that shows us how we've tried to solve things in the past. Even though that's great for survival and certainty, the truest and most powerful thing you can do is trust the unknown aspect. This is why people sometimes have a hard time trusting how something will work out— they only tap into a past memory, which provides safety, but no real solution. However, when you start to operate in the unknown, you can get into creation mode. This is a state where the unexpected happens. New energy, new opportunities, new connections, and new alignments are present. You stop fearing the unseen and the unknown. You stop trying to make everything predictable and let yourself go completely. You become a master at thriving in uncertain situations, because that's just how life is. You don't have to always have the answers, but you are able to trust that it will work out. This is your power. Start right now by asking yourself for solutions. Tell your spirit to guide you. Speak to your inner self. Ask to be led. Ask for signs. Start today.

Your spirit will not allow you to fail. You already know this. That is why you constantly strive to be better, and keep getting the strong urge to realize your potential. You can't even stop yourself. You were born to win in every situation. It's so natural.

Once you have asked, the second thing to do is listen. Just relax and trust yourself. Remember, the answers are in the thoughts that empower you and remind you of your greater purpose. The answers you're listening for come in the form of ideas that spontaneously pop into your mind. You'll know they're from your spirit because you feel moved and transformed. The noise within you will settle, and you will know how to directly access your inner treasure. You'll stop recycling doubtful thoughts and find yourself reaching new heights. Your inner power will take on a life of its own. You'll no longer be dependent on the ever-changing outer world. There will discover a natural stillness and faith. This is your secret world. Nobody knows you completely but yourself. You are the builder of your magnificent inner universe. What or whom can you trust if you don't even trust your own inner guidance? You've been putting too much power out there, trying so hard to look around, when truly, you should have been (and should now be) building from within. Your inner relationship will strengthen with this mastery program, because you'll understand who you really are to a greater and greater extent. As you start listening and receiving fresh ideas, comforting thoughts, heightened clarity, and solutions for what you need, you will become stronger, wiser, and more connected to yourself. It will feel like your life has just begun. You have received the Divine Spark, and your Inner Glimpse will light the way. This is truly your time. You have all the answers within you. Receive now.

Key Points for Day 13:

- *Mastering yourself is learning how to hone in and trust your own inner guidance.*
- *When you start to operate in the unknown, you get into creation mode. This is a state in which the*

unexpected happens. New energy, new opportunities, new connections, and new alignments take place. You stop fearing the unseen and the unknown.

- *Listening to and trusting your inner voice has a lot to do with letting yourself relax—and letting the need to control everything go.*
- *Nothing is a mistake. You might have been through some hurdles, but each moment has made you a better listener to your own inner self, allowing you to trust yourself more and more.*
- *You don't need to always have the answers, but you trust that it will work out. This is your power. Start right now by asking yourself for solutions.*
- *Remember, the answers are in the thoughts that empower you and remind you of your greater purpose.*
- *This is truly your time. You have all the answers within you. Receive now.*

Day 14 – Making an Impact – Following Your Spirit

You'll receive more life force, energy, light, and abundance for making an impact on your own life and the lives of others. You are a walking influence for the betterment and advancement of humanity. Your single force can make a difference. Your existence is needed.

You came here for a reason. There is nothing coincidental or random about your existence. Begin to follow your spirit to discover your purpose. Don't treat your talent like a hobby. You are gifted at what you're good at because you came here to express yourself. You can't go through years of your life not following your passion. No more excuses. No more talking yourself out of your greatness. Only you can offer what you offer, even if there are a million and one other people doing what you're doing. There's a unique touch you offer the world. There's a lane, a path, and a clear direction for you. Get into the habit of following your spirit and letting your impact be felt. There's so much life and energy in making a difference. It is the thread of hope, compassion, and love that connects us all. We find an instant opening of the heart and mind when we use our gift to impact the world. Don't think only of what others are doing for the world; think of what you came here to do. Your life is grand, too. People are living their purpose, and there are great rewards in following one's true spirit. You have to stop playing it small, and own the grandness of your spirit and who you are. Perfect your craft. Let it flow out of you. Let yourself be influential. You can impact one person or millions, simply by being you. This is natural when you are aligned. You don't need to look around and wonder why only others are making their dream a reality. You have no idea how much is going on in their inner worlds, or how long they have been building. The external is just the results of what takes place within. Once you stop comparing and wondering why some people are receiving so much, you'll begin to enter a world of abundance.

What are you good at? If you could be doing what your heart yearns for, what would that be? What is your passion? What makes you move? The answer is anything with high energy connected to it and pure bliss as its purpose. It will be revealed to you. You already know this. Stop getting technical and asking *how* you'll make it happen. You will, and you must operate on pure faith. Your idea coming to life is not any different from anyone else making his or her vision a reality. If any other human can do something, you can, too. You just have to do it your way. There's no stopping your energy and drive once you start following your spirit.

How can you impact your community? What value do you have that you can share with the world? What can you teach that can make a difference? You are very influential, and you can make wonderful things happen. I want you to stop looking at your potential as a mere dream, and start seeing it as a reality that is totally possible. Making an impact starts at home. You can serve as an example through your actions and results. Remember, your inner world is where you are initially building from. As your mind gets stronger and you start to believe deeply in yourself, you stop looking for external understanding and move at a high speed of expression. Your impact starts to actually make people around you feel inspired naturally. They will want to know how you're doing it...and that is your first impact. You never need to convince anyone or try hard to prove a point. Your impact will be felt no matter what. You will change lives just by being you, and that is the most wonderful thing about following your spirit. Your presence, energy, and work will illuminate the world, one person at a time.

Lesson for Day 14:

Making an Impact – Following Your Spirit

How can you begin making an impact today? Let's start by asking yourself if what you're doing now in your life is giving you more energy and excitement. I am sure you've heard many people say their work doesn't feel like a job because they are passionate about it. What are you passionate about? What is holding you back from making the transition to fully living your life while expressing your highest creativity and energy? Have you been listening to your own Inner Glimpse? You can't let your dreams stay hidden inside of you. You can't be afraid of the birthing process of bringing your vision to life. You will do it, and you'll look back and be filled with so much gratitude that you actually followed your heart and listened to your spirit. Begin today, and discover your passion. Find out what you have always wanted to do. It's evident in the dreams you had as a child, and that deep inner knowing that you came here to do one specific thing. What is that for you? The more you start to follow the wisdom of your own spiritual purpose, the more you'll start to witness an undeniable flow in your life. You will receive so much abundance and energy, so many resources to continue to do more. You won't ever have to worry about how all of this will come together. It will, because that is why you came here. Start trusting, believing, and expressing your divine truth. I wish you great success in this lifetime. I know your impact will carry an unstoppable energy that will surpass your wildest imaginings. You will serve as an inspiration that anything and everything is possible. Your story will move others into purpose. Shine brightly!

Key Points for Day 14:

- *You came here for a reason. There is nothing coincidental or random about your existence. You have to begin to follow your spirit to discover your purpose.*
- *You can't go through years of your life without following your passion. No more excuses. No more talking yourself out of your greatness.*
- *There's a unique touch you offer. There's a lane, a path, and a clear direction for you. Get into the*

habit of following your spirit and letting your impact be felt.

- *You have to stop playing it small. Own the grandness of your spirit and who you are.*
- *Once you stop comparing and wondering why some people are receiving so much, you'll begin to enter a world of abundance.*
- *As your mind gets stronger and you start to deeply believe in yourself, you'll stop looking for external understanding and begin to move at a high speed of expression. Your impact will start to actually make people around you feel inspired naturally.*
- *The more you follow the wisdom of your own spiritual purpose, the more you'll see an undeniable flow in your life. You will receive so much abundance and energy, so many resources to continue to do more.*
- *Your story will move others into purpose.*

Day 15 – Expanding Your Light – Unstoppable Momentum

You are now gaining momentum in energy, creativity, power, and awareness. You have officially created the shift, and it will now ripple throughout the entire universe and be felt by many.

Now that you have reached the final day of the Self-Mastery Program, let's close by discussing how you can further expand your light and gain unstoppable momentum in your creativity, vision, health, and overall wellness. It's all about balance. You have learned so much in this program. You have discovered your inner power, and it is now time to live your life in an expanded manner, radiating even more brightly and exercising the momentum that comes from within. You have done the inner work, and now it will begin to show. Understand that when you are living your truth, you generate a strong aura that expands further. Each person with whom you come into contact will feel your undeniable power. You will bring joy into people's lives by simply being you. That is what it means to have a powerful presence. You will also build a momentum that becomes unstoppable, to the point that you find yourself completing what you have always intended to finish. You'll feel a sense of things just naturally working out for you. You are truly magical, and everything about you is expanding from this moment on. Claim this. Feel it. You are the only one who can make declarations about your life. You have the free will to do this. Nobody can stop you. Keep this private and sacred. Like the seed that silently flourishes in the darkness, let your beauty speak for itself. This is where the balance lies. You create in darkness. This is your private world. Your imagination is a blank canvas that you get to paint on. Make your story artistic. Don't be afraid of the darkness or the unknown. You flourish in all states, and your radiance and energy will speak for themselves.

Lesson for Day 15:

Expanding Your Light – Unstoppable Momentum

Do what allows your heart to expand. Do what you are afraid of. Live your life trusting that this is the greatest experience. Create momentum around you by doing what you want to...boldly. Movement creates unstoppable energy. Do what you must, and retreat when you need to. Either way, each moment serves a great purpose for your self-mastery. In this book and program, I honor the resting phase as well as the creation phase. Don't miss out on the simple things: the joy and laughter you share with others, the smiles you bring to so many faces, the stories and adventures you create. This is expanding your light further. You enrich yourself with all that life has to offer. You no longer confine your spirit to cycles that keep you small. You are free. You have broken free from all the illusions, and you begin to live only according to the ideas you agree to. Nothing is holding you back. Allow your spirit to expand. Fly high in every way. Fill yourself with energy by tapping into your inner resources. From this moment on, you will have unstoppable momentum. This is so natural for you. Think exponentially, and feel expansion as your truth. You have what it takes.

Key Points for Day 15:

- *Understand that when you are living your truth, you generate a strong aura that expands further. Each person with whom you come into contact will feel your undeniable power.*
- *You are truly magical, and everything about you is expanding from this moment on. Claim this. Feel it.*
- *You are the only one who can make declarations over your life. You have the free will to do this. Nobody can stop you.*
- *Your imagination is a blank canvas that you get to paint on. Make your story artistic.*
- *You have broken free from all the illusions, and you now live according to ideas you agree to. Nothing is holding you back.*
- *You no longer confine your spirit to cycles that keep you small. You are free.*
- *From this moment on, you will have unstoppable momentum. This is so natural for you.*

The success you'll experience from this Self-Mastery Program will originate in your acceptance of your divine nature. This is just a return to what you already know. That is why these words resonate so deeply. It is not necessarily new to you, but a reminder of what your inner self already understands. You have felt a surge of energy, confidence, and life-changing emotion with every word. The power of making this program work for you isn't something that will require work. It is effortless. You know this. Step into it. True shifts take a moment to integrate. It's like switching a light on: Everything becomes clear. I wrote this book to make your adventure more enjoyable, and to help you feel more at ease as you begin to trust yourself and receive guidance from within. Use this as a tool and reference point to snap yourself back into a state of a deep inner knowing and powerful conviction that you can make the greatest of things happen. I truly believe in you, and know that you believing in yourself will make the world a better place. It is an honor to share this with you. May you experience growth, success, and evolution in every area of your life.

5

REIMAGINING – YOUR IDENTITY

Reimagining is the ability to free yourself from the identities you attach yourself to that no longer serve your new, current self. Each moment is a new experience for you to imagine something greater. If you spend most of your time thinking of what happened to you in the past and continue to feel victimized, you'll remain stagnant when your spirit actually wants to soar higher into new dimensions of life. You can be and do so many great things in your lifetime. This chapter is intended not only to free you from past thoughts and attachments, but also to learn and explore your creative ability to be free in the moment so you can create experiences that will enrich your life. Remember, all is mental. What you constantly imagine is what you're playing out emotionally and creating into your life. Your ability to imagine is your creative power to see new visions and find solutions that you can integrate. When you use your imagination to remain in fear or play the past over and over again, you create an emotional attachment and stagnation that prevent you from seeing who you really are. One thing you must understand is that what has happened is now over. Take that in for a moment. You are in a new state that's filled with so much life and possibility.

Imagine what could happen for you if you just stopped doubting yourself and started reclaiming your true power. You would be completely unstoppable. Your ideas would manifest. Your impact would be great. Your expression would be divine. All of this is within you right now. Claim it.

You can't spend another moment living in the past, imagining what went wrong or the regrets you once had. Snap out of it. You have the ability, right now, to see yourself in a new light. Who are you today? What is your current vision for yourself? How are you using the power of your imagination? What story are you telling about your life? Are you constantly victimizing yourself in conversation? Are you painting a picture of "poor me," or are you speaking greater power over your life? This is your turning point. This is where you step it up and stop playing yourself. You are a powerhouse. You can create a new shift in your life. You were meant to learn from your past, and each moment has served a great purpose. Don't allow yourself to be limited by what someone did to you, or what went wrong. Don't spend another day saying "I should have" or "I could have." What will you do now? Starting today, reimagine a new you. Release the emotional charge of the past by reimagining a new outcome in your mind. See an image of yourself no longer attaching so many current emotions to past experiences. Things happened as they did, but you are renewed now. You are born again every single day. You are rejuvenated. The only thing that stays the same is a mind that chooses to ponder what was instead of what is and what will be. You decide every single second how you can turn it around. Your identity and experience can be renewed. I am sure you have experienced moments when you looked back and said to yourself, "I can't believe I used to do that or think that way." This is what I mean by a new identity. You are constantly recreating yourself, to the point where things from your past start to look unfamiliar. Your spirit is extremely intelligent. You are designed, supported, and connected to the greatest source. You are evolving every second. The speed of your evolution is different than in the past. What used to take months or years is happening in days and weeks. Things are shifting instantly now, and you are feeling it.

Imagine the best for yourself. See it all happening for you. Feel good about it, and watch how things in your life begin to shift in your favor.

Who Are You?

Whoever you want to be. You can wake up and decide to completely turn your life around. You can take a new path. You can alter and shift any aspect of your life. Who you are is unrelated to the last moment or the next. It is a blank state for you to decide every second. This happens in such a subtle way that sometimes, you might not notice your own evolution. This understanding will allow you to remember that you, as a spirit, are beyond the physical. No matter what has happened to you in the past, it does not dictate who you can become. The past was just a moment in time that brought you to your current state, but it was never meant to play out in a way that continues to confine your potential. You are free from the past. Keep your energy light from these types of burdens. Anytime you feel restricted by a past thought, you are choosing to attach your identity to an experience that's no longer here. How someone treated you or what happened before is all gone now. The only way it can remain is if you bring a projection of it into your imagination and attach it with strong emotion. That turns it into a cycle that seems like it's real. Once again, you are free. You can choose to replay the past and recreate it, or you can make peace with it and count your blessings so that you can have a new chance at life.

You are always imagining. Why not imagine something great: a best-case scenario, the possibility of something working out, a "what if" that goes right? Busy yourself by using your mental energy to create the best life for yourself. Each moment is another chance.

Never let anyone try to tell you who you are. Believing other people's ideas of who they think you are confines your potential. How can you allow the words or thoughts of others to enter your sacred mind and plant seeds? They can't...and you won't allow them. You will never again be limited by the words of others. You will never again allow anyone or anything to tell you that you can't. You are now owning your power, and understanding that what anyone says is just empty energy. It only becomes real when you start to overthink it and put what *they* think on a pedestal. Don't let anyone make you feel guilty for following your dreams or building your vision. Don't let anyone try to bring up some image they have of who you were in the past. You will no longer be confined. You will no longer feel guilty. You are brand new. You are pure greatness. You are who you want to be. You were born to imagine the best for yourself and make an impact. As a child, you always felt like you could do anything. Someone or something tried to tell you otherwise, and you are now remembering that you still have that within you. Your Inner Glimpse is reminding you of all your potential. You feel so free, so full of energy, and so alive.

Inner Glimpse Reminders

What we imagine is just as real as what we see in the physical. Bring your wildest dreams to life. Your vision is valid.

You are feeling a surge of power that's connected to a greater truth. You are starting to feel free every single day. These are reminders from your spirit, which you already understand. Inner Glimpse reminders always come at the right time. When you feel like you have been pushed to the limit or feel great pressure, something within reminds you that you can prevail. You become stronger and more refined. You start to see who you are, and a level of faith awakens within you that helps you get through those trying moments. Your life gets shaken up sometimes so you can start reimagining greater. Instead of remaining in a cycle that depletes you, you feel a newfound freedom and empowerment that lifts you higher and higher. Don't be afraid of moments that test you. You are literally being born into a new light, because you have received an Inner Glimpse reminder that you have immense strength to come out on top. Don't be afraid of life. Don't judge yourself by the fact that things happened to you. It makes you greater, and you can actually look back and be thankful that you have now recreated a whole new experience. The main thing you must always remember is that you can imagine greater for yourself. Whatever happens, think from a greater perspective so no situation has the power to limit you.

It Can All Be So Different Right Now

Imagine the best version of yourself, and begin acting, thinking, and feeling as if this is who you are right now. The power of being and owning the state of your desired reality is what aligns you to attract everything.

What are you currently imagining? Do you believe that it can all be so different for you? It can—and you can see everything from a new perspective. Your imagination is your powerhouse. Each image you call upon brings in a whole world of thoughts, feelings, and ideas attached to that one vision. I am sure you have experienced moments of feeling so positive that all you could imagine, see, and feel were great emotions and experiences. When this happens, it's like your entire world has a cover of bliss over it. No matter what is happening, you just can't see it any other way than what you have imagined. This is the power you have. One thought or vision attracts other thoughts and images that paint your world the way you see it from within. Things on the outside reflect these images in your mind. Think of how much you have changed in a month or a year. All of this is evolving in your inner world, and you alter your external experience as you begin to realize who you really are. Knowing this, how can the present moment be different for you? You can start by changing what you are imagining right now.

Reimagining Protocol

The Reimagining Protocol consists of specific steps that have worked miracles in my life. Instead of looking at every situation as is, I have changed how I see what is happening around me. This has turned everything around in my life in such a positive way that I have decided to share it with you. You can start using this tool as a way to hone in your mental powers and redirect your emotional state into a desirable one. You will no longer be swayed left or right emotionally. You'll start to think in terms of solutions instead of problems. You'll notice your mind operating in a way that allows you to be naturally optimistic no matter what life throws your way. My hope is that you build strength, awareness, and an understanding that you can redirect yourself and your mental state at any time. You don't have to stay stagnant or get lost in things that are happening to the point that you lose yourself. What's real is how you choose to feel and see things, not what it is trying to provoke you. You have a choice at every moment. Start deciding.

Turn Any Situation in Your Favor

Imagine that everything suddenly shifted in a positive direction for you.

Is there something that's happening in your life right now that you want to change? You can. Start reimagining the experience the way you want it to be instead of how it is. Your reimagining power lets you see the world the way you want it to be by visualizing a new path instead of accepting your external experience as final. For example, let's say there's something you want to happen for you, and a situation comes up that makes it seem like the outcome you want is impossible. Instead of accepting this, reimagine the situation working out for you. This changes the results you get. Don't accept rejection as final if you feel it in your heart that something better was meant for you. Instead of limiting yourself to that one experience, bless what or who tried to make it seem like it wouldn't work for you, and turn the situation in your favor. Too many people give up on their dreams just because of a perceived rejection. You can't stop your vision. It was planted in you. Begin living your life by mentally seeing your world the way you want to experience it physically. Use this technique as often as you can. You'll start to notice a new energy of optimism and determination that can't be stopped. Anyone who has succeeded in life has learned that a no is not a final answer. You can turn any situation in your favor. Start now. See life how you want it, and watch everything around you shift.

See Yourself in a New Light

Imagine yourself as a healthy, positive, vibrant, energetic, magnetic, loving being. Let your mind be filled with strong, positive visions of yourself. You are greatness. You are strong. You are whole and complete already. Accept it, and allow yourself to have this mindset.

How do you see yourself? How do you define who you are? Is there potential in your self-image? Is it positive? The way you look at yourself and what you silently affirm is constantly producing your outcome. You no longer have to downplay your greatness or play the role of pretending to be small just to fit in. You are pure greatness. Accept this, and allow that feeling to flow through you. When you are empowered, self-assured, and positive about who you are, you can impact others and the world in a magical way. You can be the voice that reminds people that they, too, can accept their greatness. The way you see yourself is the most important thing you'll work on in your lifetime. Your self-image impacts your mental and emotional wellness. Start seeing yourself how you want to be. Reimagining a desired state begins with knowing that you can always get better. Create the most positive self-image by loving who you are. Don't spend another moment acting against yourself. Don't let limiting self-judgment thoughts keep you low. See yourself in a new light. Imagine yourself at your goal, as if it is already done. This recreating and reimagining doesn't mean that you are lying to yourself. You know what is a lie? When you doubt yourself. When you create false fears. When you think of worst-case scenarios. All of these things require your imagination and mind to concoct them. Instead, let's switch it up and imagine the best. It all requires the same energy, so you might as well see yourself in a new, positive light that nourishes you and supports your inner wellness.

Put Love Where There Was Once Pain

Don't let situations make you bitter. Keep your heart open through it all. Let go of all grudges. Release the past. Forgive yourself. Do it for your physical, mental, and spiritual health. You deserve your inner peace and clarity more than anything else. Welcome it right now.

Take your power back right now by putting love where there was once pain. This pain can be from yesterday or years ago. No matter what, think love. When you put love into situations that try to take your mental and emotional energy, you automatically free yourself from the repetitive, hypnotic cycle that keeps you stuck. Reimagining love instead of pain is your power to shift your inner world. This changes everything for you. All heartbreak, regret, guilty feelings, and trauma automatically lose power. You no longer allow them to fester inside of you. You put love where there was once pain. This love comes from understanding that you are not that identity or experience of what once was. You are renewed today, and free to forgive yourself. Each time a negative thought or feeling comes up, automatically project love toward the image in your mind. You'll start to notice how liberating this is, and how much stronger you become by taking your power back through love. Elevate, and begin to reach new heights. You are free from it all.

Have Hope in All Situations

One thing I have realized is that everything always ends up working out— sometimes even bigger and better than you could have imagined. Remember this when you feel like you're in a hard place or when you're being challenged the most. Believe in where you're headed. See the bigger picture.

The ability to have hope during the toughest situations and circumstances shows just how resilient and strong your spirit is. It is so easy to assume that something is going badly or won't work out simply because of external appearances. As a person of strong faith, you can never allow tangible things to influence your internal faith. You are the visionary, the seer, and the believer in great possibilities. Your power to alter your experiences is to have hope in all situations. You can start doing this right now. How do you see your current situation? Is there something going on in your life right now that you can put the power of hope behind? Today is the day to begin having hope in all situations. This will naturally alter how you experience life, because you won't rush to the emotion of doubt. Instead, you'll find yourself rising above any illusions that try to bring you down into fear. You can access your inner super-power of hope anytime you need it by changing your perspective on what's happening in your life. Always have hope in all situations.

Constantly Reimagining

The entire universe supports you; your expression, your vision, your goals, and your dreams. There's so much energy being given to you right now. You have the power to do something great with it. Refocus, reimagine, and recreate everything.

The goal of this chapter is to help you free yourself of mental images that create fear and doubt in your life. It begins when you stop living in the past by reimagining everything from a greater perspective. Once thing I have realized is that people focus too much on the negative when they picture what is possible for them. You are always using your energy to create scenarios in your mind. Why not see the results you want? You truly can. Stop the overthinking right at this moment, and see the opposite of any draining thought. The more you constantly alter your inner world (thoughts and feelings), the more you'll start to see how natural it is for you to change anything in your life. Imagine the best for yourself. Take your mental power back, and see the world exactly how you want it to be.

Key Points

- *Each moment is a new experience for you to imagine something greater.*
- *Remember, all is mental. What you constantly imagine is what you're playing out emotionally and creating into your life.*
- *You can't spend another moment living in the past and imagining what went wrong and the regrets you once had. Snap out of it. You have the ability right now to see yourself in a new light.*
- *You are designed, supported, and connected to the greatest source.*
- *Keep your energy light instead of focusing on the burdens of the past. Anytime you feel restricted by a past thought, you are choosing to attach your identity to an experience that's no longer there.*
- *You can see the world how you want it to be by visualizing a new way instead of accepting the external experience as final.*
- *Imagine yourself at your goal, as if it is already done.*
- *Don't spend another moment acting against yourself. Don't let those limiting self-judgments keep you low.*
- *Take your power back right now by putting love where there was once pain.*
- *The ability to have hope during the toughest situations and circumstances shows just how strong and resilient your spirit is.*
- *Imagine the best for yourself. Take your mental power back, and see the world exactly how you want it to be.*

6

Living the Accelerated Life

Living the accelerated life is when you enter the vortex of miracles and blessings knowing that you are a spirit and a powerhouse. You claim your divinity and connection to the Source that provides you with every single breath. You become aligned with your spirit and live your purpose from your heart. You are no longer playing the game of competition and lack, or even thinking in terms of scarcity. You know you are abundant and infinite, with access to free energy outside of space and time. The accelerated life is all about gratitude and awareness for the depth and richness of life. You have to know that you already have the key and the connection. You are already chosen and gifted. You are a genius and a creative force. You have to start living your life knowing this. You were born this way, and you know this deep within you. Once again, this is all just a reminder to get activated so you can claim what has always been there for you. Living the accelerated life is a choice. The energy state you're in creates a strong magnetic field around you that matches how you think and feel. Are you fully aware that you are unique? Do you know that nobody can do what you came here to do? Are you following your heart daily? Do you listen to your inner guidance? Are you in a state of gratitude for life? Do you notice the subtle energy beaming through your body and all around you? Do you notice the synchronicities and signs? Ponder these questions for a moment. Feel who you really are. Feel your essence, and see how energized you become. This is the accelerated life.

Things will start to accelerate in your favor in every area of your life. Be ready for it, and start being grateful today.

When you acknowledge your divine nature and accept who you are, you start to move differently. You start to think and feel in a way that gives you so much energy to live your life fully. You start to appreciate the little things, and find greater meaning in making an impact and sharing your light with the world. Living the accelerated life is acknowledging who you already are. Somewhere down the line, you forgot that you are a powerful spirit, and that things were always magical when you were a dreamer. When you were a child, anything was possible. You still know this deep within. Your ability to imagine is your superpower. You can make a great difference by knowing and accepting this. You will feel empowered to live your life fully. All stagnation is removed when you accept living the accelerated life as a natural state for you. This is something you're remembering and beginning to accept. I am sure you have noticed things miraculously working out for you when you just believed in them and felt good about them. What you naturally believe must happen for you...and it always does. The accelerated life is living by faith and trusting the unseen. You'll feel a surge of new energy that propels you forward because you have decided to accept your divine nature as a powerful spirit who can make great miracles happen.

Great things are happening for you at an accelerated rate. Even things that seem to be going wrong or ending are just a redirection toward something bigger and better. Allow the emotional, mental, and spiritual clearing to take place so you can be renewed.

Starting today, you will accept yourself and love who you are. You will forgive yourself and begin to accept instant healing. Your heart and mind will expand; you will discover a greater meaning in life and a deep desire to express your purpose. When you start to rise out of the mental ashes that try to keep you in the darkness, you begin to see more clearly. You gain a new perspective and a sudden drive to be the best you can be. Your total self-acceptance right now will liberate you. Living the accelerated life also means you have reduced and removed excess mental and emotional weight that has kept you blind to your natural state. This can no longer go on. We need someone like you to dream, imagine, and be a part of what humanity needs right now. We need more activated people who love themselves and have recognized their divine power to make an impact. The more we are stronger within, the more we can change, empower, and restore our communities, country, and the globe as a whole. Individual impact starts within. The changes you make on the mental and emotional level ripple out into the world and alter the energy field of the planet. You have to understand how impactful you truly are. You can create momentum and shifts simply by being you.

You Have Officially Entered the Accelerated Life

Your path is being cleared right now. All blocks are officially removed. It is only upward from here. You're going to experience an unstoppable acceleration. It's time to start receiving.

Starting today, you have officially entered the accelerated life of miracles and great blessings. This new state of living comes from knowing that your divine nature is already blessed. This mindset is about loving yourself so the energy in your mind, body, and spirit work in unison to provide deep inner changes to expand your natural state of being. Entering the accelerated life is speaking power over all situations, every single day. No matter what is happening, you feel hopeful and optimistic. You have so much enthusiasm for life. You walk by faith as a magical being. Everyone around you feels this from you. You become a sign of hope for others, and they feel that anything is possible for them when they are around you. Living the accelerated life impacts your energy in such a way that you radiate love, compassion, purpose, and understanding. This is not a process. This is who you are when you accept yourself right now. Always think, feel, and believe that you are living the accelerated life, with so much energy to do whatever you want in your lifetime. Be the example of richness, beauty, excellence, love, and wisdom. Shine your inner light, and others will remember that they, too, were born great.

All Situations Work in Your Favor

The accelerated life means every single thing, good or bad, is always working in your favor. This is a mindset shift that you can proclaim daily. You can change your perspective about any situation at any time. Feel this feeling right now: Everything is working in your favor. Even in the midst of what appears to be a crisis is a realignment for something greater. If you dwell on things solely as they appear without the wisdom that it is all working in your favor, you can become too caught up in external appearances rather than the mental images and spiritual faith you naturally have. What we see on the outside requires meaning from within us. We are constantly interacting with the outside world by attaching meaning, thoughts, and perspectives to what we see. Even though what is happening might not be how you see it, your choice in how you choose to perceive it influences how you respond. In the accelerated life, you consciously decide what everything means for you from a greater perspective. You'll go from being triggered and overreacting to having wisdom and understanding that help you remain optimistic and hopeful. There is no rejection or end. Everything is always reshuffling to bring you to a greater place. That is the perspective to nurture when you see things on the outside that might not fully support your inner vision/goals. From this moment on, say to yourself on a daily basis, "All situations are working in my favor!" This can be your declaration over anything at any time.

Daily Blessings

You are always blessed. You have to feel this way and speak it boldly. You are extremely blessed. Living the accelerated life means you see the blessings that are happening in your life at every single moment. Not only do you recognize and acknowledge these blessings, you always feel that you are naturally a highly blessed individual. Everything you touch, partake in, and intend to do always has the energy of blessings surrounding it. You feel this feeling right now, and it reminds you of your natural essence. You are a miracle. Think about how long you have been receiving. Think about all that's taking place in your life at every moment, everything that's filled with reminders of the source that sustains you. Blessed people are always grateful and to the whole world. They appear lucky. We all see people on the outside, but understand that we each have our own unique inner world that has an energy signature we project outward. What are you radiating? Do you project blessings? Do you shine a bright light of enthusiasm and hope? Blessed people impact others as a way of sharing the overflow. You will always receive because you live the accelerated life of miracles and great blessings.

You Win at Everything You Do

Feel like a winner every single day. No matter what your past or what has happened to you, never feel like you have failed. Start looking at everything as a learning experience so it can take you to the next level. So many people spend so much precious energy judging themselves about what didn't work or what went wrong. It is also a perspective and a choice if you are deciding to give your attention and energy to a negative outlook. When you see your life as blessed and you choose to live the accelerated life, you know that you are a winner in every way. All that you touch is golden. Feeling like a winner at all times, you acknowledge yourself as capable of magnificent things. This is the kind of energy that will propel you forward and retrain your mindset to see things as potential instead of loss. The more your mind gravitates toward what you can learn from a situation, the more you gain a solution-oriented mindset. The rate at which you succeed is connected to how much you have started to accept yourself as a winner already. Nothing in life is as bad as it seems when you remember that you are filled with so much potential to make a difference right now. You can completely shift your entire life in this moment, starting with your mindset and taking action forward. The accelerated life is all about powerful declarations and self-belief that you are destined for greatness because you were born with this ability. The difference between you and anyone else doing incredible things in this world can be found in your level of faith, self-belief, and dedication to daily action to be the best you can be. We all have the power to express our God-given talent. The source has provided us with all the codes. Start feeling like a winner daily. At every moment, make that your affirmation, and own it as your truth. You have already won just by being here. You are magnificently designed and optimal in every way. You were chosen for this. Feel that energy, and start moving like the winner you are.

You Thrive in the Areas of Health, Mindset, Business, and Relationships

You naturally thrive in every way. Think about the fact that you can decide to get better at every moment, and the entire universe will support you. Thriving is a part of your DNA. You have this upward energy that makes all your connections very special. Once you understand the importance of your inner wellness, you thrive externally. I want you to take some time to recognize your own divinity and who you are. Dedicate yourself to thriving in your health by accepting that you are already healthy. The inner you is filled with a strong support system that is working every single second to make sure you are together. Now, let's get your mind in that state, as well. You are completely okay and thriving in every way. Let your mind accept that for a moment. Make this your predominant thought so you can step to the side and walk in your power. You can make the choice right now to be the best you can be by thinking and feeling that you are always thriving. Once you feel comfortable in this state, you will begin to see things around you take a positive turn for the better. You become a better example as a leader in your business, community, and work environments. You create a better home and even healthier relationships simply by thinking and feeling that you are always thriving. Your mental inner shift creates a whole new world for you. You don't have to wait for the outside world to change to start feeling that you're moving upward. Expand from within, and let that energy move all around you.

Accelerated Manifestation

When you've accepted that you are living the accelerated life, you will start to notice instant manifestations and signs around you that project the thoughts and feelings you're having. Things accelerating in your life begin with you understanding that there is no separation energetically between you and the state you desire. You go from merely thinking about it to actually owning your desired reality as your truth right now. You stop seeing your life as a future destination, and proclaim it as your now. This is when things begin to accelerate. With a combination of self-love and openness in your heart, you begin to create a vortex of possibilities that pulls everything forward. You really believe in your dreams. You'll notice how quickly your thoughts are coming to life. This will happen in conversations. You'll see things showing up all around you. You'll notice how the world is starting to reflect your inner state of being because you are aware of it now and intentionally empowered. You feel so alive and so motivated to be aware of all this. You have newfound hope, and you are even beginning to dream bigger. You will start to notice your imagination waking up again, proceeding from limitations to unlimited possibilities. This will be a time you receive so many ideas to make an impact, both in your life and in the world. You'll find yourself wanting to make a difference in how you live, what you allow, and the things you tolerate. You know you are manifesting instantly and seeing miracles daily. You are living the accelerated life. You can't really explain just how it is all happening, but your faith in yourself is pulling major strings and creating incredible alignments. Start noticing how your inner shift provides a whole new world all around you. Recognizing your inner creations and seeing them manifest is where you start to feel the most empowered. This will create a feeling within you that you can't describe in words. For a moment, you have stepped outside the structure of how things seem to be and entered the way they truly are: complete inner freedom. There is no *they*, or any idea of someone stopping you. It is all in your mind to own who you are and live the life you want. Break free from the concept of mental limitation, and manifest/create the life you want intentionally.

Accelerated State of Mind

You no longer have time to partake in limiting conversations. You can no longer talk down to yourself. This is a no-go for you. You have entered the accelerated state of mind that moves you into thinking and feeling the life you want into existence. Each thought pulls to you the feelings and energy that matches it. This is why, when you feel negative, you see the world as doom and gloom. When you feel alive and positive about yourself, you see the brightness, possibilities, and ability you have within you. To maintain an accelerated state of mind, you must stop yourself in your tracks when you find yourself being pessimistic or negative about life. Do not allow these energies to occupy your inner world. You are precious, powerful, and pure. You know this already because you were born with it. All of that mental chatter, doubt, and overthinking is the biggest illusion that distracts you from living the life you deserve to live. It's time to put this to an end. Anything that doesn't show you your own true potential is a lie to distract your energy from who you are. Reclaim your accelerated mind. When you take back your power, you start to see that you are thinking differently about how you see the world. You become part of the solution and stop creating unnecessary problems that don't exist. You start to see humanity in a new way. You remember that we are all sharing this experience together, and things aren't as heavy as they initially seemed. This new state will provide you with fresh ideas and new opportunities. You'll notice that you get your work done more efficiently and find yourself with a desire for life and creativity. You are a part of this vast universe. You have a purpose here, so start thinking in the accelerated state of mind.

Every Situation Is a Blessed One

One of the most liberating feelings is knowing that all is just. There are things that happen in life that we can't explain. The outer world is a manifestation of the inner world. When you see someone having a certain experience, you shouldn't judge it whether it seems good or bad to you based upon outer appearances. You have no idea what they are learning from that situation, or what is going on in their inner world. You can choose to start seeing everything as just. All is working toward the highest good, for each individual and for the collective. The more you stop trying to control every little detail of life, the more you create trust within yourself that every situation is blessed. We have all been in situations that initially seemed "bad," when truly, they ended up turning in your favor. This is why, when you think and feel blessed, you put that energy out into the world. Don't burden yourself with trying to decipher why something happened the way it did. Just breathe and move forward. You are always blessed, always uncovering a new direction. Try looking at the toughest situations as blessings trying to reveal themselves to you. This accelerated way of thinking keeps you out of the negative mindset and helps you move more faithfully.

Your Life Will Seem Like a Miracle to the World

The accelerated life starts within. This is an inner world that only you can initially see when you are optimizing yourself and evolving. All of the inner work you do and the love you create within yourself will begin to manifest in how you live, treat others, and create in this world. You are always building your inner foundation, and this gets projected into the world. A lot of the time, we only see the results of what someone has created; we never see the depth, the transformations, the inner alchemical transmutations taking place. This is why the success of others appears like a dream. They are literally dreaming it into existence, and we only see the outside. It is the same for your success. All the wisdom you have gained will open inner doors for you that make you stronger, wiser, and more connected to yourself...and more blessed on the outside. You become an example of what the source can provide when we decide to believe in ourselves. This new way of living will make it seem like you have discovered a secret possessed by only a few, when in reality, you have simply accepted who you are and remembered your true inner power. You are a powerful spirit, and you came here with a great purpose. You will walk the Earth reminding others that they, too, can do it. We all share a strong connection that creates motivation. This is not just for a small group of people. This is for you, too. You can have what is possible because *you* are the miracle. Literally take a moment to take that in. You are the miracle in this life, and feeling this as your truth will help you reclaim your natural state today. This is the beginning of your accelerated life. If you have already been living it, congratulations! There are more blessings in store for you. Be ready.

Key Points

- *Living the accelerated life happens when you enter the vortex of miracles and blessings, knowing that you are a spirit and a powerhouse.*
- *Know that you already have the key and the connection. You are already chosen and gifted. You are a genius and a creative force. You have to start living your life knowing this.*
- *When you acknowledge your divine nature and accept who you are, you start to move differently. You start to think and feel in a way that gives you so much energy to live your life fully. You start to appreciate the little things, and find greater meaning in making an impact and sharing your light with the world.*
- *Starting today, you will accept yourself and love who you are. You will forgive yourself and begin to accept instant healing. Your heart and mind will expand, and you will discover greater meaning in life and a deep desire to express your purpose.*
- *You are always blessed. You have to feel this way and speak it boldly. You are extremely blessed. Living the accelerated life means you see the blessings that are happening in your life every single moment.*
- *Feel like a winner every single day. No matter what your past was or what has happened to you, never feel like you have failed. Start looking at everything as a learning experience so it can take you to the next level.*
- *Thriving is part of your DNA.*
- *You don't have to wait for the outside world to change to start feeling like you're moving upward. Expand from within, and let that energy move all around you.*

- *When you see someone having a certain experience, you shouldn't judge whether it seems good or bad to you based upon outer appearances. You have no idea what they are learning from that situation, or what is going on in their inner world.*
- *You have entered the accelerated state of mind, and you are moving toward thinking and feeling the life you want into existence.*
- *You are the miracle in this life, and feeling this as your truth will help you reclaim your natural state today.*

7

YOUR MENTAL ECOSYSTEM

We have discussed many times the importance of mental health and wellness. I wanted to incorporate something crucial in this book: the concept of managing your mental ecosystem. What is your mental ecosystem? What are the ideas, thoughts, and beliefs that dictate your experience and how you represent yourself and use your energy on a daily basis? There's more to who you are than meets the eye. You are constantly renewing yourself through your mental world when you learn new things, read new books, and expand your horizons. The deep desire to evolve opens your imagination and activates your ability to dream once again. The most important lesson, I believe, is learning how to balance your inner and outer worlds. Understanding yourself, your thoughts, and how you can alter them opens you up to a world of possibility. You don't have to live your entire life in a loop of repeated behavior and thoughts. Don't claim a mere state of mind as who you are. You can get better at any second. You already have access to unlimited wisdom. Listening, connecting, and tuning in with yourself brings you back to your natural state. We live in a world that is constantly tugging at your attention to focus on everything outside of yourself, to the point where you attach your identity and meaning to something that is fleeting. Everything all around you is constantly changing. Nothing is as solid as it appears. Inner stability, self-development, and recognition of your divinity come from remembering that your mental ecosystem belongs only to you. When you manage your inner world with powerful self-belief, a strong spiritual nature, and faith in the unseen, you become unstoppable. Everything on the outside becomes second nature to your strong stance. The strength of a tree comes from the depth of its roots. This is why you must cultivate, discover, and understand yourself first.

Rule Your Inner World – Build Your Inner Architecture

How do you treat yourself? Do you dream big on a consistent basis? Does your imagination show you possibilities? Your inner world is the one you get to build for yourself, with the wisdom and understanding that you can create the life you want. Understanding how powerful you are comes from recognizing that the life force is present within you right now. It is constantly giving to you. You must start by realizing your spiritual nature and your essence. There's so much more to you. Your mind only currently sees what you believe to be your truth. Everywhere around you, there are people who think and feel trillions of different things. There are so many different inner realities taking place. You have to know that your inner world is a sacred space. Who created the inner world you are currently agreeing to? Are these your own thoughts? Have you built up your own mental ecosystem the way you want it? Do you feel good about yourself? Are you always optimistic and hopeful? If not, who told you to doubt yourself? Why can you so easily give in to the possibility of something going wrong instead of right? These are reflective questions meant to help you ponder just how much you are actually dictating your inner foundation. When you see how you are representing your most sacred, special, and private inner world, you will start to automatically shift. You'll think for yourself, realizing that you don't have to agree with thoughts that are actually limiting. You are free to stop thinking that they are real, or that they are something you must abide by. You no longer have to agree with negative thoughts or ideas of yourself that do not belong in your mental ecosystem. When you don't have strong inner roots, refinement, and strength to build from the inside out, you easily can allow others to decide what this state is for you through suggestion or influence. The fact that someone's opinion or words can easily shift your inner world in any way shows that you're still allowing the outside world to constantly sway you left and right.

You're getting better daily. A new you is coming alive. You feel it happening in every area of your life. So many inner shifts are occurring to help you reach new heights. You're evolving daily. You can no longer hide from your greatness. You can't deny your power.

What you need to know right now is that you are extremely powerful. You have an essence within you that is all about live giving, dreaming, evolving, imagining, health, abundance, and major blessings. You are a walking blessing. Just think of all that went into your design, your biological existence, your mental ability, and your aliveness. The balance of the inner and outer worlds is perfectly sustained. You were chosen and designed in an immaculate way that demonstrates expansion. If you don't stop to recognize these basic things, you won't be able to see or experience miracles, because you'll focus on what's missing instead of celebrating, accepting, and acknowledging your pure greatness. These aren't just words; this is deep truth that resonates with everyone who can see beyond the illusion that something is wrong with them.

Don't think your life is a coincidence. You're here for a great reason. You are the light that will impact the world. See beyond the illusions and limitations. Let yourself feel empowered. Claim your divine state as your truth. Anything else is unworthy. Be great!

If you don't believe that you were created as a whole, complete being at the core level, you'll remain open to outside impressions that will give you the illusion that something is missing from you. When that illusion is impressed upon your mind, you'll feel a sense of lack, when in reality, you are already complete. All has already been given to you. You gain access to this through recognition of self and praising the gift of life. This becomes a turning point for you because you understand your basic divine powers. When you don't see who you really are, you allow the world and/or society to tell you who you are. So many people will try to sell you an identity, when honestly, it's all about simply accepting your greatness. The source has provided all that you need within you. Once you get the mental aspect in order by remembering your own nature, you open the inner doors, and the blessings start to pour in nonstop. You are always blessed and provided for. Anytime your life has changed, it has always started with a new thought about yourself that goes back to remembering that you have this power. There's always a sudden rush of energy that snaps you out of mundane self-judgment and lets you step into liberating self-empowerment. This is the foundation of your mental ecosystem. You always can—

and you always will—do anything and everything you imagine is possible.

Your Own Inner Life Laws

What do you live by? What is your life motto? What dictates your level of faith? How much do you believe in yourself? What do you allow in your life? What are your standards? Have you created your own life laws? When we talk about building your inner mental ecosystem, the most important questions that arise have to do with what you have allowed to dictate your life. If nothing is real but what we choose to agree to as truth, what can you reflect on right now, then remove or recreate? What ideas are you binding yourself to? Remember, you are free to do and be who you want to be. You can provide the greatest value to humanity knowing your inner divinity. Your inner life laws come from what you declare governs your inner world. For example, I like to say that my life law is that I believe in myself in all situations, no matter what is happening. This life law helps me see beyond current circumstances as final. It allows my spirit to remember that all is just a moment, and that greater solutions will present themselves. The point of this is that I have declared in my mental state that I believe in myself, no matter what is happening externally. This declaration allows me to receive greater solutions in any situation instead of getting caught up in appearances. In your private journal, I want you to make your own declarations and life laws to live by to support your expansion. You can write as many as you want. If you were to create a mental world right now, what would you allow? These laws aren't meant to keep you confined. They are reference points that help you remember things. *I am someone who always believes that I can manifest what I want. I treat myself with the highest respect, and I allow only respect into my life. I am naturally blessed. I am connected.* Life laws are fun. If

my life law is that I am naturally always blessed, can you imagine the thoughts I am always having, and what I am
feeling inside? You become untouchable, and your mental
ecosystem strengthens with great power.

*You might keep getting a recurring
thought or feeling that you are worthy of so
much more. You might even be receiving
signs that it is time to finally do something
about it. It is time to finally take your power
back by declaring and deciding how you
choose to live your life. It all begins right now.*

You decide your inner truth. If something or someone
makes you feel limited, eliminate that from your mental
ecosystem. Override how you feel, react, and respond to it
in that moment. You no longer have to give power to opinions. That is a thing of the past. All you need to do is see if
something resonates with your truth in order to expand,
evolve, and become better as a spirit. Anything that comes
with limitation is an illusion. By now, you already know
this, and you are building a strong mental state free from
ideas that do not serve your growth and ability to express
your creativity. Anyone or anything that says you can't do
something is simply lying to you. You have creative abilities, and you can imagine/dream for a reason. You can
even alter how you respond to and treat past experience.
Positive or negative, things tend to replay in your mind,
which means that they live on within you even if they are
no longer happening in the physical state. If something is
recurring mentally, you can now choose to remove it from
your inner world or alter how you respond to it, removing
its energy charge.

One major question I always receive from people is how they can free themselves from some past event or thought they picked up that continues to limit them. If someone told you that you weren't good enough before, and you still believe it, that is a choice. You mind belongs to you. Your emotions are your private inner world. You can decide right now that you won't believe what someone has said about you or to you in the past. Do you know how free you'd be to live your best life every moment if you took your energy back on the mental level from these past events? You can free yourself right now. Don't waste another second replaying any degrading experiences or words. You are way too powerful. You have superpowers to alter your mental state, experiences, and vision toward a renewed and recreated you. Building your mental ecosystem also means revamping, reconstructing, and rebuilding using fresh, new material and ideas. It's all about enhancing who you are.

Your Mental Ecosystem Builds Your Energy Field

Everything is energy. Your thoughts and emotions all happen in a space outside of what you can see. This is something that can be felt in such a subtle way that we can't fully explain or understand the depths of it. You've probably already had the experience of picking up on the energy of someone before you could even communicate in words. There are subtle signs we're always sensing in many different ways. Our mind and body project what we have cultivated within us. If someone is feeling angry or sad, we can automatically pick up on those cues. We can read them—and most of the time, we feel them.

Things aren't as they appear physically. There are layers to people and situations that are usually made up of what they have built within their mental ecosystem. Understanding this will help you know how real their energy is and how we are constantly projecting our inner world outward. The mental ecosystem you have created becomes your energy field. You automatically start to signal what you feel and think. People all around you, near and far, feel the energy you are radiating. This is something that makes you attract your inner world to yourself. These attractions show you want you want to see. You're always looking for what resonates with your own inner beliefs or core values. Once you shift what you think and feel, you enter another world of connections, alignments, and manifestations. Just like anything else that is happening in your life, when you are fed up with something or someone, you decide that you want better or that you deserve better. When you see external situations not working out for you, you reawaken and reenergize yourself to do better. What is the first thing you should do? Go within, and say to yourself, "I can do better. I deserve better." This is what the Inner Glimpse is all about. You return to your natural state and build up from there.

The things we overcome only make us stronger and more powerful, if we choose to focus on the lesson and the gain, not the loss and what's coming to an end. There's something brighter, greater, and more promising in all situations. Focus on the bright side today. Stay positive about everything.

When we don't agree with the external results that we have been manifesting or experiencing, we take it as a lesson to learn and evolve. You can agree with the life you're currently living if you feel like it is balanced in terms of creating what you want, or you can switch things up and say,

"This isn't final—I can create better, because it all starts within me!" When you speak that boldly, you regain your power. Nothing is final. Make that your life motto. You'll go from being affected by all that is happening to observing and altering things to your liking. Remember, your mind seeks what validates its beliefs. You always gravitate toward what resonates with your vision. You make friends with people who think like you, people with whom you share a similar mental ecosystem. This is why, when you decide to evolve or change something about yourself, it triggers the relationships you already have. People may assume that you have changed. They may make it seem like it's negative, but what they are really saying is, "Hey, our mental concepts no longer align." Relationships and friendships are mostly maintained through values and ideas that connect people together.

In your evolution, you shift what you feel defines who you are, and that automatically puts you in a new world of experiences. You can literally choose what you want to experience. The only thing that maintains your current reality and experience is the mental states you have affirmed or agreed to as truth. This can be momentary, because we have all seen people change for the better. You can see someone go from the bottom to the top simply by deciding that it is time to do better for themselves. They can wake up one day and say, "I am tired of the way I'm living," and decide to change. That strong, firm stance is what creates energetic movement of life and possibility within them. They become unstoppable because they have started to demand better from themselves. You, too, can do that at any time. You are not attached to past identities or mishaps. You aren't mistakes or trauma. You are who you choose to be at every second. You wake up every day to reaffirm a past state or create a new one. If you like what you have been doing thus far, go ahead and keep thriving. If you feel tired and want to do better, you can choose that right now. I am not just telling you this. I am promising you that you have greatness, power, and infinite possibilities within you waiting to be expressed. You are a creative genius as a spirit, a being alive to experience this. You are a part of the vast universe, and it is no mistake or coincidence that you have arrived here. Stop allowing the illusion of what seems solid to keep you from what could be. Decide right now to build your mental ecosystem with the firm foundation that you can do, be, and accomplish anything you want. Make it fun. Keep it light, and most definitely be consistent. These words are breaking up anything within you that tries, even for a single second, to create doubt within you. You feel a newfound power and surge of energy for more life, more blessings, and more ideas. You are here to make a difference in yourself and the world. Nothing would be the same if you didn't exist. Remember that.

The universe is opening up for you. Everything is moving out of your way. You'll start to notice sudden shifts in creative energy, health, abundance, happiness, love, and peace. It's time for you to start receiving in a major way. Be open, and be grateful.

Your energy field will now begin to get stronger. People will feel connected to your magnetic energy, and you will remind all who encounter you that anything is possible. What you share with the world will show and be felt from you. You have what it takes, and this is why I want you to build from the inside out. I want you to be the strongest you have ever been. I want you to believe more than you have ever believed. I want everything within you to come alive so you can finally claim what has always been yours. You were chosen, and you are perfectly designed. You have been created to show what you can do with your imagination, mind, and vision. You can make wonderful things happen when you remember that everything starts within you. You are a powerful spirit, and you are not only remembering this, but accepting it as your truth. This removes all layers of doubt. It breaks all past energy that has been on your mind. You are instantly liberated, because all depends on what you choose in this moment. You have chosen to take your power back. You are no longer waiting for external validation. You are now walking with purpose, power, and great self-belief. These words alone magnify your Inner Glimpse. You are automatically being liberated and reconnected to what you already know. This is only the beginning for you.

What are you radiating?

What are you currently projecting, mentally and emotionally? What is the main signal radiating from your mind? Remember, everything is felt and sensed. Everything is produced by your inner projection of how you see things and how you respond to them. The most authentic way to live your life is to live from your inner truth. So many people create an inner secret world and think people won't feel it. They assume the world isn't reflecting what they predominantly think and believe. Being true to yourself and building a strong inner foundation reflects what you radiate to the world. Sometimes, you'll meet people and have no idea why you like them so much. There's something magnetic, positive, and light about them. You naturally gravitate toward them for a reason, and it feels good being around them. There are also people you have met who you quickly repel. There's nothing wrong with any of these states, because everyone is living out their inner own ecosystem, and the energy reflects that. The point I am making here is that you naturally pick up on these cues without words.

Now think of what you're radiating. What you put out isn't what you think people should believe about you. It's what you believe and build within yourself. People agree to your authentic state because you own it unapologetically. You're not waiting to change yourself in order for others to accept you. That's the most uncomfortable place to be. I'm sure you have experienced a situation in which you might have changed yourself for someone and later regretted it, because that one person still did what he or she wanted despite making you believe otherwise. You'll never be happy over the long term trying so hard to hide your true nature from someone just to be accepted. You have to accept who you are and be real about it.

You don't even realize the greatness that's waiting for you when you decide you want better for yourself. The declaration and choice you make is the catalyst that alters and shifts everything you attract to yourself. Start with your mindset. Start now.

The whole point of being the best you can possibly be is staying true to your inner self and what you have built. You can always alter things in order to get better. It makes sense for your evolution, but you never have to create resistance or restrictions, which only slow down your improvement. You must radiate your truth. You must reflect and decide if what you are currently projecting matches what you want to attract and experience in your world. You are the center of everything that comes into your life. Everything teaches you something about yourself, and most situations bring you closer to understanding that everything starts within you. No matter where you are in your life, you will get to a moment where this hits you, and you'll begin to make inner changes that soon reflect in your outer world. We all have seen it happen, whether you have gained new insight or new knowledge about self-improvement. When the mind shifts, reality shifts. It literally all starts with you.

What are you currently attracting?

Does your inner mental ecosystem reflect what you are currently attracting? If not, you can change that. You have to start believing that your inner world reflects your outer world. If you silently doubt yourself or speak negatively about what is possible for you, you automatically create dissonance between what is going on and what you expect to attract. You have to stop assuming that the outside will change on its own. You can no longer live your life building your inner world with weak, broken energy. You can't keep playing negative thoughts in a loop and wonder why things aren't changing and moving in your favor. You are 100% better off imagining possibilities and speaking power over your life than repeating unworthiness. You are pure greatness. You are a powerful spirit. The greatest investment will be to replace what is going on within you instead of being worried about how you are perceived. People spend way too much time working on the external alone in hopes of gaining approval, validation, and appreciation when they haven't gotten their inner selves together. You are better off building, revamping, and recreating what you want from the inside out so you can be stronger, wiser, and more connected to the pure resources of your spirit.

Everything on the outside is constantly changing. The people you meet, relationships, and your work life is always being altered from the inside out. The best thing is to create a healthy, mentally stable, optimistic you from the inside out. You'll start to see how much your life will change. Things will feel lighter, and you will feel the flow. You are no longer wearing a mask or hiding your truth. Speak boldly, move truthfully, and live authentically. What you attract shifts, because you are no longer trying to maintain an image. You are starting to be yourself and live your purpose. This is when you start to see magical things happen in your life. You begin to thrive. You'll feel an unstoppable momentum that propels you forward. You will begin to naturally feel at peace without even trying, because you know it is already there. Just accepting yourself automatically brings healing. It is not in the future, or "one day." It is now.

All is being felt energetically.

The world feels you. Everything within you goes out into the world, and you see what validates your core beliefs. If you know that your energy is being picked up on, what do you want your signature to be? What you put out magnetically finds you. This is very obvious, and I am sure you have experienced it many times. It feels as if things are happening more quickly the more we become aware of it. The projection of subtle energy makes you go back within yourself and be real with who you are. That is why it is the most important thing you can do. We have to be real with ourselves and stand up for what we believe. Your dreams should be projected so that everything can align for you. All that is moving within you is moving toward you. Let yourself be who and what you want to be, and allow it all to come together for you. Don't live a double life in which you feel and think one way about yourself, and try to play the opposite with everyone and everything. Step back and discover who you are and what you want, and believe that all is possible for you. The more you get clear, the better you become at receiving. You're not sending out mixed signals or uncertainty. Stand strong, no matter how long it takes you. You are a firm believer, and you will imagine greatness into existence each moment.

Strong Mental State

What is your current mental state? How do you feel about yourself? Reflect from within, and ask yourself these questions. Are you living in regret? Are you overthinking a situation? Do you believe you can dream your life into existence? Are you motivated to take action to get the results you want? You can start right now to have the mental strength to believe in yourself. You never have to be timid again, or concerned with things going wrong. Yes, things do happen in life, but what gets us through is our mental strength and inner foundation to fly higher each time we face adversity. The point of this whole book is for you to start cultivating undisturbed strength that comes from your spirit, to the point that you see clear solutions where there seem to be problems. You will never again be weakened by situations, or pushed to your wits' end out of fear or overthinking. You have now arrived, and with this arrival comes a new outlook on what seems to be happening in your life and what you choose to feel and think as a result. You'll find a sense of lightness, even in the heaviest situations.

Your mind will start to operate differently, because how you perceive life has changed. You'll start to have hope where you once felt hopeless. You'll start to feel possibility where there were once thoughts of limitation. You'll start to see beyond the structure of how things are, and begin to dream things into existence. Your strong mental state comes from self-value, self-belief, and self-determination. You are realizing that all is okay. You are taking the charge away from overreacting and overwhelm, and putting it toward attention to messages from your spirit. You stop allowing yourself to be controlled by small, fleeting things. What problem has ever lasted? Think about all you have lived through. The only thing that has lasted is what you have decided to continue to play in your mind. Some thoughts are long overdue for release. It's time to give them up. Can you just give them up right now? Do it for yourself. Let it finally go. It's time to make peace with yourself and open your energy to this new moment. We have lived and learned, and now is the time to move upward into our natural state and welcome the great blessings and peace that have always been here.

Consistent self-forgiveness frees up mental energy.

Make peace with yourself so your heart can expand and your mind can be at ease. Self-forgiveness is knowing that you are not defined by your past. Every moment is a brand-new start for you to recreate, reimagine, and redesign your life. Your potential is unlimited.

You know what depletes mental energy? Constantly being hard on yourself, and constantly criticizing/judging yourself about everything. Living in regret steals your life force and creative energy. You have no idea how great you're doing with each passing moment, but being hard on yourself takes away from your victories and accomplishments. You have improved in many ways and overcome so much. You are growing and evolving daily. Do you even recognize that? Do you even see who you have become over these years? What moves you forward is getting out of regret and into self-forgiveness. I practice self-forgiveness on a consistent basis. No matter what is happening in my life, I always take some time to forgive myself and tell myself that I can come back stronger. I automatically get an energy boost and feel so alive, knowing that all that matters is this moment. I free myself from it by making a declaration of forgiveness as often as possible. If you spend all your time in self-judgment, it creates a seed of doubt that you're not good enough, when in reality, you are a powerful sprit.

What moves you forward is acknowledging and making peace with what has happened so that you can do better today. It's not about what was. It's all about what can be in every moment. Start right now, and free up your mental energy. Let go of anything from the past (or even the last second) that has tried to deplete you. Switch up how you see it, and ask your spirit for solutions so you can feel the peace in this moment. May you experience a complete release from your past, and may you experience a renewal—mentally, physically, spiritually, and energetically, on the cellular level. You are forgiven for all of it right now. Allow yourself that forgiveness, and open your heart to receive your peace. It's a new moment for you.

Self-love empowers your mental state.

The biggest energy boost is loving who you are. This means fully accepting yourself and constantly giving your attention to all the good that is happening within you and all around you. Too many people base their worth on what others accept about them or their position in life. To wait until the distant future to accept your greatness or acknowledge the divine power within you takes away from this moment. You have to start loving every part of your being. Look in the mirror and see how alive you are. See how present you are. You are here in this moment, and you will no longer spend another second at war with yourself. You will no longer hide your potential. You will no longer dim your light. You will love the body you're in, no matter what your stage of evolution. You will not attach self-love to the outside. Imagine the millions of people who have lived life here on Earth. Where are they now? Will all the little details they stressed over matter today? It all dissipates. It all ceases to exist one day. Why not spend your time on Earth celebrating yourself? Celebrating how you see yourself, not how others see you? You are so beautiful and magnificent, and what makes you so great is beyond the physical. Create memories worth feeling, sharing, and learning from. Express yourself freely and openly. What is there to be afraid of? Nothing is confining you but a made-up idea in your head that you can't...when you actually can. All that you accomplish in this life creates an impact you leave behind—a touch of your energy.

Self-love will heal you, empower you, restore you, and open up new worlds within you and all around you. Self-love is the key to your mental, spiritual, and emotional health. Every aspect of your life thrives when you love who you are and accept yourself. It all begins with you.

Every little thing you overthink or worry about will pass. It will all be so far gone. Why spend another day in your mind wondering if you are good enough? Why not claim it instead? Why not be free and express your creativity? We need more people loving who they are so they can truly project the inner peace and love they feel out into the world. Be the example of self-love. The more someone accepts who they are, the more they allow creative energy to flow through them. Spending less time judging yourself opens your mind to creating, moving, expressing, and being what you came here to do. Whatever tried to limit you was lying to you. Whoever tried to make you question your worth did the same. Nothing and nobody can ever stop you or take away what is already in your spirit. You are lifted higher now, and you are completely remembering your greatness. You were chosen for this. Feel the love in your body, and shine more brightly.

A new you is born each moment.

Every second, you are renewed. Your body is constantly creating new cells. Your skin is being rejuvenated. Your organs are being renewed. The environment goes through seasons. Every day, we are born again. Every moment, we are recreated. The only thing that stays the same is the thoughts we hold onto in order to define ourselves. What are those thoughts? How can you start today to allow a mental renewal and accept your daily rebirth? You can start fresh every morning...or even every second. When you train yourself to live like this, you will recognize the power of the moment. What we do right now has unlimited potential when we are fully present and engaged. The way to live in the now and remain fully present is to accept that you are instantaneously renewed. You can build your inner world from the idea of affirming a new state. Anything that keeps you trapped in past thoughts is stealing from your current potential. Repeating those thoughts uses old material to build a new moment. Is it even worth it?

You are renewed every moment. Accept the new energy.

The body is so intelligent as it builds new cells from new material. You, too, can use new words, new beliefs, new ideas, and new thoughts to build up your mental ecosystem. Why be on repeat if it's not paying off? How are your current recurring thoughts expanding you? How are you being renewed if you are holding onto past identities that keep you stuck in negativity or make you feel like you're not good enough? Let go. Accept renewal right now. You have been given the free will to decide on new energy or remain the same. It is all a choice—consistent energy to allow newness in each moment. Begin today to speak power over every situation that is happening in your life. Visualize a new state, and ask yourself, "Who can I be right now?" You will discover an astounding amount of energy and inner power that really shows you what it means to live in the moment. You might have read about it before, but now, you will know through experience the power of now.

You are okay.

It is all okay. Up or down, good or bad. It is all okay, and we have to stop trying so hard to be connected to one moment to the point of chasing another. Things happen. We should believe it is okay, and that everything is refining us to be the best we can be. Good things are happening...as they should be. We celebrate and love who we are either way. Giving too much power to one side creates fear of the other, or yearning for goodness when you are, in fact, always okay. Think about that for a moment. You are okay right now. Breathe, and feel that sense within you. Every day, you do things to feel okay and at peace with yourself, and the truth is, that ability is always there. You might feel like you have to work hard to obtain it, and that is an idea. Things are always okay. If you make it your life's mission to try to make things okay, you are searching for what is there, but that outside search creates a feeling that is only fleeting, even when you are close to getting what you want or feel like you have received it. Feeling okay about everything creates within you a stabilized mood that can't be taken from you by the ebb and flow of life. You just know that you are okay and that all is well, no matter what is happening.

You can alter anything at any time.

You don't even realize the greatness that's waiting for you when you decide you want better for yourself. The declarations and choices you make are the catalyst that alters and shifts everything you attract to yourself. Start with your mindset.

As you begin to build yourself up, make sure to stay open to altering yourself at any time. Life is always about learning and growing. You are where you are so you can experience what you have and learn to become better. The exact moment you open yourself up to growing and moving forward teaches you so much about life. You will find

153

yourself evolving faster now. There's an acceleration that's happening in your life. You feel like the entire universe is opening up for you. It calls for an opening of the mind and heart to allow massive change. You are transforming in each moment, and the wisdom you had last month, or even last week, will seem so different today because you're learning at a level that seems out of this world. Most of your wisdom and insight will become intuitive. You'll find yourself trusting your own insight. You'll find that books and outer guidance only bring you back to yourself. Things will start to become more about listening to your spirit rather than thinking you have to go on a search in order to discover.

Now, things just naturally come to your mind, and you find yourself feeling things out more. This is going to require acceptance on your end. Trust yourself instead of questioning if something is random or a coincidence. More is being revealed to you now, and you must remain open in spirit and mind to altering what you think and believe at all times. Staying open means that you are allowing. Nothing is ever final, and that's what makes life exciting. Imagine if you were still holding onto beliefs from years ago. You would remain stagnant in those old ideals, even though you were evolving. It seems as though we are all returning to our natural state, which is trusting our own inner guidance, wisdom, and voice. This is an ancient understanding that is so natural to us. The more you trust yourself and believe in your visions, the greater the number of new paths that will open up within you and outside of you.

Constantly check in with yourself.

Make sure you're always checking in with yourself so that you remain balanced. Anytime you are feeling overwhelmed, take a break and recharge yourself. The most important thing I do consistently is self-care. Taking care of myself can mean going for a walk, spending time with people I laugh with, reading a book I enjoy, or watching a favorite movie. Look at the beauty and creation all around you. Appreciate people, since everyone you're sharing this experience with is a spirit. Think beyond what you see, and look deeper when it comes to life. There's so much happening within you and all around you, and sometimes, you need to spend time daydreaming, pondering, and just being. It's so important to know how to unwind and not overthink everything. Don't judge if you're doing anything right. Just appreciate where you are and move forward. Finding a balance between producing, creating, and dreaming is so important.

You're being healed and restored on the cellular level — spiritually, physically, and mentally. A new you is emerging, so be patient with yourself. You are transforming in so many ways. This is only the beginning of a grand life filled with strength, wisdom, love, and understanding.

When you are transforming, you need time to integrate all that you're learning. Everything doesn't have to be so structured and rigid. Do things the way you must, and do what feels fitting to your spirit. Listen to yourself and move with that inner energy. The days I feel like taking things in and relaxing give me even more energy the next day to express my ideas. I don't consider any moment a waste of time. Our creativity expands when we are relaxed. Too many people want to work every second, and feel uncomfortable when they are not busy. This is okay to do, but it is also okay to pause for a moment and recharge. Do what is fitting. Everything has its timing when you're in the flow.

When you want to relax, relax. There's nothing wrong with that. Find a balance, and continue being the best you can be.

See how you have been maintaining, building, and designing yourself.

Take a moment to see the results you've been getting. It is always so refreshing to see how much you have improved, no matter how big or small the changes have been. When you take a moment to acknowledge the results you have been getting, you give power to the blessings unfolding in your life. Celebration creates the most powerful momentum, because it is a state of gratitude for life. The joy and happiness you share within and without expand your heart and mind. The universe wants to provide more of that in your life. Take in the way everything you have committed to always happens. Let's say you decide for one month to create a fitness plan for yourself, and you consistently follow it. What results would you get? How different would it be from where you are now? How would your mind and body feel? Now think about a 30-day commitment to positive thinking and optimism. What results will you get by the thirtieth day? How would that rewire your brain and change your outlook? Anything you commit to on a consistent basis must produce results. This is very obvious. It's all about making the commitment to yourself in your own unique way. It is a must that the universe provides. Look closely at the results you have gotten thus far, and ask yourself, "Have I really committed to what I want to see?" Taking a look at all that's happening in your life is actually a fun way to see how you can alter your entire experience. Don't make things heavy or hard. As long as you remain open and optimistic, you will get where you want to go. The results are evident, and you can alter them as you like.

Always evolve.

Are the ideas you're fighting for or holding onto supporting your overall wellness in mind, body, and spirit? How much of what you think comes from within you? Be open to evolving. You can even outgrow what you once thought was the final answer in your life. We have all done that many times, and even looked back and laughed at the things we thought were our truth. Constantly learn, and always hold your values at the highest level. Consistently learning and evolving allows you to be open to receive. Remember, what someone sees in their mind is possible for them. If you naturally think things are impossible when someone shares a dream with you, then you're not keeping an open mind.

Entertain new thoughts so your experiences change along with what you attract. Constantly evolve mentally, and allow spiritual intervention.

Understand that everyone has access to and a pure connection with the source of all life. When someone imagines what is possible for them in their mental world, they believe in it. That is why arguing about possibilities (or even the need for people to see your vision as possible) is a waste of time. If you believe in something, then it is possible for you. Other people see your creation when you bring it to life, and they automatically shift into awe of what is possible for them. When your concept is in its initial vision state, they might question how you will make it happen. You don't want to be that person for other people. Always keep an open mind when it comes to ideas. Let others dream, and also allow yourself to dream. We are all in our own mental world, co-creating and sharing our visions as we produce them externally. What is possible for one might seem impossible for another based on everyone's individual level of faith, creation, and trust in what can happen.

So many people are prospering. There's hope for all, and we must shift our state of mind from lack to abundance. It's okay to dream, imagine, and believe in something greater. Lift yourself into the realm of possibility where all things can happen, and bring it into the world.

How can you think one idea is valid over another? How can you think one way of doing something is all there is? This way of thinking can keep you confined and defensive. You can be closed off and easily triggered when someone chooses to see the world differently. What is possible depends on what someone chooses to believe in and how open he or she remains to their natural, unlimited potential state. Next time you hear someone speaking of his or her wildest dreams, be encouraging. Never take anything personally. Even when someone doesn't believe in your vision, don't think of it as a big deal. You know your mental world belongs to you, and that you have your own direct connection to the source of life. What is in your heart will manifest because you believe in it. All you need to make wonderful things happen in this world is to believe in yourself, even in the most challenging times. Your results will produce natural believers, and you will inspire others to also follow their dreams—because you did. Commit to your personal evolution, and be open to new ideas.

Key Points

- *You don't have to live your entire life in a loop of repetitive behavior and thoughts. Don't claim a state of mind as who you are. You can get better at any second.*

- *Listening, connecting, and tuning in with yourself brings you back to your natural state.*

- *When you don't have strong inner roots, refinement, and strength to build from the inside out, you can easily allow others to decide for you through suggestions or influence.*

- *What you need to know right now is that you are extremely powerful. You have an essence within you that is all about live giving, dreaming, evolving, imagining, health, abundance, and major blessings.*

- *Stop allowing the illusion of what seems solid to keep you from what could be. Decide right now to build your mental ecosystem with the firm foundation that you can do, be, and accomplish anything you want.*

- *Your energy field will now begin to get stronger. People will feel connected to your magnetic energy, and you will remind all who encounter you that anything is possible.*

- *Make sure you're always checking in with yourself so you remain in balance. Anytime you are feeling overwhelmed, take a break and recharge yourself.*

- *Nothing is ever final, and that's what makes life exciting.*

- *Nothing and nobody can ever stop you or take away what is already in your spirit.*

8

YOUR ULTIMATE VISION –
LIVING YOUR PURPOSE

Every single day, a part of you awakens to remember that you have so much life in you. Even at your lowest point, there was always this inner empowerment that made you feel like you could do it. There hasn't been a single moment when you felt fully defeated. There has always been some kind of hope, a small amount of faith, and an inner reminder that you can. You have been lifted higher many times. You have learned so much in so many ways. Every single experience you have had up to this point has built you up with a strong foundation that shows you how resilient you truly are. You can never say it is over. You can't give up. Your spirit will not allow you. This is why, time after time, you bounce back. You will always get better and better. This is your genetic code, and part of your human ability. We are made to survive, learn, and grow through any situation. We get creative with ideas to find solutions to complex problems. When you start to embrace the fact that all is well and remember that you can figure it out, you connect with your ultimate vision. To remember your spiritual nature, you have to accept that you can't be defeated. It is not about being worried about what can go wrong, but more about standing in faith in what can go right. Living your purpose is living in spirit. You go from seeing the world as doom and gloom to actually seeing possibilities, blessings, and hope in all situations. You can receive wisdom and answers right now, in this moment, because you are ready to. You have always had this access, but your mind takes you away sometimes and tries to make things that are an illusion seem real.

May you receive energy and ideas to bring your dreams to life. May you get a sudden drive that is unstoppable. May you be lifted into a renewed mindset that shows you all is possible. May resources, opportunities, and connections align for you right now. It is done!

Your mind is very powerful. Imagine right now that you are feeling super happy and filled with joy. Everything is going right. Perhaps someone comes to you who is actually playing a joke on you, and tells you some bad news. You have no idea that they are just playing a joke on you. What happens to you? You shift away from that blissful state of happiness and joy, and suddenly, life loses its vibrancy. This took all of one minute. The words you heard shifted your reality, but you didn't know that it was just a joke. You accepted a belief and ran with it—mentally, physically, and emotionally. Your inner world was shifted by an illusion that was meant as a joke. Now you find yourself stuck in your head, playing the bad news over and over and emotionalizing it. You start to see your environment differently, and everything changes about you biologically. All of this happens so quickly...until you're told it is a joke, and suddenly, you find yourself swinging back to your bliss after switching your perception based upon the news you just received. What is the illusion, then? What you perceive depends upon how you respond...not necessarily if it's true or not. So many people are emotionally traumatized by illusions that they have concocted in their heads—illusions of perceived obstacles created out of fear. Sometimes, these illusions can come from others telling you that you can't, and you believe it...until you snap out of it and find out for yourself that you actually can do it. Your state of awareness is a choice, and with the example above, you will realize just how much you can choose the way you respond on a daily basis.

You're going to start speaking your truth more and living your life exactly how you want. Your purpose is being revealed to you. You can no longer play it small. This is your time.

In order to live your purpose, you must be unafraid of what can go wrong, and have an inner stillness of faith and trust that all is well and things can work out. Things happen in life sometimes that seem unpredictable, but how you choose to respond will determine what you continuously feel and accept as your truth. A strong inner foundation will prepare you for your life's mission. You'll know how to discern information and see beyond the illusions. You will be so firm in your faith and self-belief that nothing will ever take away your Divine Spark.

Follow the feeling and urge to live your dreams. That leap of faith will open many doors for you. Your purpose is calling. Listen to your spirit.

Once you get your mental affairs in order and balance your emotional reactions, you open yourself up to receive greater insight. If you spend less time overthinking and worrying, you give more time to possibilities, dreams, and hope. Through openness of the mind, you allow your inner spirit to communicate with your magnificent ideas, which are your ultimate vision. This is what people mean by listening to your inner voice. All of this naturally comes when you get right within and silence the mental chatter—out of empowerment, not force. You don't have to work so hard to do this. This is what you already are, and you are learning to accept it every single day. This is also why self-love and self-acceptance free you. You go from constantly overthinking and judging yourself to an openness that lets your mind and spirit integrate with your body. You start to feel more alive, connected, and expressive. This is the most beautiful place to be in, because you realize just how much of your life depends on your inner world. This balance opens up new dimensions within you that inspire your creativity to live your ultimate vision. Every single creator who has made something come to life knows that inner chemistry has taken place. Anyone who has overcome anything knows about that inner transformation. You transmute one state to give birth to another. We all have been there, and some of us are realizing this through these words. You are resilient, just as I am. We come out strong, and we will continue to come out on top. This freedom guides us forward into birthing our ultimate vision and living our purpose.

Where are you being guided?

What is your ultimate vision and purpose? I say *ultimate* because we all have been in situations that helped us develop new passions and interests. As we get closer to listening to our inner selves and following our hearts, our ultimate vision and purpose begins to reveal itself to us. What is constantly being repeated to you? What do you feel so passionate about that you could do it every single day without feeling like it's a job? What makes your spirit come alive, and your heart sing a fine tune of bliss? Have you been talking yourself out of your creative energy? Has fear stopped you from moving forward to bring your gift to life? It's time to finally take a leap of faith and just go for it. It's time to live boldly and thrive in uncertainty. You will go from *I need to make sure I am secure* to *I am secure because I am sure*. You will not live in fear of the unknown any longer. It's time to trust yourself. It's time to turn your dreams into reality. You offer something very special that only you can bring to life. You play a unique sound, and add a twist of color to life. The way you do this is completely unique to you.

Don't talk yourself out of your greatness. You can do it. You can make it happen. You can manifest your dreams. Feed your faith right now. Believe in yourself. Create the shift in your life through your mind. All is possible for you.

You have to stop thinking that you are ordinary, or that your talent is small. The power of the individual has to be reclaimed so that we can all thrive as a whole. When more people believe in themselves, we will have many incredible innovations, solutions, and expressions that allow us to evolve to new heights. We'll have more people who care to express kindness because they feel so deeply. Creativity opens up inner portals that remind you that everything is just a moment. You go from seriousness to a sense of awe in life. The details begin to take on a new light, and you share a giving-back energy because you have received so much in so many ways. This is why people who are highly blessed understand the importance of philanthropy and giving back as a state of knowing that we are all connected. It is better to see us all thrive and be our greatest selves because we awaken that light in others. There are no scarcity or limitation. There's abundance for all. Most of us need to start looking around and feeling this abundant force that surrounds us. It is beautiful and magnificent. It is you.

Do what you love.

This is the greatest time of your life. Why? Because you have discovered so much about yourself, and are finally taking bold action to move forward in doing what you love. You have so much to offer, and you are needed here to be yourself the best way you can be. This is the time to follow your heart and live out your dreams. You might want a sense of private time to work on your craft. Don't feel pressured to ever rush yourself. With every single thing I have created, I have allowed time for it to mature within me before I was able to express it. In a world where we see people producing and creating ideas, we assume that it happens overnight. Sometimes, your creativity and expression can reach a peak hour when you receive so much and put your vision together. Doing what you love also means trusting and operating according to your own timing.

Don't feel pressured by what others are doing or when they are doing it. Don't look for external manifestation of what others are creating to compare it to yourself. Look at other ideas as inspiration of what is possible. If they can do it, so can you, in your own unique way. Go within, and focus on cultivating and pulling together your own inner forces so your gift shines with your touch. Doing what you love means it comes from your heart and you enjoy every it step of the way, no matter what it takes or what happens. You are always learning, and more is always being revealed to you. Listen to your spirit and take the time you need.

There's no rush or pressure at all. Let your soul come alive. Shine your inner light.

Your ultimate vision is calling.

You can feel that tug of energy when your spirit is calling you to step into your authenticity. It is not about what others think about your dreams and ideas. It is all about what you are willing to do right now to listen to yourself and move into what has always been within you. I am just here to remind you of your greatness so you can receive this message as hope and a call to action to follow your heart. Living your purpose will mean so much to you. It is what you have always known and wanted to experience. No matter what has happened in the past, today is a new day to make the choice to claim your talent and express yourself boldly. The people who understand will show up. The resources will arrive. The opportunities will present themselves. It is all just waiting for you to decide.

If your decision means taking a risk to step outside the social norm, this is what you must do. If that means some people will be surprised or shocked by your bold move, well, that's also fine, too. You can't live another day carrying this creative genius within you that so badly wants to be expressed. You have received so much within you for a reason. You can't hide from this calling. It is coming alive, and wants to run the world as a beam of light that will touch every person who experiences your creative energy. You carry that right now. This is the time to start really thinking about what you want out of life. Don't let your mind talk you out of your greatness. Fear creates comfort in living in the mundane. There's heaviness when you don't bring what's brewing inside you to life. Your ultimate vision is calling. Please answer, and the rest will take care of itself.

Guidance

Ask, ask, ask! I can never stress this enough. Go within, anytime, and ask for guidance. Ask for things to be revealed to you. Every single day, if there is something you need a breakthrough on, or if you need answers for something that's on your mind, write down your request on a piece of paper and keep it with you. Once you ask, feel that the answer is coming. You can ask your inner self for guidance on your purpose, family, relationships, business…anything you feel you need clarity on. There hasn't been a single time I have not received an answer when I needed it the most. I took a few moments to really immerse myself in the moment of what I wanted to know, and sent out my request for guidance. You always have access to it as a greater vision, but when you forget that it is there within you, you experience stress, which creates the illusion of disconnection.

You have to start operating in the realm of possibility. Nothing is as solid as it appears. There's a life force energy and power surging silently in all of space. You are connected. You have access. Start believing in your inner power. Start accepting your inner gift. You are extremely valuable and blessed.

You are always connected. You are just coming to realize this. I am sure you have done this before through prayer, sometimes even when you felt like you were at your breaking point. We all know how to do this; we have always been doing it. Now you will do it confidently instead of always seeking outside advice on everything. You have access to the greatest teacher and guidance within you. You have access to answers that are perfectly tailored to you, which nobody else can fully understand. You are very complex, and your inner world is utterly sacred. No one will ever 100% know who you are and what makes up your way of thinking and feeling. Words don't even do this expression justice. Asking for divine guidance gives a clearer answer, and you can ask anytime you want. Feel safe, loved, and connected. You are never alone on this adventure. Celebrate that feeling.

Celebrate Your Life

Living your ultimate vision and purpose doesn't mean you're consumed with your own creation. It also means that you have a way of honoring other minds around you that are also bringing wonderful ideas to life. See and feel all that surrounds you. Enjoy all the variations and beauty that life has to offer. Everything has its own unique expression. Look at people as spirits with so much life in them, and honor the moments you share. We are all here together. There's joy in looking into someone's eyes and seeing that life force within them. We are always interconnected at the core. Sometimes, it's hard to imagine the vastness of the universe and how, in this moment, we all share this space together. Your life will continue to be enriched as you see the life in all things.

Lift your thoughts higher. Lift your vision higher. Lift yourself and others higher.

You'll continue to learn and co-create with others. Imagine the possibilities if we all encouraged expression, even if we didn't fully agree. The point is not to like or dislike something. Things are just the way they are. People will do what they do. How you feel about it only takes place within you, and the inner conversation you have exposes you to those thoughts. Everyone is living out his or her inner world, no matter what you think about it. The more you understand this, the more you'll learn how to just embrace expression, not necessarily how you feel about what is being expressed. This will save you so much time and make your connection with others more adventurous as you stay open to the creative life force. Look for ways to celebrate life and enjoy the blessings you have always been given. The ability to understand these messages and feel inspired, moved, and activated is truly a signal that you get it. You are connecting with your Inner Glimpse and reclaiming your Divine Spark right now.

Key Points

- *Every single experience you have had up to this point has built you up with a strong foundation that shows you how resilient you truly are. You can never say it is over. You can't give up. Your spirit will not allow you to. This is why, time after time, you bounce back. You will always get better and better.*
- *Once you get your mental affairs in order and balance your emotional reactions, you open yourself up to receiving greater insight. If you spend less time overthinking and worrying, you give more time to possibilities, dreams, and hope.*
- *It's time to finally take a leap of faith and just go for it. It's time to live boldly and thrive on uncertainty.*
- *There is no scarcity, and there are no limitations. There's abundance for all. Most of us need to start looking around and feeling the abundant force that surrounds us. It is beautiful and magnificent. It is you.*
- *You offer something very special that only you can bring to life.*

- *You are always learning, and more is always being revealed to you. Listen to your spirit and take the time you need. There's no rush, and there's no pressure. Let your soul come alive. Shine your inner light.*
- *Feel safe, loved, and connected. You are never alone on this adventure. Celebrate that feeling.*
- *Enjoy all the variations and beauty that life has to offer. Everything has its own unique expression.*

9

STREAMING – WHAT ARE YOU TUNING INTO?

What are you constantly giving your energy to? Everything is a stream of energy. In order to become aware of something, you have to choose to tune into it. One thing I have realized based upon personal experience is how much the existence of anything depends on the attention and energy we give it. I remember experimenting with the concept of completely taking my attention off of something that was happening, and realizing that it no longer existed in my world. I was so surprised to find out that my inner senses and point of attraction had completely removed me from even bringing it to my awareness. I was absolutely in awe of the fact that what is real in our world requires our consistent energy to validate it as real or as truth. When you are removed from it, it no longer has any meaning for you. Just think of how many things are happening all at once. There are so many realities, ideas, and concepts constantly flowing. You could have a conversation with someone new, and they might never have heard of something you are aware of. Biologically, we love to create associations that support what we think and believe in. It's like your mind goes on a search to validate the reality you have chosen by exposing more of it to you. It is up to you to decide what you want to tune into. Each time you choose to expand your awareness, you shift what you bring into your reality.

What are you focused on?

How do you see the world? How do you see your life? You must reflect on these thoughts for a moment to see if your outlook supports your vision. Sometimes, the greatest thing you can do is confront your inner views so you can see what is hindering you from growth, evolution, and great transformation. What are you constantly streaming about your own self? Your thoughts paint the world a certain way. Only you will see the world from that perspective. Think for a moment about a time when you were having a bad day and could only see negativity all around you. Things might have seemed dull; the vibrancy of life didn't exist in that state of mind. Now think of a moment when you felt great joy inside, and just saw life and beauty in the world. You probably felt energized and filled with so much hope. The only difference is within you. The outside world continues to be.

Even on your up days, someone near you might see the world as down; on your down days, someone else might see so many great things happening. All of this is taking place within you, and the way to alter it is to never take anything so personally that you feel drained or hopeless. We are always learning and moving higher. We are always evolving. The goal is to constantly shift your focus to the outcome you want so you don't remain in a negative state or take on a doom-and-gloom mentality. You have to remember how powerful you are. You can't just think all of this is random. Every single moment is beaming with so much life force. Every single thought is filled with so much potential. It's time to reclaim your view from the inside out and see all the miracles that surround you.

You attract what you primarily talk about and focus on. Nothing is a coincidence.

174

You have a choice right now to switch things up. How do you want to see your life? What is the vision you have about the world? Do you see possibilities all around you? Do you believe you have access to unlimited resources right now? Do you think things can change for you today? Think about these questions. The more you realize what you are putting your focus on, the more you'll start to see what is lifting you up or holding you back. Sometimes people assume the world is one way, when in reality, it is only that way for that person, based upon their choice to remain in a certain pattern of thoughts and habits. We all have seen people rise up from the darkest moments and lowest states. We have all seen miracles happen in the lives of others because they have decided to stop being victims and start reclaiming their divine rights. So many people have demonstrated the power of changing their mindset, habits, and thought stream. Other people's triumphs are only reminders for you to know and understand that you, too, can be lifted higher. You, too, can change your mindset and reclaim your power now. You have no idea just how much is happening in your favor. You have no idea how much you were designed to thrive, succeed, and win at life.

You're not a victim. You're not the past. You're not any past mistakes. Let the guilt go. Don't keep yourself mentally and emotionally bound to what has passed. Each moment, you are renewed and have the chance to recreate yourself. You are free to start over with a new mindset and a new attitude.

Starting right now, put an end to the self-victimization and the illusion that "they" or "someone" is holding you back. Nobody is standing in your way but the thoughts and habits you choose to entertain or agree to. Snap out of any trance that has kept you low, and step into what has always been present within you: your true divinity as a powerful spirit. You honestly know this already, and sometimes, that back-and-forth gives you an Inner Glimpse of what is possible. You experience a period when you revert back. You can no longer play this game with yourself. It is time to fully step into your power and lead your life by example. Focus on the positive, loving, and gifted aspects of who you are. Give that focus some time, and be repetitive about it. In the mental world, what we focus upon multiplies. It attracts other thoughts and emotions that match that state of being. You'll find yourself initially "trying," then eventually just being in that state. It will become natural for you to focus on the positive aspects of everything. You'll find yourself feeling completely hopeful and optimistic, even when you are faced with challenging situations. You'll start to see that you're not as worried and stressed out by outcomes. You're now moving in faith. You are empowered on a whole new level, and this time, it can't be taken from you by experiences. This only comes from within you, and you have finally realized this. Your focus is your power. Switch things up from this moment on, and paint your reality exactly how you want to see it. You can make that choice right now, and it can get better and better.

What are your natural reactions, thoughts, beliefs, and ideas about the world?

Does what you think belong to you, or are you reacting to things based upon ideas that someone else has shared with you? Are you really against or for something because you understand the depth of it, or have you been easily swayed into thoughts that seem appealing? Is what you stand for adding value to your life or making you angry? What comes up inside when you stream certain thoughts that are presented to you? I ask these questions so you can start to really think for yourself about what is happening all around you. How much of what you think of is swayed by a trending topic versus logic or even intuition? The more you remain clear about what you are tuning into and how that affects your inner world, the more you can steer clear of unwanted ideas that trigger emotional responses for no reason.

Stand for what you believe in, but also make sure you truly understand what you are representing. Make sure it is not segregating you or creating a personal hierarchy. All ideas serve a purpose. Even when you don't agree with someone else, you can still have an understanding that doesn't cause inner turbulence. Nothing is personal, so you can choose to see another's opinions as a point of reality for them, not yourself. Everyone is constantly choosing the thoughts they stream. Just because you don't agree with others doesn't mean it will affect their inner views. Everyone is entitled to his or her own point of view. The more you understand this, the less you'll be concerned with other people's opinions of you or certain situations. You can agree or disagree, but never be pulled into anger or outrage just because of someone else's thoughts.

Your energy is too precious to waste overthinking, overacting, and overcomplicating things that were meant to be simple. Let it go. Let your mind be open to new possibilities so you can start to receive answers that bring greater solutions.

You can be hopeful about the world and where you are headed, or you can see it crumbling. Every single thought is a choice, and it will paint for you how you choose to see the world. You can see things thriving. You can see progress. You can see advancement. How is everything making you feel? If you are feeling down and unmotivated because of your perspective on the world, you are blocking yourself off from what could be. Just because you see the world one way doesn't mean that's how it is. The world you choose to see is the one you will experience. As we are all learning and discovering ourselves through this experience, we can all have hope that everything is working itself out. We can take action on a daily basis to project thoughts of optimism and give energy to the spirit of life. This allows us to continue to move forward in our own thinking and entice our imagination with greater solutions. When we believe and have hope, we bring new ideas to life. We are naturally creative and have the ability to solve huge problems. When the mind is driven toward solutions, answers eventually come. The future depends upon our current thinking. It is our minds that bring forth the next experience. We must take action according to how we think. We might not have all the answers right now, but we should never lose hope in the revelations of our deep desire to receive greater guidance based upon our vision for a brighter future today. Vision will carry us through, and action will support us through it all. Believe in yourself, and have faith in humanity.

Your awareness becomes your reality.

Sometimes, you can be so involved in all that's happening around you that you might forget to take a step back to actually take everything in. What you are experiencing is never final. You can enjoy what opens your heart and makes you thrive and expand. However, anything that continuously keeps you in a gloomy state is not forever. You can always choose better. You can get out of it. You can break free from that one habit. You can completely recreate yourself at any second. So many people forget this access. You're not forced to change, but sometimes, circumstances push you toward greater development so you can move forward from unhealthy habits that keep you the same. You have the choice every single second to decide what you give your mental energy to.

No matter what happened yesterday or even a few seconds ago, you should never feel defined or limited by it. You should always see hope, potential, and possibility in yourself so you can keep soaring higher through all adversity. There is literally nothing you cannot overcome. Your strength is unmatched, and your determination can become unstoppable. Your spirit has all the answers, and as you read this, you are realizing so much about yourself. You're remembering that you can make a choice. You're remembering that what you see and experience is never final. You're remembering that you have the inner strength to prevail and overcome it all. You are filled and whole already. You have access right now.

You have the greatest connection within you. Ideas, resources, and creative energy are just a mental shift away. Visualize the best, and believe it is happening now.

Think about the thoughts you give your energy to all day long. Are they from the past? Is there some of kind of regret or guilty feeling associated with them? Are you always judging yourself for the smallest things and being hard on yourself? Where does all of this come from? What

179

if you switched things up, and decided to become aware of the vast abilities that lie within you? What if you switched your focus from lack to possibility? Why is it so easy to doubt yourself? There's a finer essence to life that's filled with so much energy and so many miracles. You are a part of that miracle. You can switch your awareness today to start reclaiming the fact that you *are* a miracle, and that life is filled with hope.

Don't let the things around you paint a world of negativity. Don't let people try to doubt you. Don't let anyone try to dim your light by creating a structure in a world of possibility. You have to continue to dream. You have to constantly access your imagination and visualize the best. People will try to tell you what's real, but the truth is, what you choose to believe in and see from within is your reality. You get to impact the world from a state of awareness that is all about self-value, self-worth, and self-belief. You will see the light in all situations. You'll start to receive ideas that will guide you into new territory that shatters all illusions from the past. Fear will fall apart because you have stood in faith and faced yourself.

You have no idea how much is happening for you in spaces and places you can't see. All that you have intended, visualized, prayed for, and spoken into the universe is at work right now. Your action is unfolding itself. The results are showing up. It doesn't matter how or when. Just believe.

Start today by choosing to see everything the way you want to live it. See the changes you want to see. Start feeling the energy you want to experience. Nothing is as solid as it appears. If everything is energy and we are spirits, then we are not confined to what used to be. We can be and do anything we choose in this lifetime. All lessons refine you. You become stronger every moment, and with all the realizations you have gained, a new world of what could be has arisen within you. Don't let your awareness be taken by your past or the things someone else wants you to believe in. Your mind belongs to you, and every single thought that no longer serves you can be released.

Snap out of the repetitive trance that keeps you in habitual thinking and makes you question your worth. You are already very valuable. You are already a miracle and a blessing. If this is your awareness on a daily basis, imagine the inner and outer doors you can open. Imagine how your consciousness will expand into infinity. We have to step up how we think and feel about ourselves and the world around us. Our awareness is what will lift us higher when we discover that we are not held to one state. It can all be so different at any given time. You are intelligent, and you are a natural-born winner. Always remember that.

How you react to what you perceive....

We are constantly interacting with the world around us. We see many storylines taking place. Even things you have no clue about are happening right now. The magical thing about perception is that it changes as soon as you change your mind about how you respond to the outside world. You influence the environment around you and it also influences you, depending upon how you guide and filter what enters your state of awareness. Imagine how a single conversation can redirect your mind to new awareness. Think of how a movie or a book can impact your outlook. The things you see on social media sway your thoughts. Who are you when you clear all of that out of your mind? What is your level of thought and awareness? What inspires your viewpoint? Who is guiding the way you think? Too many people assume that what is happening outwardly is reality.

The reality and experience of the outer world is always changing. It is fluid, and can be molded into any state you desire. If all of your thoughts are dictated by what's happening and not what you want to see, you become created by the outside instead of creating yourself. Too many people accept conditions based upon how they appear. You can choose to deny what doesn't relate to your vision. If you accept a certain state or get into the mindset of acknowledging it as a real thing, then you start to give it life force. Your energy and attention are your power. You have the ability to imagine for a reason: so you can dream a new world, a new experience, and a new state of being. Your fears are a lie. It is all in your mind, and sometimes, you have to move boldly into areas that scare you, just so you can stop holding your own self back from your greatness.

Allow yourself to accept your own greatness by remembering that you already have everything within you. Affirm: I am whole, complete, and perfectly designed by the Most High. I am good enough. I accept myself, and starting with this moment, I will always claim power, health, abundance, and peace over my life.

Who you are is not a collection of thoughts you have picked up over the years. Some thoughts can make you doubt yourself, or even amplify what you fear. The mind without direction, self-value, self-awareness, and self-belief waits for the outside to be the sole director of identity. This is where insecurities can arise, and where you can forget how worthy you are. The Inner Glimpse is something that's deep within you and shines through any state that tries to make you forget who you are. Your spirit comes alive and helps you snap out of all repetitive thoughts and habits that bind you to things that don't resonate with your higher ideals. Building your inner world— refining yourself—gives you insight and strength that can never be found anywhere else. When you realize that everything starts within you, you'll never end up comparing yourself or giving away your power to doubt and or habitual overthinking. Look at the choices you make. How many of them are influenced by the last thing you read or saw? How many of them are influenced by your friends or what you saw on social media? What we look at becomes part of our consciousness. The point is to self-reflect so that you're not comparing yourself when you were born unique and great. Make sure you're not questioning your abilities when you are fully capable of unimaginably great things.

Don't be controlled by external situations. Don't find yourself always reacting to things you see on social media out of anger or fear. Things are happening all over the world in so many different ways. It is all unfolding, and you are the center and point of creation that decides when you will make an impact by managing yourself, your inner world, and how you respond to what you perceive. Remember, the way we see things depends upon our perceptions and how we choose to relate to them. Two people looking at the same exact thing always process and perceive it differently. This is what gives you your own unique perspective. You don't have to convince anyone to see things from your perspective.

There should be an understanding and allowing of shared ideas and thoughts. Either way, people will think the way they want, see the world in the way that is fitting for them, and continue to create based upon their own personal ideals. Knowing this will free you from becoming reactive to what you see. You'll go into things with more of an understanding that everyone is expressing the power of their own free will to think, do, and feel as they please. People are very complex and multidimensional. There's so much going on within them that you can't fully understand or perceive through external examination alone. Don't waste your energy judging, condemning, or trying to force others to think like you. Avoiding this pattern will completely change how you live your life and alter your relationships with others for the better.

What you look at on a consistent basis becomes real in your world.

Have you noticed that anytime you start to cultivate a new awareness, you find videos, books, and people that are also in that state of awareness? It seems like what you focus on is amplified in your world. You get into streaming thoughts similar to your own. There are probably so many people out there who have never heard of what you're into, but that doesn't mean it doesn't exist, or that it is not real. The point of this section is to help you realize just how quickly you can change what you perceive in your network. You actually have done this so many times before. There might have been a habit you were into at one time, and that habit connected you to experiences, people, and environments that aligned with it. Suddenly, you decided that you wanted to do better and change one troublesome habit. You found yourself stepping outside of one world (like an energy network or community) and entering another state better suited to your new thoughts and choices. The previous habit now appears completely different, and you might ask yourself how you even did that at one point. Even when you run into people you used to share past habits or connections with, it all seems so unfamiliar. People still in the field of energy that resonates with that habit or thought pattern might accuse you of changing up on them. What really took place is that you shifted out of what was and created new networks, connections, and energy alignments that matched your new state of thought. Think about this for a moment: If you acted on that habit so many times before, can you imagine what you could do with all the awareness you have now?

You have the power to change any circumstance or set of challenges in your favor. It's never over, and nothing is ever final. It can all have a new beginning, and things can get brighter for you. You can and will prevail.

Is what you focus on uplifting? Motivating? Inspiring? Positive? Are your connections speaking positively about the world, or does everything seem like doom and gloom? Do you see solutions or problems? Are the habits you share with the people around you life-giving, thriving, and amplifying your energy field and state of mind for the better? Are you holding onto past connections just because it feels like an obligation? Are you open to new thoughts? Are you open to meeting new people? Are you open to new experiences? New books? New ideas that are different from yours? These are all questions you should reflect upon for a moment and be honest with yourself about. Adventure and curiosity don't really mean you're seeking meaning or answers. You're just enriching yourself and your spiritual experience as you continue to evolve, learn, and grow. There's so much beauty, variation, and newness that exists in the world. Be open to experiencing something new on a consistent basis.

Test it. Stream new things and see what happens.

You can actually put this to the test. Starting today, change something you focus on and watch how it completely leaves your state of awareness. This test can be something you're always thinking, doing, or watching. It can be done in many ways. You can clear out your social media accounts and what you follow. You can declutter your mind of excess thoughts that don't support your vision and goals. You will start to see that where you direct your mental energy is more important than what is present in front of you. You are the one who chooses, at the end of the day. This will help you see certain habits more clearly. Instead of focusing on what others are doing and comparing yourself, try reading inspiring new books and spending time with people who motivate you instead. One thing I love doing is reading autobiographies. I love reading books on resilience that show our human power to break free of dire situations. I love scientific books and articles that explore expansion of the mind and the energy field of human potential. I love movies with messages I can decode. I notice that every time I expose myself to what is possible or look at humans who have lived life on the verge of cosmic breakthroughs and divine intervention, something within me comes alive. Remember, we are very imaginative, and we play out scenes and stories in our minds. Our ability to do this puts us in the frame of experiencing what is being read or watched. This is why movies, shows, books, art, and what you observe all have a direct impact on the thoughts you think, the words you utter, and the way you act. It becomes you, and you become it. This alone will alter your experience instantly.

You don't even realize the greatness that's waiting for you when you decide that you want better for yourself. The declaration and

186

choice you make is the catalyst that alters and shifts everything you attract to yourself. Start with your mindset. Start now.

The moment you start focusing on what you want, entering the mental world of possibility you have access to every single second, who you are comes alive. Your Inner Glimpse of light awakens, and your spirit is inspired to remember. Everything brings you back to yourself. Times when you learned so much have revealed more to you about yourself. Layers were removed so you could see clearly and feel deeply. It's okay if you didn't know this before. You were always in it, and you are now more aware. The timing is just right. Your energy will no longer be dissipated by judging others or yourself, comparing who you are, or overthinking what you can change. You have entered a state in which you surround yourself with content, visuals, and people that match what you intend to experience. You have also discovered that you can create everything within you. You can see the images, experiences, and outcomes you wish to have. It all begins to happen instantly.

Once you see it, it becomes as real as your vision. It becomes one with you, and almost starts to feel as if you've stepped into a virtual reality of possibilities. You have the understanding right now that you are always interacting with and integrating all that happens around you. Your mind and state of awareness pull toward you everything that is the truth, even though what seems like the truth for a moment changes with every new awareness you adopt. This is why it is so important to always be open to new possibilities, even if they contradict your previous beliefs. Openness enriches your life to see, feel, and move in a new way. It gives you a stronger connection and trust in the divine that miraculously designed you and everything surrounding you. It is all genius, and if you see the universe this way, you'll ignite your own Divine Spark to remember that you are beyond all illusion and limitation.

Key Points

- *Everything is a stream of energy, and in order to become aware of something, you have to be the one who chooses to tune into it.*
- *Each time you choose to expand your awareness, you shift what you bring into your reality.*
- *Stand for what you believe in, but also make sure you truly understand what you are representing. Make sure it is not segregating you or creating a personal hierarchy. All ideas serve a purpose. Even when you don't agree with someone else, you can still have an understanding that doesn't cause inner turbulence.*
- *You can agree or disagree, but never be pulled into anger or outrage just because of someone else's thoughts.*
- *No matter what happened yesterday or even few seconds ago, you should never feel defined or limited by it. Always see hope, potential, and possibility in yourself so you can keep soaring higher through all adversity.*
- *Don't let the people and things around you paint a world of negativity. Don't let people doubt you. Don't let anyone try to dim your light by creating structure in a world of possibility. You have to continue to dream.*
- *Be open to experiencing something new on a consistent basis.*
- *Starting today, change something you focus on, and watch how the old thought completely leaves your state of awareness.*

10

FIVE POWERFUL METHODS: ALTER HOW YOU EXPERIENCE REALITY

In this chapter, I will share with you five powerful methods you can use every single day to change any experience and alter how you respond to, interact with, and see the world around you. When I first discovered these methods, it came about through reflection and introspection in terms of my day-to-day experiences. I had no idea how much my energy and focus were putting together what I saw all around me. I was seeing more of what I was thinking...in a way that reassured me about what I wanted to see. It seemed as if my inner state was always being magnified through the outside world. It wasn't about attracting or seeing something as good or bad...it was just a way for my mind to make my outer experience match the ideas I had about myself and the world around me.

The fascinating thing is that nothing is as it appears, and nothing is as stagnant or final as it seems. Your beliefs can change right now, and this can propel you in a new direction. You can change one habit and suddenly find yourself living in a whole new way. The point I want you to recognize and acknowledge here is that there can be multiple outcomes at any given time. These outcomes relate back to what you think, how you see things, how you react, and what you constantly repeat to yourself about yourself. They are connected to every single choice you make.

Don't let negativity distract you from your power to create a new state. You have the ability to transform anything—most importantly, how you see things. A shift in mindset is a shift in lifestyle, reality, and outcome. You are very powerful. Stay focused on that.

Remember, nothing is as solid as it appears. Nothing holds you to a single idea or thought but yourself. It is as if you've created a mental world from ideas about who you are, and now you live by rules and laws you designed for yourself (or at least accepted). This can either confine you or expand you. The methods that I am about to share with you will help you step into a new dimension of thinking. This is where you will alter and decide what comes next. These methods are meant for you to move into the highest and greatest you. You already know about the Inner Glimpses you have been receiving, and sometimes, these insights literally pull you out of what was and directly into what could be. It is like you're navigating your mental world and seeing the outcomes you want. Your Inner Glimpse is no joke. It is your spirit showing you the way when you feel like things aren't making sense. It can be a rush of creativity or solutions to a dire or complex problem. The Inner Glimpse brings certainty in uncertain situations so you can have the energy to be motivated, inspired, and determined to see your way through.

The Look Method

Your eyes play a major role in collecting data from the world around you. Not only do you receive information to process, but you also project in order to see what you want.

The Look Method came to me when I realized that what I was looking at the most kept showing up in my life. It was like a mental algorithm that wanted to pull into my world the things I thought I wanted to see. This is very similar to advertising algorithms and the way you see more on the Internet of what you have been recently looking at and viewing. A good example is YouTube videos. The ones you watch gather other related YouTube videos. The same goes for the content all over the Internet. One interesting thing is seeing in the digital world the conversations you could have been having. The digital space gathering your interests, the information you focus on, and what you give your attention to are no different from how your mind looks for things to match what you are thinking, feeling, and wanting to experience.

The Look Method is about altering what you randomly give your energy to so you can have a more precise outlook on what you want to see. You will change what you attract as you change what you focus on. This could be in your mind (thoughts) or events in the physical (what you spend time looking at repeatedly.) Thoughts, as I mentioned, are habitual (such as physical behaviors). You might already be used to something, and this can seem normal because you have done it for so long. When you step back and apply The Look Method, however, you'll start to see how much of what you give your life force to attracts your experience.

Don't give away your mental energy so freely. Your focus and attention are your power.

When you apply this new way of focusing on what you want based upon what you're always looking at, reading, and scrolling through, you'll understand the power of your attention. Your attention is very valuable. You are a living energy that gives to and interacts with everything you experience. You give meaning to things based upon how you rank them in your mind. The value of anything is based upon what you think of it, not what it actually appears to be. You have to know how powerful you are. Stop thinking that everything is so random and coincidental, and start honing your power of attention and decide what you want to do with it. Don't let what you look at have so much control over how you respond in terms of reactivity or lack of thoughtfulness. Think things through, and give value to what expands you and evolves you. You might be scrolling through social media, overvaluing things and/or undervaluing yourself based upon what you perceive or put on a pedestal.

Things aren't as they appear, and if you don't make a decision about how you want to experience this reality and be bold about it, you'll just get pulled into other people's storylines. Remember, you have the ability to completely shift how you see things when you use the Look Method. Give your attention and energy to what evolves you. Don't undervalue yourself by comparing yourself to how things appear. What someone else is doing with his or her life is their creation, and they will paint their picture the way they want. You are only a bystander when it comes to other people's realities, and you are the main actor, director, and creator of yours. Start tuning into what you want to see more of. Look for things that help you grow, and learn from experiences instead of reacting to them or being controlled by them. You are way too powerful to be swayed left and right.

The Speak It Method

The Speak It Method will give you your power back by helping you recognize how much your conversation and inner self-talk creates what you attract. Words narrate your life. It is like a script and a bond when you speak something over your life. This is why I talk about the importance of positive self-talk, affirmations, and speaking things into existence. This isn't just something that is only for people who has realized their ability to do this. We all have been doing it, and will continue to do so whether we are conscious of it or not. We have been using the power of words for all of human existence through prayers, chants, and conversations. Words can transform relationships and build powerful connections. Words create feelings and associations. They can trigger a memory or draw a vivid image in your imagination. If you knew the power of your words right now, you would be more aware of how you use your verbal energy.

Once you see a vision or speak something into existence, it is already yours.

The Speak It Method is fun, and it produces instant results. It will keep your focus on speaking power to yourself and over your life—consistently. This method will also teach you the impact your voice can have on how you make others feel, and what you can co-create when you tell your story. Sometimes people use words and don't really think about how much energy is associated with them. You are the one who feels the words and holds onto them. You choose to repeat them and be defined by them. The Speak It Method opens your world up so you can enter a space where you analyze how you identify yourself as a person and the words you constantly speak to yourself. You have to remember that you are making habitual changes on a thought level, and this can start on the inside. It can be a train of thought that builds you up based on how you choose to direct it. Everything that is happening within you is your personal movie. You are feeling everything and thinking it. You can have emotions and thoughts that people never know about, but this inner world starts to reflect in your face, skin, attitude, body language, and state of being. You can feel what you radiate from within, and that becomes the signal you send out to the world.

It all starts within you, so speak power into every situation.

The Speak It Method helps you acknowledge that your voice is much more powerful than you know in terms of making an inner impact on yourself and others. I want you to be the best you. I want you to shine brightly and radiate like never before. I want your confidence to show because you have discovered how to speak to yourself and maintain that state. I want you to start having conversations with others that not only build them up, but build you up, as well. We are always exchanging energy and becoming more of who we are through interactions. Every single person has an imagination, and most people associate you with what you tell them. They imagine you to be the words you are constantly speaking. That is basically how we give insight to each other. We unravel ourselves in our interactions, and this sometimes becomes the identity people perceive. Who are you to yourself? What are you constantly saying about yourself to others? People only have the insights you share. Is your sharing reflective of your vision and true self? Remember, the words you speak over your life radiate into the world. You are not obligated to be defined by the past and continuously speak that. No amount of challenge or pain can stop your spirit. You were literally chosen to be here. You were designed for this, and your words about yourself must match that reality. I want you to start your inner work now. This is the point where things will turn around for you.

Imagine what could happen for you if you stopped doubting yourself and started re-claiming your true power. You would be completely unstoppable. Your ideas would manifest. Your impact would be great. Your expression would be divine. All of this is within you right now. Claim it!

Which words do you want to use to represent who you are? You have to begin to realize that the inner noise that has been making you forget who you really are is going to get so much clarity and direction with the Speak It Method. You will no longer randomly judge or be hard on yourself. Doubts and fears have stopped you from so many dreams. This is now going to come to an end. Your spirit is coming alive now, reminding you of the importance of your gift. You will begin to use repetitive words to bring your dream and ideal vision into reality. You will start to represent your highest and greatest self every single second. Your words will be filled with energy and magnetism. You will look at yourself directly, and notice all the changes taking place on the outside because you have altered how you speak to and think about yourself. Day by day, things keep coming to-gether for you. The image you have been creating within yourself becomes your experience. Your confidence, self-love, and charisma will open doors you have only dreamed of. Self-acceptance allows you to move differently. You are able to do more, live your purpose, impact others, love unconditionally, and be all that you can be just by accepting who you are. The more people see their light and inner gifts, the more we can change humanity.

You are being lifted out of all negative situations right now, and you are entering a new state of possibility, hope, miracles, and unstoppable life force that propels you forward. You feel a new energy, and you are dreaming bigger for yourself. It is all within you.

You will need patience with yourself as things begin to change for you. You are creating a new way of being that is clearing things out and bringing you back to the greatness you have always been. These moments create a momentum that will allow you to let go of words and thoughts that do not represent your spirit. There's no rush or timeline to this. You have to be consistent with yourself, even on the days when you feel like the past is resurfacing to test you. These challenges can be faced with the tools you have picked up. You have the power to speak something greater over any circumstance. When words of self-judgment enter, you can deny them and let them go. Too many people want great results but judge themselves for small things that come up when their strength, wisdom, and resilience have shown them, time after time, that they will always prevail. In the moments when a negative thought or pessimistic attitude shows up, loudly and boldly speak words that completely alter that state. Things can enter, but it is up to you to redirect yourself using all the tools and insights you have. You have to really understand how powerful, strong, able, and unstoppable you are. You cannot let a few words or thoughts keep you small. It's an illusion, and you are starting to realize this. You are becoming free, and it feels good to know this.

You're becoming more powerful every day. You're starting to see who you really are. You're realizing what you deserve. Your light is turning on, and you can feel an Inner Glimpse of hope that everything is going to be okay.

Applying this method must begin now. Start catching yourself when you silently put yourself down or find yourself playing the comparison game. Catch the thoughts that try to tell you that you can't. You have great ideas to move into your dreams. Nothing can stop your purpose. Every single day, tell yourself how much you love who you are and that you can do it. This will become your natural state as you remember to reclaim your inner self with words that empower you. The only thing stopping you is your own self. This practice will free you from the cycle of repetitive thoughts that try to dim your light. We are all dreamers and creators, and we all have a vision. Some of us make our dreams reality because we have decided not to believe in a false narrative that doesn't represent where we are headed or the vision we have of ourselves. You, too, can do this. You can be anything you want. These tools will always continue to refine you, because no matter how successful you become or what you do in this world, there's nothing more peaceful than loving and accepting who you are.

Step into It Method

Are you ready to step into any state you desire? You live in a world of possibility. You have access to unlimited wisdom, knowledge, books, opportunities, and hidden talents. You can decide right now to become anything you want. Sometimes, we get caught up in what we think we should be based upon what someone once told us. We might silence our Inner Glimpse, which never stops trying to awaken within us our own true gift. You can no longer deny what is possible for you. Think about how existence alone is unexplainable and truly magical. There are so many miracles taking place every second to keep you intact and keep things in order as you play on this big playground called Earth. You have an imagination for a reason, and you can visualize something greater than you have ever imagined before. What stopped you all along was thinking that you couldn't, because in your mind, you had made it all seem bigger than yourself. Just take that in for a moment. Nothing is impossible in this reality. Any thought that limits your way of thinking only keeps you confined to concepts that are not your natural state of freedom. You are limitless!

Think higher and greater of yourself. See yourself growing and expanding in every way. Own how powerful you are by acknowledging your strengths, divine abilities, and power to turn any negative situation into a positive opportunity. You can change your perspective at any time.

Nothing is greater than moving thought and the passion in someone's heart. You are alive for a reason, and you are learning how to use your thoughts to maximize your superpowers. You have it all within you. I wrote this book solely to remind you and activate within you what you have always known. Your spirit understands, and this is why there's great joy and a surge of energy happening within you right now as you read each word. This powerful method I am going to share with you will allow you to start stepping into what you want. You will see your ideal self and the things you desire most happening in this moment. This could be a new talent or an expansion of your ability to learn, process, and apply information. There's no limit. Just thinking about it gives me chills.

The Step Into It Method is basically choosing any experience that is already a complete vision of your desired state. You take this image and bring it to life inside of your mind. It is almost like meeting yourself, but as a person who has already accomplished your specific desire. When you visualize this inner you, imagine it as if you are about to sit down with your own accomplished self and receive wisdom, insight, and guidance. This is an extremely powerful method that will shift your entire life toward stepping into your dreams.

Let's get back to the vision in your mind. When you have a dream or want to see yourself fully living out your talent, understand that it is already done. You have created in your mental world an image of that possibility existing, and it does exist...right now. What does the accomplished you look like? What do they know? How do they think, feel, and talk? What wisdom can they share with you right now? Ask for things to be revealed to you. Pick up on the energy you feel from your own ideas and thoughts.

With this method, you will step into what you want instead of imagining it as "one day" or outside of yourself. For example, let's say you want to create a successful business or develop an idea you feel will make an impact. Imagine yourself in that state by stepping into that person (your imagined self): a successful businessperson with multiple successful ideas that are changing the world. This imagined self is here now. This is you already. Instead of looking at it like some kind of distant state, look at it as now. Don't let your mind start running into how, when, why, or timelines. It is all now, and this whole time, you have been pushing your dreams into the future, thinking you couldn't step into them in the moment and own the energy. Do it now, and see how fast things start moving for you.

May all doubt and fear be removed from your mind.

When you step into this state, you will find yourself working and moving differently. You'll find that you have more energy, more determination, and more motivation to suddenly see it through. It's like you have become activated. You have turned the codes on and shifted the direction of your life. You are going to feel unstoppable, and this will create so much success in your life. Insight will naturally flow to you. Alignments will suddenly happen. You are living a miraculous life, and this is when you will start to reclaim what has always been within you. The Step Into It method will change your life like never before. You will look at all situations from a new perspective. You will find yourself stepping into health, balance, and peace, doing what you love most. You can change any circumstance by changing how you see it. Once again, things aren't as solid and static as they appear. There is an energy within you and all around you that's so alive and waiting for direction. You can jump timelines and enter a completely new reality and way of living. Don't be held back by the past or repetitive thoughts that make life seem daunting. Things seemed heavy and unbearable because you might not have known about the power you have. You might have been responding to how things appeared without really being in the creation state of doing what you love. Thoughts about things being impossible are just a comfort zone that doesn't challenge your thinking or what you believe in. You were meant to be free, and if your thoughts aren't in the right place, you'll reflect that in how you move, feel, and behave. Your spirit knows there's more to who you are and what you can do. When you're not living this way, you can get overwhelmed with day-to-day life. Even the most accomplished person wants to feel alive and activated. We all want to know what we can do. We all want to follow our hearts. We all want to live our dreams. You can actually do it. You can really, truly step into it. Dream bigger!

The Edit Method

You have the power to change your perspective on things. This method is very interesting, because it helps free you from past experiences that took so much of your mental energy. Do you find yourself playing out scenarios in your mind of something that could have been or should have been? Do you try to create new ways of seeing what happened? The thing is, you have been using the Edit Method: imagining a situation in your mind and changing the outcome or what you could have said or done. The thing I want you to understand is that you might have done this from a place of regret or being hard on yourself.

First things first. Everything happened the way it did for a reason. Now that we are clear about that, we can move into how you can free yourself from past traumas, heartbreaks, regrets, and things you simply wish to edit or alter. Using the Edit Method teaches you that your mind is free, in this moment, to be liberated from the past. The only reason these experiences last longer than they should is because you keep them alive by playing them out consistently. The Edit Method will allow you to remove the storylines that keep popping up in your mind by editing how you see them. Things only have power over you when you imagine yourself as a victim, or someone who wishes they had proven themselves more. With the Edit Method, you will see yourself in a new light. See yourself as someone who doesn't get triggered by past thoughts. Instead, create a new feeling around your imagined state.

It happened the way it did so you could evolve from it. See the greatness that came out of you instead of questioning why things happened the way they did. A simple shift in your perspective opens you up to new opportunities and helps you attract new blessings filled with great experiences.

Remember, you are always editing things in your mind in your own way. Now I want you to edit what you keep playing over and over, creating mental scenarios you want instead of keeping things as they are. Every moment is filled with possibility for a new outcome. Your mind and body have been through so many changes just in the last second. Now, why would you allow yourself to wallow in something that happened years ago, or even last week? Why give a negative imagined state that much power over you? Edit it out, and create a new feeling of worthiness and empowerment when you find the past trying to show up. Too many of us want to think things are as real as they seem, and that somehow, you are bound to a past self or some situation that happened. You can decide in this moment to be renewed, revived, and recreated just by switching your thoughts. Past thoughts required mental energy. But your new thoughts can be fed with the realization that you are actually free of them. You can edit the situation and see it from a greater perspective, with new emotions and a positive outlook. You are already at peace if you claim it now. You are already healed if you claim it now and step into it. The possibilities are endless, so why hold yourself to something that doesn't represent the new you today? Edit often and release daily. Every moment is another chance for a new you! Claim it!

The "What If It Does Work Out?" Method

This is one of my favorite methods. For so long, I have been writing about the attention we constantly give to the possibility of something going wrong instead of imagining it going right. I have been using this method for quite some time now, and it has helped me create a new state of mind that focuses on things actually working out when thoughts come in that want to stop me from being positive and optimistic. I love all things about mind power. It begins with understanding habitual thoughts and why they seem so natural to us, when in reality, they have only been a hindrance. Writing on this subject helps me convey the importance of introspection so you can catch what's constantly playing out.

I am sure you have had the experience of coming up with a wonderful idea, then finding a hundred and one thoughts trying to convince you of the worst-case scenario. This is not real. This is just fear of true success and accomplishment. You know how powerful you truly are? Maybe you play this game of slowing yourself down by using your mental energy to overthink and judge what could be. I want you to switch that up right now. For every doubt, affirm: *What if it does work out instead?* This method can be used in any situation where you find yourself going against your own vision. You can put an end to it by saying, "What if it does work out?" This creates a new energy within you and all around you. At the same time, you get into an optimistic mindset and attitude that propels you forward.

Change your language to "What if it does work out?" Believe in possibilities. Think of the best-case scenario. Retraining your mind will lift you higher, out of the overthinking, stress, and worry of negative habitual thoughts. Change starts with your mindset. Shift it. Switch it.

I want you to start thinking of best-case scenarios and imagining things working out for you. Go boldly into your vision, and move faithfully. You can no longer stop yourself. Your spirit has been planting the seeds of incredible ideas in your mind. You know those sudden thoughts when you feel like you are having an *a-ha* moment, and you feel deep inspiration? That is your Inner Glimpse. Too often, pessimistic thoughts have held you back from your own greatness and the seeds of amazing ideas flourishing. You might have thought the ideas you were getting were too great or impossible, when in reality, they came to you because you have the ability to see them through. Nothing you can imagine is too far out there. The things that come to mind lift your spirit up and come from a higher place of guidance. This is why this method will assist you to begin speaking and thinking differently. You will now begin to entertain thoughts that expand your dreams. You will welcome in the feeling of things suddenly working out for you. Remember, no dream is too big, and no idea is too grand. It is all possible, and the more you understand that, the more magic you can create in this lifetime. I want you to be the best you can be, and have the right tools in your hands to conquer your mental space and feel liberated to express your spirit. You have what it takes. This is your turning point!

Key Points

- *Remember, nothing is as solid as it appears. Nothing is holding you to a single idea or thought but yourself. It is as if you have created a mental world with ideas about who you are, and you now live by rules and laws you designed for yourself.*
- *The Look Method is about altering what you randomly give your energy to so you can develop a more precise outlook on what you want to see. You will change what you attract by changing what you focus on.*
- *Things aren't as they appear, and if you don't make a decision about how you want to experience this reality and be bold about it, you'll just get pulled into other people's storylines.*
- *You are way too powerful to keep being swayed left and right.*

- *The Speak It Method will give you your power back by helping you recognize how much your conversation and inner self-talk create so much of what you attract.*
- *Words narrate your life.*
- *Nothing is greater than moving thought and the passion in someone's heart. You are alive for a reason, and you are learning how to use your thoughts to maximize your superpowers.*
- *The Step Into It Method is basically choosing any experience that is already a complete vision of your desired state.*
- *Don't let your mind start running into how, when, why, or timelines. It is all now. This whole time, you have been pushing your dreams into the future, thinking you can't step into it at this moment and own the energy.*
- *You have the power to change your perspective.*
- *The possibilities are endless, so why hold yourself to something that doesn't represent the new you right now?*
- *For every thought of doubt, affirm: What if it does work out instead? This method can be used in any situation where you find yourself going against your own vision.*
- *I want you to start thinking of best-case scenarios and imagining things working out for you. Go boldly into your vision, and move faithfully. You can no longer stop yourself.*

11

THE UNIVERSAL SUPPLY

Asking – Receiving – Accepting Divine Gifts

Do you realize how much you are receiving every single second? The universe provides for all without a single error. It is the ultimate tool created by the Most High to assure that we are taken care of at all times. We are provided for on multiple levels, from subtle cellular energy to the magnificent miracles that take place in our lives on a daily basis. Where is your mind? What are you focused on? Do you see, feel, and recognize the divine gifts that are available to you? You have a choice to start seeing how blessed you are right now, so you can go from struggling with self-esteem to bringing ideas to life and breaking free from mundane cycles that try to belittle your great energy.

Moving into this chapter, you have to be prepared for a serious mental and spiritual shift. You're about to remember what is divinely yours, and you will start walking in your power and reclaiming your divine gifts. Every single one of us is loved, supported, and connected beyond what is imaginable. You have to start seeing through a new lens. What gives you this vision is the state of mind you're in right now. Anything can change, and this is what makes life exciting. It is a thrill to know that we can completely alter our current state.

Your connection to the provider is very sacred. You actually have always been connected, and every single word in this book is meant to help you remember what has always been within you. You have always received Inner Glimpses in the most trying and most joyous times of your life. You spirit has always given you nudges through visions, signs, and a sudden feeling that arises for you to remember that you can make it through. I want you to receive all there is, and all that you truly desire. There's no difference between you and someone else who seems to have it all. There is no comparison involved in terms of what you can do and imagine into existence. The focus here is to ask boldly, act intently, and accept freely!

The Universal Supply You Receive Daily

Affirm: I welcome the infinite supply of the universe into my life. I accept it. I recognize it and see it surrounding me. The air I breathe is constant and consistent. I am being nourished and provided for. I celebrate the subtle miracles happening in my life right now. I am so blessed!

You are connected to the supply of the universe no matter what you do, where you are, or who you are. From the moment you were created, you have always been supported. Your mind must recognize this connection to remember the access you have. Think of how intelligently your body was designed...all the subtle energy it takes to sustain you every moment. You breathe so effortlessly, and your cellular community works day in and day out in your favor without interrupting you as you live your life. You have access to great healing and a loving, caring support system. It is so obvious, but we are used to it—and when you get used to things, you forget how miraculous you are. Take a moment to recognize how magical your existence is. This appreciation for life opens your mind to a new dimension of blessings, giving you a vision that wasn't there before.

Be ready for the good energy that's about to enter your life. Everything is getting ready to shift in a positive way for you. You're about to be released from all that has been holding you back so you can start shifting your inner light. You are a powerful being.

A shift in awareness starts with a realization that moves your spirit. I want you to start living your life in praise of the power of the Source, which continuously provides for you. You have been given the ability to imagine new ideas, see new possibilities, and create new experiences. With every single thought or desire you have, you can sense a new way being made for you. The path opens up, and opportunities start to present themselves. This is where asking comes in. Some of the most powerful moments for me have come through prayer, intently asking for guidance, or asking for the way to be made clear for a desire or a vision to manifest. There hasn't been a single moment that asking has failed me. To read about this is one thing, but when you get into the mental, emotional, and spiritual place where you start to ask from the depths of your heart, you create an instant shift and catalyst to receive divine gifts. We are always heard, and the time that elapses between when we have asked and when we have received is only a difference in alignment.

Inner Wellness and Peace Now

You can have inner peace and wellness. You can be in vibrant health, filled with energy to overcome anything and create what you love in this life. When you think you need something in order to be well or to feel peace, attach it to an object, or a certain time, place, or experience. Don't put what is possible for you so far from yourself. It is all here right now for you to welcome and step into. The universal supply gives abundantly, and all you need to do is be open to it. Let go of resistance to ideas of how you can receive it. Instead, feel it, welcome it, and speak it into your life. Get out of the chasing mindset that happiness, wellness, and peace are fleeting. Nothing will run away from you or leave you when you remain open in heart and mind. Your spirit is very much present and alive. You are a great source of power, and you are beaming, thriving, and shining with so much life.

Focus on all the things that bring you peace. Your inner wellness is your priority.

Too many situations have made you forget your true gifts of guidance, and sometimes, the more you are tested, tried, and put through hardship, the more you become hardened by the struggles of what happens instead of remembering who you truly are. Don't let obstacles steal from you. Don't let challenges make you forget who you really are. You will walk this earth from this moment on with a fierce attitude of knowing your divine truth. You have the spark now, and it can't be taken from you. No matter what gets thrown your way, you come out on top, and this is what makes life so miraculous. Day by day, you learn that you can't be broken. You learn how resilient you are. You discover how much God has always been there with you. Every little thing brings you back to how connected you are. Think about how much your body has withstood. You can create new, healthy habits and suddenly create new cells, a new environment, and a new body that supports the new you. You are a miracle walking, and that alone should begin the inner activation of peace and wellness. Allow yourself to surrender and trust. Allow yourself to recognize the subtle energy that is working for you every second. You are a powerhouse!

Your Presence Is the Supply

You have to accept that you are already connected to the supply. You are the connection, and the flow is constant. The only thing that has been hindering you is the fact that you have probably been thinking that you must become something else or work very hard to try to get to the place you have always been. The supply is a state of mind first. So many people do physical things without shifting their inner understanding of where the supply comes from and how to begin to receive it. This is why it can feel tiring or overwhelming. Once you start to acknowledge that you are connected and that you *are* the connection, the way things happen in your life changes. You'll start to notice an effortless flow, and a feeling that you're at the right place at the right time. Everything is what you decide to think of it or what you associate it with. There's a level of liberation that lifts you out of any hardships or challenges, altering how you experience everything around you. You have to start thinking, feeling, and being the supply. Every single breath indicates life. Every single movement is creative energy in flow. The world around you is what you have imagined into existence, and you mold what you want into what you desire. Nothing in your experience is random. It always connects back to something you have thought or felt in some way. It's like connecting pieces of the puzzle, and at times, there will be *aha* moments that make you feel the magical aspects of existence.

The same energy that's managing the entire universe with such precision is working with you. You are connected to the source of unlimited wisdom, abundance, beauty, love, supply, and infinite support. You are being guided. You are loved. Listen to your inner voice. Trust yourself.

It's time to claim your natural gifts by knowing that you already have access. The Inner Glimpse is just a reminder of what is already within you. It's the understanding and the nudge to start claiming your divine nature. The signs are clear, and it is up to you to start feeling the subtle aspects and recognizing how much has been happening for you since you were born. Don't be timid or afraid of life. Don't think you're going to be stuck in a routine or held by ideas of the past. You are free to be who you want to be today. No matter what your dreams, they are valid. You have the opportunity to declare for yourself a better life, and you can start by accepting yourself. When you feel good about who you are, you remember your connection. Even if you have had moments of uncertainty, there is no disconnection. Each moment, you are supported, and the more you start to accept this, the more incredible and unimaginable things will begin to happen in your life. You are very abundant, no matter what is happening in your life right now. You can be going through the most challenging thing, but the moment you remember that your presence is the supply, things alter in your favor. Step into your truth, and get out of the mindset that things are final. You have what it takes, and you are the one who can make a difference in your life.

Things will change for you when you real-ize your supply comes from the invisible. Don't let what you see distract you from what can happen for you. Conditions are momen-tary. Challenges don't last. Obstacles aren't forever. Strengthen your faith. Imagine it. Feel it. Trust it. Believe it.

When you remember your connection, you move differently. You stop overthinking everything and begin trusting more. You start to become a positive influence in other people's lives. Your new way of thinking and being reminds them that they, too, can do it. Living your dreams inspires others that great things are possible for them, too. We are all reminders to each other. If you have overcome something or simply applied yourself to step into a new state, people will feel that, and the supply will start to flow from you and into other people's lives. Treat your life like a dream. Nothing is a coincidence, and no situation is final. You are going from looking around for the supply on the outside to declaring and expecting it to happen from within. You are a magical being. It comes through you and from you. Being alive is a gift, and it will only continue to give to you when you begin to remember, reclaim, and accept the divine gift of life. Everything you do from this moment on will activate nothing but abundance all around you. Your presence is the supply!

Your Mind Will Take You Places

You have imagined so many great blessings into existence. You have dreamed and believed in yourself, even when you have been pushed into a dark place. You have learned, evolved, and grown in so many ways. What is this thing within you that lifts you out of all situations? You could be going through something that you feel like you can't handle, and suddenly, you get this Inner Glimpse of hope that you can. You have incredible ideas and flashes of invention. Your imagination is very powerful. You are a natural problem-solver, and you're solution-oriented. You can take your mind anywhere. That is what dreaming and visualizing are all about. You are the one who has the ability to see a new state by choice, and most of the time, our inner self gives us a glimpse of hope when we are in a dire situation. We are always receiving.

You're going places. New worlds. New dimensions. New creations. New ideas. New experiences. All is coming to life for you. You're the master of your reality. Own your truth, and feel more confident. The universe responds to how you feel about yourself. Feel good, be great, and attract the best.

Allow your mind to see beyond the physical. Mold your reality, speak it into existence, and have fun with it. Go into an optimal state and create what you have always wanted. Don't wait around for "one day." Make that choice in this moment, and start living from within. There are no rules or limits when you imagine. Anything that tries to stop you from dreaming is not real. What is real is seeing yourself doing what you love. Do things that make your heart expand and your spirit shine. This also means doing things for yourself, not just for the world to see. Remain true to your art and your talent. Your passion will inspire the world because you are having fun with it. Don't try so hard or take everything so seriously. There are unexpected miracles in openness that allow powerful things to happen in your life. When you're so structured and rigid in your thinking, you try to reason away everything. If you allow yourself to just be open, you will notice a different kind of movement in your life.

Things are aligning for you in places and spaces you can't see. Don't give up assuming that it isn't working. It actually is. In a major way.

Some of the greatest ideas have come to creators through a glimpse, a dream, or a sudden insight. I am sure you have had some ideas pop into your mind and probably thought they were too great for you to do or bring to life. You have to understand that nothing comes to your mind randomly without there being a reason for expressing that idea. You are connected to the universal supply, which also provides ideas. You are always receiving, and I am sure you've noticed that when you feel like things won't let up, they suddenly shift in your favor. Your mind operates differently when you're in situations that cause your emotions and energy to charge up. There's great power in urgency and the feeling that you want things to happen for you. This can also happen when you feel really passionate about something. When energy is charged up, it is in expression mode, and it almost feels like you are creating at high speed. I am sure you have felt that. I know I have experienced miraculous blessings when my passion was higher for what I was doing or intending to bring to fruition. This is also the reason you can feel things into existence. The more you cultivate a higher energy of emotion behind your dreams, the more quickly they seem to manifest.

Every moment that you believe in yourself, you create a powerful momentum for your vision to come to life.

Start believing in yourself again. Start believing in your ideas. Start trusting yourself. Your mind will take you places because you have the ability to dream up solutions and take action. You are being guided from within, and what you see all around you starts to form into the ideas you desire. It all starts within, and you are the turning point when you go inside and deeply believe in who you are. Don't ask how or when. Don't think of what didn't work before. You are renewed every moment to start believing again. Don't allow any pessimistic thoughts to pull you down from the supernatural abilities that are your birthright.

Create the shift in your life through your mind. All is possible for you!

If you find yourself trying to talk yourself out of your greatness, snap out of it. It is truly an illusion. If life itself is a miracle, what makes you think your ideas can't happen? What makes you think your mind can't take you places? Just look at the universal supply. It continuously gives. Think of how much has happened for you effortlessly, day in and day out. If you keep denying yourself blessings because of what someone told you or said to you, you are giving away your power. It is far better to believe in what is possible than what is not possible. Doubt and worry require the same energy, which is the life force you use to invest in what can happen or can't happen. If you notice, both require you to visualize and feel things into existence. You can decide to stay stagnant, or you can allow your mind to take you places that become physically tangible. Think greater, and dream bigger. You cannot be stopped!

Vortex of blessings: I receive universal gifts daily.

Wake up every single day feeling like you are about to receive a gift. If you stay open, the miracles find you, and it will start to feel natural. I always believe that I am surrounded by and operating in a vortex of blessings that continuously provides and supports me. No matter what is happening, my mind goes back to this: *What is this moment bringing me, and where is this experience taking me?* You have to stop feeling down or victimized by what is happening around you. The mindset shift you're experiencing—going from *poor me* to *I am blessed* in every situation—will be the greatest turning point in your life. What is happening around you can't stop your miracles. The only thing you have, at every moment, is where you allow your focus to stay. Get into the mindset of transmuting energy from *why me?* to *I've got this.* The vortex of blessings will never fail you. You'll notice how every experience is unfolding into a greater one for you. Every single thought and emotion has brought you to where you are, and even at this moment, you can transcend into newer and greater thoughts. You're always building, recreating, and sometimes even starting over. The supply will never abandon you, even when you have forgotten your connection. The gift of life will continue to give to you, and the moment you come back to remembering this, it will amplify and fill every area of your life. Be grateful for everything, and recognize who you are.

Vortex of blessings: I receive daily breakthroughs.

The answers are here, the signs are obvious, and the clarity is present. You can receive daily breakthroughs in all areas of your life. If you feel like you need something to happen for you, start thinking and feeling the affirmation above. When you expect daily breakthroughs, they happen. Sometimes, it's not about what we do to get a breakthrough, it's what we speak that creates the breakthrough. If you focus on what is wrong or why something isn't happening for you, you feed the concept of impossibility, which makes you forget that you are operating in the vortex of blessings. If you are busy expecting daily breakthroughs, your mindset will look for solutions, and you will remain open to receive from the universal supply. It will feel sudden, even happening when you least expect it. The whole point is that you think and operate in a receiving energy that wants to provide for you. This state of mind will become so natural to you that no matter what is happening, you will get through it.

Vortex of blessings: Unexplainable things just miraculously happen for me.

When you know that you are operating in the vortex of blessings, you will experience some of the most unexplainable miracles that seem like they're from out of this world. These are the kind of miracles that you just can't put into words, and they put you into a state of gratitude that lifts you higher. The universe is a mystery filled with possibilities. When you think you know it all and try to create a step-by-step plan for how it will happen for you, you close yourself off from unexplainable miracles. Dream big, and allow yourself to stay open. Some of the greatest things that have happened in my life have come in ways I still can't put into words. We have all been there, and this is what it means to ride the wave. Believe that your entire life can suddenly change for the better. Believe that one idea you receive can take you to a whole new level. Someone might walk into your life right now, and your direction could completely change for the better. You have no idea what is possible for you when you live your life as if everything is a blessing. You call upon the greatest source, and things start to move in your favor. Always affirm: *Unexplainable things just miraculously happen for me.* Watch how things start popping up into your life.

Recognize the Miracles All Around You

You are the miracle! Do you feel it? Think for a moment about how much goes into being alive...the way you process everything and how much energy you're given on a daily basis. You have so many incredible talents and wonderful abilities that you may be overlooking, thinking you have to do and be what someone else is doing. You forget who you are when you are busy focusing on what you're not or what you don't have. A nurturing state of mind lets you know that all is possible for you. There's nothing stopping you. The more you give your attention to miracles, the more they show themselves to you.

You were divinely chosen to be here, and to be of value. You have something rare and special to offer that can only be uniquely expressed by you. Don't think that things are a coincidence or random. It is all perfectly constructed. You are the miracle.

Think of how vast the universe is, and think of all the life that lives within it. Nature will show us many reminders of great miracles if we go from trying to define it to actually feeling it. You can get used to these blessings by explaining them away. The sun can just be the sun…or you can rejoice in the rays and power behind it. You can feel the wind and acknowledge the life that roams the planet. Everything is provided for. I love looking at the universal supply at work and observing how nature continuously provides. Start acknowledging the many miracles in your life, especially the ones surrounding you. If you are busy giving praise to who you are and what surrounds you, what you focus upon will expand. Many miracles will now begin to be shown to you, and abundance will start to multiply in your life.

The Power of Accepting from the Universal Supply

Stop denying yourself the gifts of the universe. Stop being so timid and shy about what you ask for and speak into existence. If you ask for a little, you get small amounts. If you dare to demand greater, you'll receive that, too. The universe is always giving freely and abundantly. I've noticed that people have a hard time accepting favors or gifts. They think they have to be humble and deny the blessings trying to enter their lives. When someone offers you something or gives you an opportunity that aligns with what you have been asking for, be open to accept it, because the universe works through others, as well. It is all aligned for expression, connection, and blessings. There is no shortage of supply. There's no limitation. What you have can also be given to billions of people if they, too, want it and are open to receiving. There's a flow, and it is constant.

Everything in your life will now begin to propel forward. You'll notice a shift from stagnation to flow, from lack to abundance, from confusion to clarity, from pain to peace. This is your turning point.

You can also be a symbol of the universal supply. You can give freely, knowing that you are already connected. There is no stopping the flow, and the more you bless others, the more it multiplies in your life. Give like there's no end and no shortage. Radiate abundance, and show others that the supply is constant. This will open people's minds and allow their spirit to remember that they, too, are connected. Be the example in how you think, give, and receive. You don't have to attach so much meaning or a personal story to what you are doing. Just be it, exemplify it, and allow it. Be the reflection of the universal supply. This will show you how freely it pours into your life in exchange for being so open and free with it all. There is absolutely no shortage! Give and receive!

You're going to be telling a different story very soon. A story of how miracles have found you. A success story filled with so much inspiration. You will give hope to so many people when they see just how much you have overcome, and still, you are standing strong enough to come out on top. Your life is an incredible movie!

Don't apply boundaries to how the supply can enter your life. When you limit the avenues by which blessings arrive, you create a block. The universe wants to give freely and abundantly to you. Allow yourself to stay open. Speak about what you want to experience, but let the concept of overthinking go. It will happen in a way that will restore your faith in believing that anything is possible for you. The universe is on your side!

Congratulations! You have now entered the ultimate connection with the universal supply.

From this moment on, you are aware of your connection to the universal supply. You can never forget it and the number of blessings it will now start to give to you. You are so blessed in so many ways, and this energy surrounds your life. Things will now start to move in new ways that once seemed impossible. What has changed is your mindset and acknowledgement of your connection. This is the beginning of a wonderful time for you. Anytime you need to be reminded, come back to this paragraph and activate your connection. It has always been there, and it will always be there. Sometimes, things that create a cloud of uncertainty and doubt are only an accumulation of negative energy and thoughts. This state can be removed instantly by reminding yourself of who you are, how miraculous your life truly is, and how connected you are. Don't let one moment blur your vision. The universe silently and earnestly provides, even when you forget the connection is there.

Key Points

- *Every single one of us is loved, supported, and connected beyond what is imaginable. You have to start seeing through a new lens. What gives you that vision is the state of mind you're in right now. Anything can change, and this is what makes life exciting.*

- *There is no comparison that involves what you can do and imagine into existence. The focus here is to ask boldly, act intently, and accept freely!*
- *You are connected to the supply of the universe no matter what you do, where you are, or who you are. From the moment you were created, you have always been supported. Your mind must recognize this connection to remember the access you have.*
- *You have been given the ability to imagine new ideas, see new possibilities, and create new experiences. With every single thought or desire, you can sense a new way being made clear for you.*
- *You can have inner peace and wellness. You can be in such vibrant health and filled with so much energy that you can overcome anything and create what you love in this life.*
- *Get out of the chasing mindset that happiness, wellness, and peace are fleeting. Nothing will run away from you or leave you when you remain open in heart and mind. Your spirit is very much present and alive. You are a great source of power, and you are beaming, thriving, and shining with so much life.*
- *You are a miracle walking, and that alone should begin the inner activation of peace and wellness.*
- *You have to accept that you are already connected to the supply. You are the connection, and the flow is constant.*
- *Allow your mind to see beyond the physical. Mold your reality, speak it into existence, and have fun with it. Go into an optimal state where you have created what you've always wanted.*
- *The answers are here, the signs are obvious, and the clarity is present. You can receive daily breakthroughs in all areas of your life.*

- *Dream big, and allow yourself to stay open.*
- *You are the miracle!*
- *Many miracles will now begin to be shown to you, and abundance will start to multiply in your life.*
- *Stop denying yourself the gifts of the universe. Stop being so timid and shy about what you ask for and what you speak into existence.*
- *There is absolutely no shortage! Give and receive!*
- *This is the beginning of a wonderful time for you.*

12

YOUR LIFE IS YOUR MOVIE

Narrate your life story! This is your chance to stop playing a background character or an extra in your own movie. This is your chance to start understanding your position and power. Narrating is using your inner voice to empower yourself so you can create, design, and do whatever it is that you want. Stop giving away your power and acting like a victim. Stop thinking that things won't change for the better. All is possible in this world, and anything that says otherwise is only keeping you away from what you can do, have, and be. It is all an inner declaration based upon how you decide to write your movie. This analogy is simply something that came to me when I was thinking of different experiences in my life that literally seemed like a movie. It is only when you look back that you can fully understand it. You might have had certain people in your life at specific times who showed you something about yourself that took you to the next level. Once the lesson was learned, you moved on. This can happen in many ways: jobs, cities, countries, and everyday experiences. At the end of the day, you are the one who remains within your own self. You are the one who experiences everything and keeps the experiences of all things within your mind. It feels like you're moving through scenes, and every aspect of it leads you back to something that ignites the light and understanding within yourself that you are not only powerful, but also the center of what you are creating.

Pray deeply and passionately, but also be trusting of the timing, because things are always unfolding for you. There's divine order and divine timing in every situation. Trust it. Trust yourself. Believe it until you see it all manifest for you.

You should always have the understanding that things are unfolding, and your trust in this is what allows you to carry on, no matter what is happening. You can stop holding onto one aspect of your storyline. You can stop fantasizing about what once was and feeling guilty about who you are today. It's all an experience, and there's so much you're learning that's bringing you back to you reclaiming your divinity. This is a different level of freedom, because you stop feeling like a victim and condemning yourself; you stop judging, comparing, and limiting your spirit to what used to be. Your potential is on fire, and every single word in this book is meant to ignite that remembrance and activate the memory that you can do what you want and still be at peace with yourself. My goal is for you to start acknowledging the subtle aspects of life—your essence, energy, and aliveness—but at the same time, have a greater perspective that allows you to stay clear, open, and inspired to be all you can be. You can make the choice right now to switch things up. You can tell a new story that supports you. You can be aligned in mind, body, and spirit!

Narrate Your Story

You can literally narrate every aspect of your life. Your words and thoughts support this because you believe in it. This is not a new concept for you. You have always been speaking, thinking, and feeling things into existence. This is your natural state, and you do it so effortlessly that you don't even realize it. There's nothing happening in your life right now that did not stem from your imagination: a thought, or even a desire, for something greater. Sometimes people say, "I didn't manifest any of this chaos or misfortune that's happening in my life." The point isn't if you manifested it or not. The lesson is, what did you intend? What did you speak? What did you imagine? What was your attention constantly on? This can be in conversations when you are telling your life story to others. What is the main tone in your energy? Are you optimistic or pessimistic? Do you speak to people in a way that shows you are dreaming big, or do you put yourself down to play the humble role so everyone around you can be comfortable? Manifesting is a much subtler energy than you might realize. It can even be your predominant ideas and views about the world. Your mental movie is only going to attract to you what supports your current state of awareness and mindset.

You are here for a reason. You are a work in progress. You are magically unfolding. You are continuously growing and getting better.

The big shift happens when you declare that you deserve better. This always happens when you are feeling pressure or overwhelm, and you suddenly charge your energy through the feeling that you want better. The answer comes in ways that you least expect, and sometimes, it might initially appear as a loss. This is why you should always take responsibility for what is happening so you can release it and enter a new state with greater command. If you blame others or any situation outside of yourself, you will lose the power to alter your reality. This creates an inner distortion that someone else is narrating your life. You always have to be the one making the decision. This is a very intimate inner experience. What's happening all around you shows you myriad possibilities in terms of what has already been created. Everyone is internally narrating their lives and going after what they want. Don't hand your story over by getting triggered at every moment by what someone else is doing or why something is happening the way it is. The point of narrating your life movie is to speak power over any situation. It is about switching things up and turning it in your favor on all levels. You can be at peace with yourself by looking at everything as a learning experience, even when you do have those moments when you get emotionally caught up.

The power of narrating isn't only to guide your personal experiences and turn them around just as you would want them to be. It is also seeing everything from the greater perspective that things always have a way of working out, even when it feels like they are falling apart. If you look back at your life, there might have been moments when you had no way of knowing what was next; but somehow, you made it through. The end of something brought you greater clarity, insight, and the power to do better. Things always add up. Start today by stepping back from everything as it appears, and begin to see how things are playing out. What is it that you truly want? How does it feel to live your vision? Who do you see yourself sharing the moment (or scene) with? Be detailed and playful.

Allow yourself to create new energy that completely shifts what's happening because you have changed how you see it. This takes so much pressure off of you and gives you back so much energy, which you can redirect into narrating your life movie. When you are narrating, be free with it. Treat it like you are watching a movie on the big screen. Make every moment emotionally charged with bliss. Smile about it as you do...because it is fun. Let your body and mind be relaxed. This is something you can do at any time, in any place or situation. You can decide to mentally see experiences you want and live through them as if you're already there. Narrating can happen through images, words, writing, and feelings. It is all up to you to decide what makes you feel open and fluid.

Direct Your Movie

Treat this experience the same way you would if you were writing a story for a movie. You are the main character. What do you see around you? How do you see things playing out? My favorite aspect of this is that you can do it right now, and in any situation. If you give people or things around you more power, that determines how they affect you. You never want to lose yourself to the point where you are stuck in cycles and habits that do not lift you higher. Remember, you are directing, producing, writing, and creating what you want at all times. You are in the flow when you allow yourself to understand where you stand in your creative process. Start switching things up and turning every aspect of your reality in your favor. Don't be held back by past experiences or fear of future ones. Directing your movie is about having fun with your creations and enjoying the process as it unfolds.

You're not behind. It's not too late. You're exactly where you're supposed to be. Everything is unfolding as it should be. Don't judge yourself or be hard on yourself about how long something is taking to happen. Your time is coming. Just be thankful that you made it this far.

Let's say you're in a current situation that you feel like is causing you to overthink or worry so much. What you're really doing is taking a particular scene in your mind, whether it is from the past or the future, and choosing to amplify its power over you. You play out the details and see yourself in it. You think of the could haves, would haves, and should haves. This is literally a way of directing your movie, but it isn't in your favor. It's interesting how easy it is for someone to doubt him- or herself or imagine the worst, when it takes the same amount of energy to invest in creating mental movies that support the outcomes you want. You have to understand that not believing in yourself is a habitual state. It is learned, and it is repeated until it becomes the norm. This is why, when you gain access to some kind of hope, you step out of the state of discordance and see all of your light. You get an Inner Glimpse of your true potential. This can be such an inspiring moment for you. You'll even find yourself wondering why you denied yourself all of the blessings that have always surrounded you. Take that in, and really understand that you can be anything you want. You can dream the finest dreams, and you can live them out. You have to start directing your life movie and removing the mental images and inner state that try to make you stay in a cycle of lack. Your self-love will grow. Your awareness will expand. You will unlock what has always been there through a shift in awareness.

You're getting stronger and becoming more aware every single day. You're expanding and evolving in new ways.

I want you to be the best you can be. I want you to love who you are and celebrate your life. I want you to see entire dreams manifest, and your inner light to glow so you can impact many others to remember who they really are. This is only the beginning of what you can do. There is no limit to your expression once you have been activated, and every single word in this book is meant to be a reminder for you that you have what it takes. You are not defined by what has happened to you, or any current state you're in. Now is the moment when you can step out of what was and step into what can be. You have the choice to do it, and it starts now. This is the beginning of being more empowered, more determined, and more connected to yourself. The inner war must come to an end. You are on your own team, and any thought form that has tried to stop you from seeing your truth must perish now. You were created from so much love. You are filled right now, and it will only take realizing that fact in this moment to get things moving in the right direction. I see you as mentally liberated from habitual thoughts that have kept you down for far too long. Nothing can stop you anymore. Things are shifting energetically, and you are becoming stronger than ever. You are the one who is going to command, direct, and design your experience exactly how you want. You're going to have so much insight that allows you to maneuver through anything that comes up.

Step out of Any Situation

You have the power to step out of any situation so you can gain a greater perspective. Sometimes, when you're so emotionally charged up about what is happening to you, you can have a different reaction in the moment than how you would truly feel if it didn't rile you up. If you step back and out from it, you can alter the experience instead of regretting it. Imagine something is happening that you don't like. The first thing you should do is step back and see yourself in a better situation. How would you handle it if it were happening to someone else? What advice would you give that person? This is like altering a script you have created. It is not just about what is happening in that one moment, but how you choose to move forward in your experience that provides you with a greater understanding and more peace. We can allow emotions to flow as they should, and once they clear out, we can have a clear mind to make better decisions about what's next.

Remember to ask for it. Ask for healing, clarity, peace, wisdom, insight, and guidance. Ask for abundance, creativity, light, and love. Don't be timid in your prayers or requests. Be bold. Be positive. Be grateful, as everything you're asking for is already making its way to you.

Always take some time to allow things to clear out, but don't make situations bigger than they really are. Anything can turn around at any time. The power is in how you respond, what you envision, and the direction you want to go. Never be afraid of what could go wrong or what could happen. That fear alone will take over, and you will try to force positivity just to avoid feeling what you could be holding within. The point is to know that you are always properly equipped with the wisdom and insight that this, too, shall pass. You already know this, and you have seen it happen in your life so many times. You have overcome so much, and stood strong through it all. If you have this understanding, you will never be afraid of what could happen. You will be consciously speaking power over your life at every moment.

Switch Things up

You can decide right now to switch things up. You can be and become who you imagine yourself to be. Nothing stands in your way. You can't think that things are as real as they seem. What is real is what you imagine and believe into existence. You have to start living your life from a place where you thrive in the unknown and the unseen. Too many people stay the same: afraid of change or the unknown. Any change that has happened in your life in the past has taken your growth and evolution to another level. It is no different now. You are shifting on a cellular level, and you are starting to believe again, and this is what is going to allow you to experience the freedom to be the best you. This is something that's already your natural state. Feeling these words and understanding this book is meant to create an automatic shift of empowerment in your life, to the point that you feel unstoppable. You start to see the miracles that have always surrounded you. This is your movie, and you are the one remembering, reclaiming, and recreating it all exactly how you dream it to be.

Nothing is set in stone. This is the power of switching things up in your movie. Why hold onto past characters or scenes? Why keep replaying what was? This just keeps you in a loop. Why even judge yourself for what was, or the kinds of shortcomings or mistakes you experienced in the past? That is a mental and emotional trap. I want you to be liberated from the inside out. Success won't feel the same without inner peace and mental clarity. Everything aligns when you are tuned in with yourself and feel strong enough to speak power over your life. Manifesting and creating your dreams starts with inner self-confidence and self-mastery. The more you know who you are and understand the unlimited power you have access to, the more you can trust the unknown and walk with pure faith that you can and will be all that you can be. Nothing is stopping you! Decide to start switching things up. Tell a new story. Tell a better story about yourself. Even if you have a moment where you talk about the past, talk about what it taught you, not what happened that held you back. Understand that at each moment, your mind can go in any direction. Making peace with the past isn't just running away from it. It is accepting that you have learned so much, and you are still here today to express your creative power.

Imagine what could happen for you if you stopped doubting yourself and started reclaiming your true power. You would be completely unstoppable. Your ideas would manifest. Your impact would be great. Your expression would be divine. All of this is within you right now. Claim it.

The interesting thing about reality is that what we believe is what is real for us. This is why truth is relative, and no two people experience reality the same way. One thing that has always fascinated me is how movie actors talk about how much it takes to become the character they are playing. They are fully integrating a new way of being. They have to change habits related to their diet and mindset, and spend months or even years becoming the character they intend to play. The fascinating thing about this is how much it affects the actor's life after they have stopped playing the character. Many actors have talked about seeking therapy or finding ways to cope with coming back to their reality, out of the character's world. This makes complete sense, because our minds allow us to be who we choose to be—but we don't have to return to what was. We can live out our recreated self and switch up anything that doesn't serve our evolution.

What I truly want you to receive from this chapter is that you can alter, recreate, and switch things up anytime you like. Your message to the world, and to yourself, is how you think, feel, and act. The way you carry yourself is the energy you send out into the universe. What is your personal signature? How do you tell your story? Is it one of triumph and resilience, or one of regret and pain? You are not a victim. Every particle of your existence is filled with so much life and so many possibilities. I want you to see and feel that so you can allow your spirit to shine through. There will be a natural flow to your life. Begin to love who you are, and accept that you can be at peace no matter what is happening. Remember to change anything you want at any time. Every word that comes out of your mouth should be empowering, and you should be speaking intentionally and consciously of what you want to experience. Direct your movie and live out your dreams. Anything is possible for you!

Key Points

- *You should always have the understanding that things are unfolding. Your trust in that fact is what allows you to carry on no matter what is happening.*
- *At the end of the day, you are the one who remains within your own self. You are the one experiencing everything, and having the experience of all things within your mind.*
- *You can tell a new story that supports you. You can be aligned in mind, body, and spirit!*
- *You can literally narrate every aspect of your life. Your words and thought support this because you believe in them.*

- *The big shift happens when you declare that you deserve better.*
- *The power of narrating isn't only to guide your personal experiences and turn them around just as you would want them to be. It is also seeing everything from the greater perspective that things always have a way of working out, even when it feels like they are falling apart.*
- *The end of something brings you greater clarity, insight, and power to do better. It always adds up.*
- *Allow yourself to create new energy in this moment that completely shifts what's happening because you have changed how you see it.*
- *Make every moment emotionally charged with bliss.*
- *You have to start directing your life movie and removing the mental images and inner state that try to keep you in a cycle of lack.*
- *You have the power to step out of any situation so you can see a greater perspective.*
- *Always take some time to allow things to clear out, but don't make situations bigger than they really are. Anything can turn around at any time.*
- *You can decide right now to switch things up. You can be and become who you imagine yourself to be. Nothing is standing in your way.*

13

YOUR SUPERNATURAL ABILITY TO ADAPT

There is absolutely nothing that human beings can't adapt to. No matter what the situation, we always find the ability to access higher energies that make our lifestyle appear effortless. From the outside looking in, people might see something that seems so supernatural about you, and they might wonder how you got those abilities. The truth is, what you have adapted to seems normal to you; but in reality, others are wondering, *how can you do all that you do?* Well, you have the capacity to access new energy that supports your new outlook and way of living. All is provided for anyone who can command more energy for his or her expression, creativity, and livelihood. Adaptation is something that is very much a part of our genetics. We might go into a new environment that initially seems challenging, but once we integrate, we can learn and thrive in that space. The same goes for new habits and anything else you put your mind to. Adaptation is also learning to evolve through change. You receive new thoughts and ideas that allow you to access a new level of who you are and who you can be. The most important lesson I have learned is how to continue to thrive no matter what is happening around me. Time after time, I have accessed this supernatural power of strength, wisdom, and insight, and it has never failed me. In the toughest moments, even when you have to imagine a completely new way, the answer seems to flow in. However, when you avoid the change and growth taking place, you assume a state of stagnation, which blocks your blessings.

You can't stay stagnant anymore. You're being guided to step it up and break free from past habits and repetitive cycles. It is time to soar higher and enter a new dimension of possibilities. You are ready for it.

Moving forward into all that is surfacing and learning to adapt to changes allows constant growth and new energy to continue to enter your life. There is nothing you can't adapt to or thrive in once you allow yourself to chart unknown territory. You can make the choice right now to step into all that you have been avoiding so that your mind, body, and spirit can adjust to the shift. Don't hide from your emotions. Don't overthink the past. Don't waste another second of your energy worrying about what is possible for you. All you need to do is step into it. Go right ahead and move forward with all that you feel, and you will realize it isn't as bad as it seems. You are superhuman, and you have supernatural abilities that have always been within you that allow you to overcome anything, thrive in myriad ways, and create the greatest ideas. Fear is the illusion that makes you forget your own ability to thrive. You will find out that it's not as scary as it seems when you decide to walk boldly into your dreams. No matter what your situation, you can always succeed in anything you do or put your mind to. I want your new energy to start allowing you to say, *I am supernatural, and I thrive under all circumstances.* Walk like you are powered by your spirit, think like there is no limit to what can happen for you, and feel that you are abundant and great in all ways. The more you start to understand just how powerful, gifted, and super-natural you are, the more you can express your natural creativity and step into your dreams as if they had always been right there with you. They have!

What have you adapted to that keeps you away from seeing your true self?

There might be a certain way you're thinking right now that you learned from someplace or someone which has nothing to do with you your true self. You might be re-peating a habitual thought that is keeping you in a mental loop of unworthiness or lack of self-confidence when that's not who you really are. Something might have happened before that made you forget your true light and knowledge that you are perfect, beautiful, great, and capable of all. Your true self is beyond any limiting ideas. As children, we all knew this, and we still do. All we need is a reminder for it to click, and this is what the Inner Glimpse is intended to do. You know how lively and carefree you were before that one thing happened? You know that one time when you dreamed of what was possible for you, and actually spent time imagining it? There has always been undeniable po-tential in you, and you always felt that you could pull through, even when the world was weighing you down. The debris from past experiences is getting cleared out of your energy field and mental state so you can see more clearly now. You are becoming emotionally free from the past and any concept that hinders you. You are remember-ing yourself without all the fears and illusions that try to show you something else. There's this sudden rush of relief to know that you're not alone, and that you can decide right now to reclaim who you truly are.

Feeling good about yourself attracts better and greater to you. Get your inner world in order. Balance your emotions. Get clear mentally. Let the past go. Make peace with everything so you can allow yourself to transcend limiting, draining thoughts. Declare change over your life.

If there is any thought of self-judgment—or comparison of yourself with anyone or anything—then you are not embracing your inner truth. You're spending too much time looking outward without understanding that so much is happening within all of us that creates what we project externally. Outside manifestations are simply what has been taking place in the mental and emotional world of the person. In reality, there is no comparison, but instead a deep realization of taking back your power in order to live out your dreams by owning your truth. Any thought that stops you from dreaming big, or any feeling that prevents you from taking action, is an aspect of something you have picked up through habit, outside of yourself. You have spent far too much time looking outward instead of within. You have accumulated lessons that were meant to enhance your experience as you maneuver through life, but far too often, you have allowed certain moments to limit who you really are. Why can't you have it all? Why can't you imagine it? There's nothing stopping you but what you believe, which is only in your mind—and that is something that can be changed right now. Get clear and adapt to greatness. You can make being great a habit. You can make being confident and blessed a habit. It takes the same amount of energy to decide to think that you can instead of repeating that you can't.

Imagine if you invested the same energy you use to doubt yourself into actually believing in who you are and what you can do. Imagine if you only thought of the best-case scenarios. You can start doing that now. Your mind can be retrained and guided to make you an optimistic believer.

It is time to tell a new story and think a new thought. You can stop spreading energy about yourself that signals a victim mindset. You can stop playing the struggle card, and turn every word and action into power. You truly have that within you. You always have. This is your time to take ownership of what has always been yours. No matter what has happened, what you have been through, or what is currently occurring in your life, you can turn it all around. I want you to start shifting now. I want you to forgive yourself for ever doubting yourself or questioning your potential. This is your turning point, because it is finally clicking. Being activated within your mind and spirit allows your creativity, expression, and self-love to flow. You have a great purpose here: to make an impact not only on your own life, but on your community, as well. Impact isn't about being famous or successful. It is about the compliment you give someone that lifts his or her mood. It is about the reminder that all is okay that you projected toward someone, helping him or her get activated to believe in who they are. We are constantly impacting our environment, friends, family, and even the entire universe. When we own who we are, we radiate a strong energy that helps others see and feel a sense of aliveness. It doesn't take anything but love. Never judge, or even try to change people. Simply exist as a living reminder of the inner abundance that flows through you.

241

From this moment on, you will only see expansion, growth, multiplication, abundance, and unlimited flow in your blessings, creativity, energy, and life. This is a turning point for you. This is your time to start receiving in such a divine way that it will all seem miraculous.

We are all learning, and we are all on our own adventures. You know how much it has taken to be who you are and outgrow the habits that once held you back. Give people their space and time to adapt as they need to. Whatever you think of others is only happening inside your mind. They have no idea what you think and feel about them, and if you get consumed by the energy of judgment or overthinking someone else's life, you get pulled in and create stagnation in your own field. Wish people well. Send blessings and continue to project the thoughts you want to feel and experience, even if they are for others. Send out more of what you want your life to radiate. You'll no longer waste time condemning or trying to understand why someone is the way they are. Give yourself peace, and adapt to a state of mind that allows the greater perspective that all is happening for everyone's highest good. As you continue to move forward, you will start focusing on what is taking place in your world. You will begin to conserve energy to get better at self-expression, self-development, and compassion. Everything is just a moment that will take on new meaning for you. You will be liberated to know that everything is okay.

Think more highly of yourself. See yourself growing and expanding in every way. Own how powerful you are by acknowledging your strengths, abilities, and power to turn any negative situation into a positive opportunity. You can change your perspective anytime.

This is a great time to think of the word *expansion*. Your mind is reaching new heights. Your inner growth is evolving. You are getting better and better every single day. This is a great time to start freeing yourself from anything that tries to limit your expression...even your own thoughts and ideas about who you are. You no longer have to play it small or confine your truth. Don't be afraid. The unseen space of what is next for you is safe to trust. We have always lived by faith, not knowing if we will make it to the next day...or even the next second. There's this natural trust that we will make it, even when we don't really know how. Life is very mysterious, and in order to thrive in this space, faith is needed. So go right ahead and release anything and everything that weighs heavily on your mind. Release anything that has told you that you can't. Release habits that have kept your vibrant energy stagnant. You are needed here, and you came here to remember your power so you can elevate your expression and share your gifts in your own unique way.

Initial Change

As you adapt to feeling this new energy of greatness as your norm, you will clear out a lot of whatever made you question your true abilities. It is very normal to experience clearance in the physical as tiredness, or even a boost of energy that makes you feel unstoppable. It is different for every single person, but in the end, you will walk in your power. It will start to feel normal to think positive thoughts and feel optimistic. You'll find yourself motivated and inspired in ways that once took so much effort. You will go from trying hard to being carried by this energy in such a natural way. Whatever state you feel, don't overthink it. Allow every single moment to present what it needs to show you. Remember, you're entering a world of possibility. Every aspect of your mind, body, and spirit is being activated. Don't judge yourself when it comes to timing. We all have different aspects to our inner nature that take their own time to flourish. The point is to not spend too much energy overthinking why you feel a certain way. So many people reach one little moment of discomfort when they feel unmotivated or want to take a break, and suddenly, they find themselves questioning what is wrong with them. We aren't meant to always be on the go and constantly doing. You don't always have to be searching, either. You get the most insight when you just breathe and allow yourself to trust what is coming and allow it to clear you as it should. This takes you to the next level of your growth. Be very patient with yourself. If you're getting signals that you need a break or that rest is required, follow through and take a moment to integrate.

If you're starting to feel like you deserve more or want better for yourself, you're awakening and realizing your true potential. You can no longer settle or avoid what is possible for you. You're upgrading on all levels. Welcome the change, and be patient with yourself.

As you adapt to living in the mindset that all is possible for you, and actually begin to see tangible results as a result of your inner changes, you will realize that every moment it took to get there was worth it. You're forming a new inner world of habits that help you believe that you can, you will, and you trust and believe in yourself. This mindset and energy signature is integrating and becoming a natural state for you. Let yourself adapt. This will happen more quickly than you think, because space and time are all in the now. An automatic activation will present itself. This will influence how you carry yourself, the way you treat yourself, and the energy you put out into the world. Silent, unspoken language between humans is felt on the subtle level, and this is what allows your energy to speak for itself.

Adapt to Loving Yourself

This is a new time. The old ways are passing on. Acting against yourself in your attitude, mindset, and habits is no longer acceptable. It is time to boldly love who you are and move unapologetically. There is no time for inner doubt or attaching your worth to anything or anyone outside of yourself. Your level of self-love shouldn't change based upon attention or validation. You are worthy just by being you. You are a highly valuable person. Get comfortable with owning the energy of self-love and inner empowerment. You are not defined by what someone has said to you to try to dim your light. They can't do this with their words or actions. It is only you who decides how you feel about yourself. You will begin to feel stronger and more empowered as you remember that your inner world belongs to you. Take that power back, and feel a new sense of love that is fulfilling, freeing, and rejuvenating. For once in your life, you know deeply that it all comes from within.

Receiving is extra, and giving is a bonus with the abundance that's flowing through you.

Your New Normal: You Are Blessed

From this moment on, you are working and operating within a vortex of blessings. You are surrounded by blessings. You recognize blessings. You are a blessing to others. You feel grateful about your life. No matter what is happening, you always think, feel, and speak that you are blessed. This is the state that you have adapted to. All lack and limitations have perished out of your field of reality because your attention has turned to the abundance within you and all around you. All it takes is for you to recognize it and celebrate it. You have denied this to yourself for far too long. This is a new beginning for you to start embracing life. Blessings are real, and every single day, they are working nonstop in your life. The more you feel this way, the more you start to see miracles happening in your life.

Every experience will seem supernatural. You will feel that you are being supported in ways you can't explain or express. You will be in awe, and feel an overflow of joy unlike anything you have ever felt. You will start to wonder why you ever spent time worrying when magical blessings are taking place every second. You will never ever again forget that this great field that is all around you. You will even have the vision to see it in nature and in others. A new world will open up for you, just because you have decided to switch your point of focus. Everything you touch, put your mind to, and intend to do will simply work out, no matter what. It is like you have the golden touch, and all it took to access it was normalizing how blessed you are. You are blessed simply by being, and that is a powerful declaration that will completely alter how you move.

Adapt to Habits That Support Your Vision

What are you doing every single day with your time? Your life force? With your mindset? Are your habits producing the vision you see in your mind? So many people get frustrated, wondering why their vision isn't happening for them. It's not that it can't happen; it's just that certain habits have been repeated so often, it almost feels comfortable to you to stay the same. Your vision doesn't go with that. You see yourself as healthy, vibrant, and loving because that is your Inner Glimpse into your natural state. How does that vision match with how you speak to yourself all day long? What are your predominant thoughts? A change in habit begins with your mindset. Once you believe it, a pull is created toward change in the physical. This can happen when you feel a rush of energy to no longer procrastinate or ignore your burning passion to be the best you can be. You will also experience a breakthrough in your thinking and how you use your time. Many little shifts like these will lead to great change. It all starts with adapting to habits that actually support manifesting your vision. You are shaping and molding a new creation of yourself simply by being consistent and direct on a daily basis.

Accept Your Superpower Abilities to Adapt

You now know better and feel more confident that you can adapt to any experience or change you want to make. You can go anywhere in the world and thrive. You can alter your inner state and produce magnificent results. You can smile in this moment, knowing that you have this ability. It is a superpower, and it is supernatural for you to do this. Don't ever hide from challenging moments. Every experience is refining you to know more about yourself and unravel layers of the greater potential you have. Think of how much you have learned up to this point in your life, and how much it has brought you peace. You are able to move differently because of the lessons you have received. You are able to impact others. You are able to share your wisdom. You are brighter, stronger, and even more vulnerable because you know what it took for you to get where you are. You have done it before, and you can do it again. There is no situation too grand or difficult for you to adapt to or overcome. You will now begin to shape-shift and make the best out of your life. Enjoy being free, open, and activated!

Key Points

- *There is absolutely nothing that human beings can't adapt to. No matter what the situation, we always find the ability to access higher energies that make our lifestyle appear effortless.*
- *Don't waste another second of your energy worrying about what is possible for you. All you need to do is step into it. Go right ahead and move forward with all that you feel, and you will realize it isn't as bad as it seems.*
- *You are superhuman, and you have supernatural abilities that have always been within you. They allow you to overcome anything, thrive in myriad ways, and create the greatest ideas.*
- *You are becoming emotionally free from the past and any concepts that hinder you.*
- *It is time to tell a new story and think a new thought.*
- *This is your time to take ownership of what has always been yours. No matter what has happened, what you have been through, or what is currently occurring in your life, you can turn it all around.*
- *Your mind is reaching new heights. Your inner growth is evolving. You are getting better and better every single day.*

- *Every aspect of your mind, body, and spirit is being activated.*
- *Be very patient with yourself. If you're getting signals that you need a break or that rest is required, follow through and take a moment to integrate.*
- *There is no time for inner doubt or attaching your worth to anything or anyone outside of yourself. Your level of self-love shouldn't change based upon attention or validation. You are worthy simply by being you.*
- *From this moment on, you are working and operating within a vortex of blessings. You are surrounded by blessings. You recognize blessings. You are a blessing to others. You feel grateful about your life.*
- *Everything you touch, put your mind to, and intend to do will simply work out, no matter what.*
- *There is no situation too grand or difficult for you to adapt to or overcome.*

14

STEP INTO IT TECHNIQUE - *ENTER THE DESIRED STATE NOW*

Below, I will be sharing with you a powerful technique called Step Into It. This technique will automatically alter your reality and allow you to experience incredible outcomes. You will enter a desired state of your own in terms of how you see certain situations playing out. This can literally be used for any situation you want to alter or experience you want to change. It is very powerful, because you get results right away and start to see things changing fast. It's like going into a new dimension in which you are already living the experience you want to step into. Great possibilities exist for you right now. The ones you choose to play out are the ones you will step into. The example I will give you before I share the technique will illustrate the extent to which your mind is always playing out scenarios. You are a very imaginative being.

For far too long, we have used our mental energy to play out what we might *not* want...over and over again. This is like putting yourself into an experience you don't want to have and giving it tons of your energy. Even when the situation plays out the way you have imagined it, you always say, *I knew that would happen.* Yes, you did know, because you have now imagined it into existence. Your greatest discovery isn't going to be about *knowing* how powerful your mind is, but actually *experiencing* how powerful it is. To know is one thing, but to actually experience it and feel it takes you to another level. You go from being someone who simply reads about things to someone who lives them. Nobody can tell you what is possible when you see this happen. It will give you so much confidence in who you are, and help you snap out of any thoughts and images that do not feed your vision.

Every second, you are playing out ideas of what something can be or become. You are naturally imagining and visualizing without even trying. In the past, you might have put yourself into imagined states in which things were going wrong. You played out the whole scene in your mind, and it led you into realities and outcomes you didn't want. I want you to truly start believing in yourself. I want you to feel so empowered on the mental level that it shows in your physical world. I want your mind to be clear, direct, and ever-evolving so you can master your own path. You will begin to move in a way that seems out of this world. This is your Inner Glimpse coming to life. It is your spirit transcending limitations and turning them into possibilities. You have this ability, and the *Step Into It Technique* will help you alter your experience anytime you like. It will become so natural that you will find your mindset becoming more solution-oriented. You will be open to what is possible instead of what isn't.

This technique is meant to propel you into the end result of your vision, just as if it were all happening right now. Before you begin this process, understand how powerful this technique truly is. I am sharing it with you because I want you to live out your dreams. It is powerful how fast this technique works. I might as well attach a warning message and alert you to get ready for great and positive changes. Make sure you are prepared to step it up and step into it. You can make miracles happen with this technique, and you will see instant changes in the way you think about yourself and the way feel about what is happening all around you. It will empower you like never before, and you will begin to understand what it really means to experience a breakthrough in the moment. You can even Step Into new talents and creative ideas. This technique is energetically charged, and it allows you to enter a vortex of great possibilities. The only thing I would say is don't limit yourself in what you want to step into. You can become anything you want. Think great thoughts. You can step into new solutions for any problem you might be experiencing. See it as your own personal vortex you are entering to create new outcomes. You can create a new you right now with any talents and abilities you like. You can create a new idea of yourself that allows you to have better relationships and become a better you. You can step into the physical goals you have right now. This will allow you to create an instant shift because you are using your imagination to create new mental and emotional connections.

I remember sharing this technique with a good friend of mine who was struggling with her relationship. I asked her to not tell me the details of her situation, but instead suggested that we have some fun and talk about what could be. "Let us step into a new state and change up the narrative," I said. I asked her what she wanted to look like in her relationship. Day to day, how did she want to feel about herself? After that, we talked about how her relationship now felt after she had stepped into her desired state. She was better at communicating her feelings, had more self-love and self-acceptance, and was more at peace with her own self. Something within her had shifted because she had stopped being so constricted in her feelings and opened herself up to a world of new possibilities. She had played out the *what if all is just okay?* state of mind instead of worrying so much about things going wrong. She went from looking for problems and magnifying small things to entering a world where she felt accepted by herself. A flow of love moved through her.

My friend entered a reality that became available to her within her mind, outlook, and emotions. She changed how she spoke about herself, her relationship, and the experiences she wanted to have. She knew the power of every word, but more so how she felt in her private mental world. Her fears had been playing out before, and reflected in how she expressed herself. With just one conversation, she took her power back. This stimulated her imagination to remember who she really was. She called me a few weeks later, shocked at how much a relationship she thought was over had taken a turn for the better because she had shifted how she felt about herself. She thought she would have to work very hard to overcome her past mental and emotional habits. She thought she would have to force her partner to change or argue about things that appeared to be wrong. She thought she would have to overthink whether or not she was doing some technique correctly. Instead, she was shocked—literally shocked—at how you can alter your state of being by stepping into a desired outcome. She worked on herself, and changed how she saw the outcome of her reality. Somehow, that altered what was happening around her. It was a very reflective moment. The technique allows you to go into the perfect state of mind as if it were happening right now. This literally gets rid of any negative ideas, concepts, and beliefs about what you think is happening.

I'm not really sure how it all happens on an energetic level, but what I do know is how quickly the ideas of the past fade when you decide to enter what is possible for you now. It is like you are reborn. It's a magical blessing that allows us the mental and emotional clarity to recreate anything we want. We don't have to prolong it, or make it a long process. We don't have to wait around. The universe works instantly if we free ourselves from ideas about what it will take to get the outcome we want. If you think the process is going be long and daunting, you are energetically asking the universe to place obstacles in your path that reflect just how hard it will be for you to get there. If, on the other hand, you believe in instant shifts and miracles, you allow the universe to get creative about how things are presented to you. You will feel like a highly blessed person who just knows and feels that everything always works out for you. This is what the Step Into It technique is all about. Your mind goes into a complete vision of your desired outcome, emotions, and state of being as if it were all available to you right now. This unlocks something in your memory that knows that all is now. You never have to be trapped by past memories, concepts, or ideas of what it takes to be free in this moment.

One thing I want you to truly understand is that all of the changes you experience will be instant in your mindset, energy field, and emotions. You'll notice that things are moving in a greater direction for you. It will feel like something new has taken place...and it has. The minute you decide to Step Into It, everything begins to change for you. You have so much potential energy that you can tap into at any second. When you stop telling past stories and imagining failed scenarios, you unlock a new thought that is greater than the previous habitual thoughts you thought you were stuck in. The understanding you're getting from this book alone is creating a catalyst of change within you.

It is empowering you to believe in something greater. If you can choose the direction of your mental energy, then why not choose what makes you feel so alive? I'd rather dream big than doubt myself. I'd rather believe in what could go right instead of assuming anything less. You have the power to do just that. Let's begin now, and Step Into greater outcomes.

Step Into It – Activation

I am very powerful! My mind is very powerful! Every thought and feeling has a strong energy, which I send out. I notice and see more of what I am thinking and feeling all around me. Knowing how powerful I am, I choose to start being bolder, more positive, and more direct about what I want to experience. I am now in my private vortex of blessings, miracles, and breakthroughs. This vortex surrounds me like a clear gold bubble that's beaming so brightly. I am surrounded by such positive energy, and I attract the best to myself. My vortex of blessings is constant and always around me. I can already feel things changing for me. The vortex of blessings that surrounds me is a powerful energy that opens me up to the unlimited possibilities of the universe. I can turn any situation around right now! I am feeling good about myself, knowing the kind of access I have. Everything can instantly change in my favor right now. The way I see things is more important than what is happening. How I react and respond will be from the highest level of my being, so I can always be free to think for myself and direct my mental and emotional energy toward the outcome I want. What I project is what multiplies for me. I am creating instant changes right now. I already feel uplifted! My thoughts have now been cleared from the past, and I feel a new sense of aliveness in this moment. I am victorious in all ways. My truth is that I can and will alter my reality right now. I am ready to Step Into It!

Step Into It – Command the New Outcome

My new desired state is _____! This is happening for me right now. I feel it! What is possible is what I imagine. The second I see the image, experience, and end results playing out in my mind is the second it all starts to happen instantly for me. I can put myself in a new state of mind and get the physical results I desire. I *am* the change of outcome. My mind moves and creates around me what I command as my truth. I walk in power. My new desired outcome, _____ , makes me feel _____ (enter a strong emotion you would feel if you were now living your dreams.) I am stepping into a new reality, and I already feel so different. My thoughts are now more positive, and I am more optimistic. I have a strong feeling of deeply trusting and understanding myself and who I am. I am free and open to something new. What is real is what I am feeling right now. The past is gone. What used to be is finished. I feel so alive and filled with so much potential. In this moment, I have stepped into and entered my desired outcome. I will now begin to see all around me the results that match and align with my desired outcome. I am fully activated in the realm of possibilities. In this moment, I feel an instant shift. Wow! Things have now begun to move in my direction. My vortex and magnetism are stronger than ever. I feel renewed by a surge of energy that is so positive and so promising. My vortex multiplies my ability to experience all my dreams right now. The results will now begin to show up. I already feel stronger, and I can feel the change within my mind, body, and spirit. My environment is going to produce the results of my desired outcome right now.

Step Into It – Results

The possibilities are endless. Just like that, things have literally altered for me. That one situation finally worked out! My desired outcome I commanded has actually happened for me! I knew I would get fast results using the Step Into It technique because in my imagination, all that I see happening has already taken place for me. I am finally using my thoughts to support myself in such positive ways. I am on my own winning team, because I have discovered how to step into any desired outcome I want. I have learned that I am always putting energy out, so why not support what I want to see happen? I'd rather imagine the best for myself, because the results have been incredible! I feel an instant shift and change with the Step Into It technique. I trust myself so much! The universe has revealed to me how powerful I am, and I feel so good knowing that I can start making instant changes on a mental level. What an incredible discovery! I am so blessed to know this, and to actually get results!

Now that you have received the three steps of this technique, you can begin to use it right away for any situation. Allow yourself to read through it anytime you feel like you need a new desired outcome. The first step is the activation, which is meant to automatically get your energy up. It will not matter what state you're in when you are using the Step Into It technique. You will always be activated to feel a whole new positive energy that will alter any situation for you when you read this section. Don't overthink any of this. Feel it, and be open to all the good energy you have access to. The commanding step is all about going into the desired outcome and feeling it as if it were all happening for you right now. This isn't something you're trying to make yourself do. This is an automatic change based upon reading it through and inserting your desired outcome and feeling. You can read these sections anytime you like. You can use them for new outcomes or multiple different outcomes. You can imagine this state or write it out. It all depends on what feels natural to you when you visualize. Some people like to write down the story of their desired outcome happening, and others get into the feeling by imagining the state. I personally enjoy seeing myself already in the imagined state and feeling good about it. It works every single time!

Be sure to immerse yourself in feeling and seeing positive things happening now. If your mind tries to tell you that they are not reality, you have to enhance your feelings, just as if you have received the good news. We have to get back to using our imaginative power and avoid remaining stuck in what has already been created in front of us. Everything that surrounds you has already manifested into the physical. Everything in your mind has the potential to enter your physical world, as well. Why remain stuck on what is, when you can imagine greater things into existence? Start using your imaginative abilities, and get back to dreaming up new realities. We have always done this, and we still have the power to do it.

Lastly, the results section is a strong energy that pulls you into completion of your vision. Feel every single word, and connect with it. You are going to see some magical things happening in your life because of this technique. It has helped me alter any situation and how I feel about it instead of always accepting things around myself as a final state. Enjoy your new outcomes!

15

THE GREATER VISION AND PERSPECTIVE

You have to remember that things can be the way you want them to be. When you get pulled into storylines and ideas about what is happening around you, you lose perspective on finding real solutions, and you might begin to respond to things from an emotional or fearful place. A greater vision and perspective are operating from your spirit. You no longer allow what is happening to consume you. Instead, you use spiritual wisdom and insight to navigate your life. Real answers always come when you step back from what is happening around you and decide to tune into yourself and see how things look when you're not the one experiencing them firsthand. How can something change for you if your mind, body, and spirit are reacting to what is, not what could be? You have to remember that you have a choice every second to enter another phase, but if you continue to identify with pain, problems, and regrets, you will only attract more of that. You can only enter greater things if you remove your mind from what is and enter what could be in this moment. The only person who gives value and meaning away to things is yourself. You decide what you put on a pedestal. You are the one who mentally makes something seem great, when to someone else, it is just not as important. The goal here is to help you see so clearly that you no longer need to allow yourself to get lost in situations and circumstances. You are far greater than you truly understand right now, and with every word and chapter of this book, more and more realizations will hit you and allow you to take your personal inner power back.

The vision you keep receiving isn't random or a coincidence. Your spirit is showing you what is possible. That inner empowerment is a reminder that you can. You keep getting signs. Trust them. Move forward into them. Make it happen. Your greatness will shine through.

Who you are is so much more than what you could ever imagine. You have hidden powers and abilities you might not even know of. There's so much more to you, and it is now time to start claiming what has always been there as your truth. Speak confidently. You can no longer allow your precious life force to be drained and wasted on judging yourself, overthinking situations, and letting small things occupy so much of your time. I have seen so many people identify themselves with ideas that do not represent their true power. It is so important to think about what you are constantly saying about yourself and others. The more you undervalue yourself and overvalue things outside of yourself, the more you lower your own power. You can always access your full abilities, but sometimes, they come through growth or sudden realizations that help you skip timelines and processes.

I believe in instant changes because I have seen them happen. If you were suddenly shown something that you thought was impossible your whole life, and in one moment, you got to experience the reality of it, you would never go back to denying that it could happen. You know that it can, because you have experienced it yourself. This is why I believe that each person should allow what is meant for them to be revealed instead of trying to understand whether something is actually possible or not. There might be someone out there right now making miracles happen that might seem impossible to you, but for the next person, they are totally feasible. What makes things possible is believing they can happen. To experience a greater vision, you have to stay open to possibilities. You can't have an explanation for every single thing. Things might be the way they are because you are accepting what is happening to you as final. When you stay open, something unexpected and great can happen instantly. You have so much power right now to change how you see it. You have to start giving yourself that credit instead of looking outside of yourself to find meaning and value.

Your Spirit and Mission

You might have a recurring thought of something you are meant to do. You might look back at your life and notice a recurring pattern involving a gift, talent, or something you're really good at. This is your special, unique gift. Some of us have followed through with our passions, and others have explained away their gifts by following something someone else has told them to do instead of following their own spirit's mission and calling. There is a passion you have. Are you fully living it and allowing that flow to enter your life? Your spirit is lighting up every single moment with so many glimpses to remind you to get back to your imagination and start dreaming big again. Remember who you were before things got so mentally and emotionally heavy with the duties of life? They don't have to remain that way. You can start living your dreams and activating your spirit to accept your mission of evolving, discovering, and adventuring through life. You can turn your passion into a blessing, and make a living doing what you love. Don't be afraid of how, or even tell yourself to be realistic. Anytime you try to explain away why you can't live your dreams, you create a mental block of why you can't. You are the one who creates what is real in your world. If things are overwhelming or hard for you, don't think the situation is final. You will make it through as long as you believe you can.

Your magnificence is coming alive. You feel and see your evolution every single day. You are unraveling. Your greatness is exposing itself to you. Your spirit is lighting up. This is your time!

This is the time to start following your heart and living your dreams. This is the time to start trusting yourself and making bold moves. You can no longer be timid or create blocks. You have to know you are free and fearless. Move on from your past identity and concepts of bad luck or misfortune. You are chosen to be here, and you are perfectly designed. You have been given all the codes. You just have to start accepting who you are and following your heart, even when it doesn't make sense. When you start to trust yourself, you go from looking at the outer world for answers to looking within yourself for what is possible. Too many people have been put into situations that make them overthink external reality. They have forgotten how to hear their own truth and trust their inner guidance. Doubt and fear are not our natural state, but too often, people speak impossibilities before they even can say what might be possible for them. This mental lack isn't real, but it persists when life force is given to it through believing in it. You are a prosperous genius with ideas, talents, and creativity to make an impact. If that was all you had known your whole life, you would move differently and be great. It is hard to miss someone who walks confidently, because you can just feel power emanating from them. You have this magnetic ability, as well. You just have to clear out what has told you otherwise and claim your true natural power. You were created by the Most High as a whole being.

Things will begin to accelerate for you in all areas of your life. You'll start to see the physical results of invisible power.

I am sure you are already feeling stronger and more connected to your spirit. The Inner Glimpse is meant to expand what is already within you. It is that silent guidance you have been receiving from your spirit to follow your heart and carry out your mission. Whatever that mission is, you already know. If you have a passion, follow through with it, even when you might not know how to start or what the outcome will be. So many people have dared to dream, and have created what might have seemed impossible at the time. You, too, can carry out what is in your heart and mind. You can express your creativity and have fun being you. You can inspire others through your own story. Decide to express your spirit's mission, and the way will be made. You have to start speaking more power into your life through your words—and that includes how you speak to yourself. Think from a greater perspective, and know that all you've done up to this point can be amplified into something greater. You can be renewed in many ways. Once you have decided to follow your heart, a greater vision will be implanted in your mind. It will seem like you are divinely receiving answers, guidance, and insight on what comes next. Things just begin to miraculously work for you. It will feel so natural that you will wonder why you haven't just followed your heart before.

You're getting stronger in mind and spirit. Everything that has happened was meant to help you evolve and discover your inner power. You are resilient and unstoppable!

Take some time to start asking your inner self to make your mission apparent. Tell your spirit to start giving you a greater perspective and a grander vision. Never be afraid of asking, or think that you sound silly. You will be so surprised how everything begins to align for you when start to ask. It will seem so perfect how it all comes together. Be ready for some real uplifting energy and movement to begin to occur in your life. You are no longer waiting around for the outside world to give you answers. You are now plugged in and connected to a greater power that guides you from within. The outside world becomes fun, because you know that you're the one altering your experience. Instead of thinking less of yourself, you feel more empowered. You become more responsible for what is happening in your life instead of thinking everything is so random. You know that you are way too connected, and no matter what is happening, you can shift it and switch it to a new outcome. Start using powerful words and imagining greater for yourself and those around you. See health, blessings, and miracles as a natural state for all. What you project out multiples and expands. Never accept conditions that do not represent the highest good. All conditions can be altered. All moments can be changed. Everything has the potential to be completely returned to its natural state of perfection. When you look out in nature, do you see mistakes? Do you see order and harmony? Do you see beauty and grandness? Do you see perfection? Do you see balance? All of this is created by the Most High in perfection, and it is a reminder for us to accept our natural state so we can feel the harmony flowing through.

Reminders of the Greater Perspective

All around you, there are reminders of the greatness of life. We live in a vast space of possibilities. We have the ability to remember the greatness we are made of and connected to. Think about birth, death, and life in between. Think of this planet and all its beauty. Everything is so alive and filled with energy. One of the greatest ways for me to remember that there is so much more is to simply breathe and listen to my heartbeat. There is so much life within you. Your body is constantly at work, and forgives when you decide to do something that goes against your natural harmony. It somehow brings you back to homeostasis, even if you have spent years doing the opposite. Just think of how health, abundance, and overflow of life are supported. You are protected, nurtured, and given to from such a special place, and it will take recognizing that to get out of the mindset of lack and shortage. Abundance is your natural state. Beauty belongs to you. It is all about seeing it, praising it, and being grateful for it. Don't become hardened by reality, thinking that you have to be serious or defend your identity. If you believe in something, believe in it. If it helps you be greater, then go for it. Have fun. It is all a moment. Why live your life overthinking something that's going to be a distant memory? Why miss out on having better relationships and connections with others? The paranoia of thinking that others aren't trustworthy, or that you somehow have to protect yourself, creates too much resistance in your body and mind. Let go of what was, but don't give so much power to avoiding it that it makes your experience lower or less than.

It happened the way it did so you could evolve. See the greatness that came out of you instead of questioning why things happened the way they did. A small shift in your perspective opens you up to new opportunities and helps you attract new blessings filled with great experiences.

If your energy is focused on a greater perspective, you have no time to overthink the past. You are renewed every second, and you can decide to start noticing the blessings around you instead of judging everything. You are free, and you were born this way. If you look at how kids operate, it is almost undeniable how much they interact with others simply by waving and smiling. They exude the life force of joy and connection. They aren't overthinking what someone thinks about them. They are pure expression. This is how we are supposed to be: free in our creativity and expression, moving through life and enjoying the adventures of experience. Allow yourself to loosen up a bit, and don't overthink things. The thoughts others have of you are really only in their minds. What matters is what you think of yourself, and how you feel about who you are. If you are giving away your mental energy overthinking what someone else thinks of you, you are missing out on the ability to see things from a greater perspective. It is like putting yourself in a mental prison and giving that person the key. It is an illusion to try to protect your image from what others think of you. One day, all will be a distant memory. Lift yourself higher, and lift your vision into a dimension that is filled with life. Stop playing these petty games with yourself. Stop dimming your own light and acting out a smaller version of what you can be when really, you are so grand!

Remember how blessed you are, no matter what is happening.

Spend every single day counting your blessings and noticing the miracles that surround you. Look at the sky and all around. See the life force moving through others—and even yourself. Every single thing is alive and beaming with so much energy. You have access to this same energy because it comes from within you. If you spend your day seeing the power of life, you will feel it in your own being and the lives of those around you. The difference between you and anyone else is what is going on in their mental world. The environment looks the same, but deep down, we all have our own view that paints the picture of what we choose to look for and what we decide to see happening. This is why others might turn out differently from how you imagined them; it was the idea you had of them that you enjoyed more than the person they are. We are living in our minds, and if we can integrate our experience and see a greater perspective, we can stop being victims of what is happening and become more empowered by life, with a grander vision. One thing I enjoy that gives me greater vision is being in nature and watching animals. You can feel the life force and the perfection. You can see the flow. You can see the way God always provides, no matter what. We are connected to that same source. The small things we take for granted are what give us those *aha* moments that reignite our spiritual energy. You can be renewed simply by your own thoughts. You can start to feel this happen when you get into praising yourself, the environment, and those around you. You amplify all positive energy, and the great forces of the universe suddenly begin to work in your favor.

What Will You Remember in the End?

At the end of the day, when life comes to an end, we only remember our good memories with those who are transitioning. It is like something in your mind forgets everything but the good times you have shared and experienced. Now think about what you are going through right now. Will it even last? Is it worth prolonging? Do you need to carry that emotional weight? You can be free right now, and you can choose to welcome that energy and way of living. All situations are momentary, and for us to have a greater perspective, we have to always let go so we can be free in our mind, body, and spirit. Being at peace with yourself is knowing that you can forgive yourself for anything and everything, but you can always clear things out by remembering that it is all just a moment. You will start to enter a positive state of mind. You will notice that things aren't as serious as they once seemed. You'll take the pressure off of yourself when it comes to how others see you and what you think you need to do for approval. You will begin to live out your dreams, and day by day, you will become mentally, physically, and spiritually stronger. The entire universe will support you (and is supporting you). You are now feeling more whole and free from everything that tried to stop you. You are now for yourself, and you know that you will start to win at everything you do because you are way too connected for it not to happen. You will begin to enjoy your life and stop taking things so seriously. You will see the good in others, and know that every person you encounter is a spirit. Everything is just a moment. Take it lightly, and fly higher!

Compassion/Kindness/Angelic Moments

You can start spreading kindness and reminding others that they are powerful just by being yourself. You can start speaking words of empowerment to others and lifting them higher. If you've ever had a moment when someone felt like an angel in your life because of how they treated you when you least expected it, that's exactly what this is all about. You can be a reminder of that same moment and feeling for others. It can be a shared experience of love that expands the entire universe. We all want to see change in the world, but it is up to us to be the best we can be and exemplify it in our everyday encounters. You create a ripple effect every single time you share compassion and kindness. Sometimes, it doesn't even require words; it's just a smile or a helping hand. You're doing all this because it is how you feel. This is why I focus so much on inner wellness and self-empowerment. I know that when each and every one of us feels whole and healthy, we tend to naturally radiate energy that impacts the world without a single word. Just being you is the change you can contribute to the world. It doesn't always have to be some grand movement you have to start. Your impact starts within you and the energy you give out. You are a very influential person, and you can begin, in this moment, to shift reality in a positive way.

Start encouraging others. Start encouraging your family and friends. Just as you need someone to believe in you, you can be that person who ignites hope in someone else. You are very influential, and you can start speaking powerful words into others. You can make an impact!

271

Start being an angel in other people's lives. Give out smiles, compliments, gifts, happiness, and kindness. Be a spirit that reminds others they are abundant, loving, and free to be all they can be. Be the example, and let miracles flow out of you. The more you send out energy that reminds people of their greatness, the more you'll see it all around you. You will start experiencing things that seem like a coincidence, but it is all aligned with the new energy you are putting out. When you are focused on being your greatest, you will never be in any kind of space, mind or body, that goes against your new way of moving. So many blessings will open up for you, and you will be a big part of the positive movement that teaches people to love who they are.

It Is Not About Competition

So much energy is wasted in comparing yourself to others or even judging someone else's lifestyle. Whatever someone is doing or has done came completely from within them. They dreamed that world into existence, and there's nothing the outside can do to affect their results. This goes for you, too. No amount of "negative energy" can stop your progress unless it comes from you believing in it or giving away your power to it. Our natural state is to help each other. If the concept that measures success or pushes you to try to be better and do better than others is removed, you will find yourself in the natural, creative state of wanting to work with others for a greater impact. We are not in competition with anyone. The only thing that matters is how we feel about ourselves, and what we put out based upon how much we believe in our vision. We can create supportive communities and environments using cooperation, which supports the collective thought of a group making an impact as one. More can be done if we work together on ideas we collectively believe in. Never again should you waste your time comparing anything about yourself to anyone. We are all creating every single moment, and when we spend more time working together, we harness more creative energy for greater solutions. A greater number of minds focused upon one vision is way more powerful and impactful.

Don't judge your timing, your path, or how things are unfolding for you. It is all in perfect order. Just breathe and let things flow. You're doing your best, and you have to remember that all is okay, no matter what.

Never again judge your looks, your success, your vision, or your plans against what someone else is doing. Don't feel the need to compete and restrict the abundance of ideas, creativity, and success that is available to all. There is no shortage. You are operating in a different field than people who think lack exists, and that they have to have it all before someone else does. That must be a tiring experience—to cut yourself off from the overflow of abundance and ideas. It is hard work to compete, because that energy is surrounded by fear and possibility of losing when you were already born a winner!

Be Solution-Oriented

How does your mind operate when it comes to the problems you might be facing? Do you automatically assume it can't change? Are you someone who is hopeful, optimistic, and solution-oriented? Are you always discussing what is wrong, or are you speaking about what could go right? Even if you have a solution for something, do you focus on the negative aspects of a situation you want to change, or do you move forward, toward the solutions, and make the change? You can either focus on change or look for ways to discuss problems. One thing I want you to remember is that your mind will continue to look for what you want to see. If you have something you want to change but you speak about its opposite, you enter into that which you give your energy to. The things you are thinking of, discussing, and sharing multiply and expand.

We need more dreamers: people who can imagine a brighter future and greater solutions. Those who still have faith in humanity. We need visionaries who will make local and global impact. The mind will chart us into new worlds and experiences if we dare to step into its possibilities.

Every single person with whom you discuss your problems is helping you expand them. They are creative, imaginative beings who will see the images and ideas you paint about yourself and the world around you. The example I like to use is when you haven't yet met someone but another person tells you so many negative things about him or her. Meanwhile, you have never even spoken to this person. Now, the image the other person painted of them is implanted in your mind. When you see them, you think about what they said. This could be something completely false, but in your mind, you automatically hold onto this picture of them until the statements are proven false. This is how impressionable your mind can be. Now, let's say you speak to the subject of the negative statements. Suddenly, you realize how nice they are, and your mind changes. This is how easily you can be swayed again. The point I am making is that your mind is sometimes impressionable to ideas and thoughts that are untrue, and when you don't declare a state of inner power over the direction in which you want to move, you allow others to do that for you.

Think twice about what you routinely discuss and the energy you spread about yourself and others. Every single word carries a strong energy, and it also has the ability to create ideas and plant seeds. Start being solution-oriented, and discuss more of what you want to see happen. Spread good news and be open about the direction you want to go. You can even speak your reality into existence in conversations. Make every moment worth your energy. When you want to share something about yourself, make it end on a positive note. Your optimistic and solution-oriented mindset will attract better for you.

See Beyond the Limitations and Perceive the Bigger Picture

What is every moment teaching you? What can you learn from current situations happening in your life? Are you giving more energy to what is happening, or are you looking at the bigger picture and what it is revealing to you? Everything is about perspective and how you decide to direct your energy. When you feel empowered from within, you react and respond differently. Start seeing beyond limitations. Tell yourself that you can, and speak highly of yourself. Every single word you use to describe yourself affects your mind, body, and spirit. Your words affect the environment. You are always putting out the energy of what you want to see more of. This is why you can feel your thoughts manifesting, then explain them away as something you already knew would happen. It happened because you spoke it into existence. You are very powerful, and the more you speak greatness into your life, the more miracles you will begin to notice.

May you receive more energy that keeps you inspired, motivated, and determined to live out your dreams.

All of your ideas can happen. All of your dreams can come true. Every vision that is in your mind is a seed planted by your spirit. It is not random or a coincidence that you are thinking about what is possible for you. This is what is coming from within so you can claim what is there. If you avoid these insights and keep yourself limited, you will feel stagnant energy within you. You will feel like something is off, and that you need to follow your heart. People only regret what they didn't do when they felt like they should have. The point is to stop living in regret and start following what is coming up. You have the greatest guidance inside already. There's nothing extra you have to do to have access it or feel connected. No one else is more connected than you. You are already there, but you are starting to remember what has always been available to you. In the beginning, it will feel new, but as you continue to own your inner empowerment and reclaim your ability to imagine your world as a dreamer, something awakens in you that just clicks. You'll notice high levels of inspiration and movement unlike anything you have ever felt before. It will be a familiar feeling, though. It will feel like a sudden understanding of yourself...really stepping into your own true greatness.

You keep getting better and better. You are growing so much and realizing a lot about yourself. This is only the beginning for all the greatness you came here to do. Trust your spirit.

From this moment on, walk like you are great, think like you are great, and be great just by being you. All of your ideas are manifesting. Everything that has happened to you is clearing out, and you are starting to see the great purpose each experience has served. You're feeling free from the weight of the past. Your emotions are starting to clear out. Years of regret cleanses out of you in seconds. Your cells are revitalized every moment. You have new habits and a greater passion for life and expression. Your imagination is providing you with the vision to see beyond current circumstances, and you feel so liberated. No endings define you. Any heartbreak or pain you once went through is cleared out. You are only walking this earth with lessons, wisdom, and insight that has now empowered you to be free. You are more connected to your spirit. You are receiving answers to your questions. The greatest obstacle is now forming new paths and opportunities for you. Your vision has expanded in such a way that you now have universal perspective. You are cosmically connected, and you know that all is momentary. You feel a surge of energy, drive, and purpose to be all that you can be. You feel motivated and ready to live out your dreams. You are now going to gain momentum in ways that once seemed unimaginable. All stagnation and laziness are broken from your field of energy. You are officially optimal!

Key Points

- *Real answers always come when you step back from the things that are happening around you and decide to tune into yourself and see how things look when you're not the one experiencing them firsthand.*
- *Who you are is so much more than what you can imagine. You have hidden powers and abilities you*

might not even know about. There's so much more to you, and it is now time to start claiming what has always been there as your truth.

- *To experience greater vision, you have to stay open to possibilities.*
- *Your spirit is lighting up every single moment with so many glimpses to remind you to get back to your imagination and start dreaming big again.*
- *This is the time to start following your heart and living your dreams. This is the time to start trusting yourself and making bold moves.*
- *Spend every single day counting your blessings and noticing the miracles that surround you.*
- *The Inner Glimpse is meant to expand what is already within you. It is that silent guidance that you have been receiving from your spirit to follow your heart and carry out your mission.*
- *You can be renewed simply by your own thoughts. You can start to feel this happen when you get into praising yourself, the environment, and those around you. You amplify all positive energy, and the great force of the universe suddenly begins to work in your favor.*
- *Never again judge your looks, your success, your vision, or your plans according to what someone else is doing.*
- *Think twice about what you discuss and the energy you spread about yourself and others. Every single word carries a strong energy, and it also has the ability to create ideas and plant seeds.*
- *Start being solution-oriented and discuss more of what you want to see happening.*
- *All of your ideas can happen. All of your dreams can come true. Every vision in your mind is a seed planted by your spirit. It is not random or a coincidence that you are thinking about what is possible for you.*

16

THE REALM OF POSSIBILITIES

You are now operating in the realm of possibilities. This is a mental state that completely alters all that you experience and makes a shift possible right now. In this mental space, you instantly start to notice manifestations, alignments, connections, synchronizations, and signs that you have intended into the universe. You are no longer going against the current; you are flowing. Your mental operations are streaming at high speed, and you are starting to notice that you believe in yourself more and more. Something major has happened within you, and you're thinking the best, dreaming bigger, and having stronger faith. You are operating in the realm of possibilities. This mental state is your natural state. You don't have to try hard to convince yourself that something can instantly happen for you. It *is* happening for you, and it always has. Now you're more aligned and tuned into this powerful state of mind, and you'll notice things beginning to move in your favor.

You're growing spiritually, and it's opening up new possibilities for you.

Why is it so easy for you to doubt that something is possible? What is the feeling or thought that creates fear? If you have a choice to give your energy toward something, why not invest it in your dreams and all that is possible?

You have to get back to dreaming big and trusting yourself. Anyone who has told you otherwise has forgotten their own personal power. If you now know that the realm of possibilities exists and you can create what you love, why not take that same energy and invest it into believing in yourself? Your mental state is so important, as is what you constantly speak and feel. What is your narrative? What story have you been telling the world? What energy have you been putting out? What is your self-image, and do you feel empowered to dream again? Everything requires your belief in order to happen. Even fear requires that you feed it to exist. This is where you are breaking free, because you are stepping into the realm of possibilities that has always existed within you. You are finally going to start walking in your truth and being open to great possibilities.

New beginnings are about to bring you the new energy of hope, self-love, clarity, awareness, and positivity that will lift you higher into new dimensions of possibility.

You have to start saying that you can. You have to start thinking that it will work out. Your mind will start to build a habit that supports positive outcomes instead of self-sabotage. You will encourage yourself and believe in your wildest dreams. You will move boldly to create the ideas that come to mind. You will think and feel as if miracles are a natural state for you. You will claim that you are genetically gifted, and own the feeling of being great. If you don't speak power over your own life, you will just play the state of being timid and unsure of yourself, which opens you up to external impressions that sway you left and right. Inner empowerment is the true freedom. Nothing can stop you!

Anything Can Happen for You

There's no separation between you and what you could be, what you can have, and what you will experience in this reality. You never have to go outside of yourself or try hard to experience the miracles that are at your finger-tips. The realm of possibilities includes sudden shifts and breakthroughs. It is a space that is available to you right now, and it promises access to anything you believe in. What is stopping you from creating the reality you want? What habits and thoughts are standing in the way of what could be? You have to believe that anything can happen for you at any time. It can be in this moment, or in the next second. All that matters is that you believe in yourself and understand your inner power. There are no rules, laws, or ideas that can stop your access. It is all in your mind. The boundaries you set up and the obstacles you put in front of yourself are up to you. You are free to dream big, and if you look around, so many people have dreamed their reality into existence. All is possible, and to bring greatness to life also means that you remember your natural power of in-ner freedom, empowerment, and owning your truth. Nothing outside of yourself can do that for you. Something has to awaken within you that helps you reclaim your truth. This book is meant to be the spark that ignites that inner reminder. I want you to acknowledge your Inner Glimpse and walk this Earth with so much understanding of yourself that you don't need anything external. If you are inspired from within and know what you have access to, then what can stop you? Nothing!

A miracle can happen for you right now. Believe in sudden and positive changes.

Move through every second believing that anything can happen for you. Don't go by structures or ideas of how things can happen, or what it takes for you to make it happen. If you were living in the realm of possibilities right now, and you knew that you could have anything you wanted, you wouldn't spend another second discussing what was possible. All limitations are removed from your field. You are a powerful being, and you will feel that in every cell of your being. This is no longer the time to walk around wondering what is possible for you. It is time to live in reality that anything can suddenly happen. You mind is always influencing your experience. You are always altering reality, whether you are aware of it or not. You have spent so many years questioning your abilities. You have had so many Inner Glimpses of what can happen for you. Now is the time to know for sure that anything can happen. Whatever your dreams, just know that they are possible. You are meant to live out your highest and greatest expression. Your talents and gifts will come to life the more you follow your passion and listen to your own inner voice. This is no longer the time to look for things to identify with. Everything is just an object for us to experience and mold. We aren't supposed to be defined by any one experience or limited to a single moment. You are meant to see with your own eyes what you can do.

May you gain the spiritual wisdom to overcome anything and get through everything.

Someone could tell you a million times that all is possible, or tell you to believe in yourself. However, everything changes when you actually feel it and see it happening. When you experience on a firsthand basis the power you have, you will never look back at what used to be. You will know that every moment is filled with potential. You are the one who operates in the realm of possibilities. The universe is very giving and supportive. Our birthright is the freedom to use our will how we want. If you feel like you don't want to tap into this state, you are operating from a place of repetition, reusing past thoughts or what someone has told you is possible. Your free will is your ability to do greater and ask for better. It is about showing yourself the creative genius that is within you. Never, ever speak negative words about who you are. If you have a vision, it can happen. If you have a goal, it can manifest. You are becoming free from habitual thoughts that try to make things seem greater than yourself or more real than your dreams. What is real is what you declare. What you experience is what you speak into existence. You can go from having nothing to having all you want. Free yourself from limitations of the mind and assuming things are as solid as they appear. You're supposed to be playful and take things lightly. Allow yourself to clear out any ideas that bind you to concepts that limit your mind. You will experience such a boost in confidence and attitude along with the surge of energy that supports you as you're reading this book. You are meant to be activated and remember everything you already have.

Your life has a special purpose. You're here to do magnificent things. You were chosen, and you have been given the codes already. Trust yourself. Believe in your wildest dreams.

Lack is not in your DNA! You were created by the Most High, and you were designed so perfectly that you can literally shift your life right now. The things that have become normal to you make you forget the genius that thrives within you and all around you. Think about how all of this is being orchestrated. Think of where we are, and how there seems to be an order and elegance to the movement of creation. Your mind and body can't be fully explained. You are being sustained, provided for, and supported in so many ways. Why can't your ideas be supported, too? Why can't you have access to the realm of possibilities? Why can't anything you want just happen for you? This is where what you believe in comes into play. The access you have is obvious. Never try to normalize the creative force flowing through you or forget who you are. To be powerful, you have to see the power you are connected to. Look at how it all flows so effortlessly; there's a silent dance taking place. All that has happened is meant to bring you to a place where you remember who you are. No challenge can limit you; it can only awaken you and allow you to see who you really are. This is starting to make things very clear, and it is allowing you to take back your power!

The Power within the Realm of Possibilities

Enter the realm of possibilities right now. No fear exists here. No doubt can come in. You are free to be who you want to be and ask for anything you want. There is no concept of time or how anything will happen. This is a place of unexpected blessings, with no need to worry about when or how. There is no uncertainty or fear of the unknown. This is a place of full trust and surrender. You have so much life in you right now. What is the force that keeps you going? You don't even know what wakes you up and provides you with so much energy on that level. It's much more than accepting yourself as you are. The point is to start seeing things from the realm of possibilities so you can make the greatest things come to life.

If you start recognizing how magical your life is, you will begin to move differently and think differently. Life becomes dull when you become too identified with ideas that try to stop you from being a dreamer. Things get hardened when you think that all there is to you is what surrounds you. If you look at the structure instead of the minds behind it, which are also you, you will see something completely different. The spaces around human beings were empty on a solid level until we brought in ideas and created structures. All that is around you is a creation of someone else's mind. Why be limited by structure or ideas when everything has already been created? Technically, what surrounds you is past thoughts that have manifested. If you take this in as the end all/be all, you will remain in a state of living as if it is more real than your own self. Your mind can bring ideas to life. You can create from within by truly believing and daring to dream big.

You have to start operating in the realm of possibilities. Nothing is as solid as it appears. There's a life force energy and power surging silently in all of space. You are connected. You have access. Start believing in yourself. Start speaking power over your life. You are very valuable.

We need more people to own their divine power so we can use our imaginations to see new things and create harmony in all ways. You don't have to judge what is happening around you, or even the people in your life. Everyone is literally going to be ready when they want to be. Remember, we all have free will, and the timing for us to realize that we are powerful is different for everyone. Your impact in this world can be found in living your dreams. When people see that you are operating in the realm of possibilities and that you are dreaming big, they will be very curious and naturally activated so that they, too, can live their lives the way they want. We are the example of what is happening within us. When we reflect and project possibility, it naturally creates an Inner Glimpse in others. It is like a mirror effect that shows someone else that they can, too. Don't worry about convincing anyone of anything. Real results happen when we choose to be active in what we want to experience. We light up the world when we live out our dreams. Your own personal inner change creates a ripple effect all around you.

Daily Miracles

Expect daily miracles. When you open your eyes, miracles happen. When you breathe, miracles happen. Every single day is a miracle. If you feel that and believe it, you will start to see some of the most magical things begin to unfold in your life. Why not live this way? Your whole existence is a miracle. If you are busy seeing miracles all around you and within you, you activate energy that will show you more miracles. You begin to see multiples and expansion in your life. Treat every moment like a blessing, and be grateful. No matter what is happening, always ask for miracles to be shown to you, even when you are going through something. You will see a sudden shift within your spirit and move in a new direction. You welcome greater solutions when you operate in the realm of possibilities.

Believe that a sudden positive shift can happen for you at any time.

Don't go another day living without your miracles. So many times, you have forgotten who you really are. Life may have become too dense or seemed too hard. Your focus was on what was happening instead of what could happen. Your inner vision was blurred, and that made you forget how miraculous you are. You might have taken ideas that don't belong to you too seriously, and that might have started with someone telling you what couldn't happen. Too many people's light has been dimmed, as so many have sought external validation for dreams that only come from within. You might have gotten an insight or a vision that was solely meant for you to believe in and execute. That vision was a miracle. Instead, you wanted others to see what was going on within you by sharing it, and suddenly, external chatter started going against your inner gift. Your vision is yours. Your empowerment for your vision comes from within. External validation naturally comes when people see that your vision has manifested. They will associate you with miracles because they can't understand how you do what you do. Your secret is that you expect daily miracles and operate in the realm of possibilities, where all can happen for you.

Staying positive right now will make unexpected miracles happen for you. You won't be able to fully understand why, but you will remember that you stayed positive, and that's the start of manifesting your wildest dreams. You've got this. You can.

Once your mind gets into the habit of recognizing daily miracles and expecting them, you will start to see your life differently. Your mind will naturally start to show you more of the genius that is operating within you and all around you. You will get a new outlook on life that allows you to multiply your blessings. What we see is what we choose. Our energy only goes where we direct our attention. Imagine what you will start to see all around you when you expect daily miracles as a natural state. You will unlock something so incredible that you will wonder why you spent even one second looking for anything but miracles. Prepare for your life to take a major positive turn. Your mental state is truly altering with this new thought, and it is giving you back what has always been there. You are now walking in gratitude, and this will naturally be your state of being. You will only be associated with miracles. This is the beginning of something so grand. Be ready for what you are about to experience!

Instant Results

Instant results start with the mind being completely open to unlimited possibilities. When you expect something to happen for you, don't connect it to how you expect it to happen. Stay open, and stay ready. When you allow things to unfold for you, you are placing your trust in yourself like you have never done before. To experience instant results, it all begins with a mental declaration that space and time don't depend on your results. If you think too much about how long something will take, that will create the energy of extended time. You are the one who also decides how quickly things can happen for you. If there is even a single thought that things must go through a long process before they can occur, you are limiting yourself. Understand that instant results begin when you start speaking power over your own mind so you can think, feel, and acquire all in the now. Your inner world responds to you now based upon the ideas you have about it. Believe that in the realm of possibilities, things instantly manifest. Your mental state is already attracting the vision that is literally about to show up for you right now.

Imagine what could happen for you if you stopped doubting yourself and started reclaiming your true power. You would be completely unstoppable. Your ideas would manifest. Your impact would be great. Your expression would be divine. All of this is within you right now. Claim it!

The movement of change begins when you believe, in this moment, that you can. After that, it becomes a catalyst of results. You will find yourself motivated, determined, and driven like never before. This is the gift of believing in instant results. If you project a thought that something is going to take a long time and that you will not be able to receive, you only set up barriers energetically that make you lazy and cause you to procrastinate. Instant results are the self-belief that fuels more life force in the realm of possibilities. You can get out of any state of mind that separates you from your results, and you own your results right now as if they are happening. Never again will you live your life hoping that one day, things will turn around. Spiritually, you pull in more energy when you believe that it can all happen for you right now.

If you continue to project your possibilities far away from yourself, you create hurdles and explain them away by saying you need to work extremely hard to get there. This is also true because it is what you believe. It can happen in so many ways. All I want you to know is that believing in instant results allows the universe to work for you in a different way. You will find yourself at the right place at the right time. You will bump into someone who is meant to share something you need with you. You will have chance encounters, and you will receive many signs. It will feel like you have unlocked a reality that communicates with you in a way that once seemed impossible. You could make bold statements, or you could be unsure of yourself. The point is that all is possible for you. Get into expecting instant results and allowing more energy to flow into your life to support your desired outcome. You will be in for a major awakening.

You have no idea how grand the gifts the universe has in store for you are. You're in for a magical surprise.

When you trust yourself, things begin to happen more quickly. You clear out doubt, limitations, and ideas of what can't happen from your energy field. You become so empowered that the space around you begins to alter in ways that show you what can happen. It will feel like you are living in dream world. These experiences will change your life for the better, because you will see just how connected you are. You will never lose another second wondering what could be. It is all what you want it to be. It can all happen for you. You are a powerful being, and your mind can chart new realities for you. You can unlock inner dimensions that give you access to external results that seem unimaginable. All of this begins with changing your mindset and believing that you are so much more than what appears to be your physical identity. You have so much life force and so much potential waiting to be expressed. Allow your inner light to shine through and your divine spark to be activated!

Anything Goes: Your Realm, Your World, and Your Creation

You are leaving behind the past, where you gave away so much of your power to what others thought. You may have even wondered if you were good enough to do what you came here to do. You are now giving up the false illusions that have kept you away from your dreams. Fear is coming to an end now. Your thoughts are becoming healthier because you are living out what you want. Your passion is bringing you so much peace. Your mental health is changing as you love yourself more and more every day. You're starting to see things from a spiritual place, and this liberates you to accept that anything goes in your world. You have your own sacred inner world that belongs to you. You can amplify your thoughts there. You can clear out what doesn't belong, and you can cultivate new ideas. Everything you see and feel is real to you because you are privately experiencing, responding to, and interacting with reality. What is valid for you is valid for you. If someone else doesn't believe in what you think is possible, that doesn't mean anything in your world. Things only get weak when you allow others access to think for you by believing in what they say you can't do.

Things can drastically change in a positive way for you. Believe that anything is possible.

It is now the time to start owning that anything goes for you. You are the one from whom everything stems. We are all creating in our sacred mental space and projecting into the world the ideas we want to see come to life. We are making a personal impact that has a greater influence on the world. Every idea you project ripples outward and creates its own world. The more sure you are of yourself, the stronger your ability to create becomes. It is impossible to think less than of yourself in the realm of possibilities. This is a space where you are highly empowered, strong, and able to create new ideas now. Move with this energy and live your dreams. We are all waiting for you to share your gifts. You are extremely talented, and when that realization awakens within you, you will really start to see why everything is beginning to go your way.

It Is Now Complete: It Is Already Done

Feel the end results. Feel your success happening. See yourself healthier in mind, body, and spirit. Go into every moment as if you are already living your dreams. Cultivating the state of mind that it is already done moves things differently than hoping that one day, things might change for you. The realm of possibilities is activated with the mind believes that its dreams are already done. When you automatically think that everything is already done in this moment, you get into the mindset of instant results, which shows that you trust yourself and believe your outcome is happening now. Next time you have a vision, speak the words IT IS ALREADY DONE! This is a strong activation that creates movement all around you and into the universe. You become the one who activates how things align by sending out the thought that you are confident that things are happening for you right now. This state of mind is so different from past fearful thoughts that have hindered your progress. Too many times, you put your vision out there with such low energy that it didn't amplify your power on the mental and spiritual level. You were putting it way too far into the future.

What you want is already yours. It's already done. Start counting your blessings. Start saying thank you for it. Start celebrating it.

When you feel worthy, valuable, strong, and blessed, you send out a different kind of energy into the universe. You show a confidence in your own inner power and that reflects your faith that anything is possible for you. This new way of being and thinking takes the weight and fear of the unknown out. You walk boldly now. You move right into it, even when it feels uncomfortable. You allow the mental shift to take place that allows your predominant habitual thoughts to be positive. This will feel like a new beginning for you, but what you're really doing is reclaiming your divine right to be who you have always been. So much excess will be removed from your mind, body, and spirit. It will feel like a whole new you is being reborn, and this will give you so much clarity and peace to move through life with the strong faith that you can. Anything is possible for you. You have mastered the realm of possibilities!

Key Points

- *Your mental processes are streaming at high speed, and you are starting to notice that you believe in yourself more and more.*
- *Now that you're more aligned and tuned into this powerful state of mind, you'll notice things beginning to move in your favor.*
- *The realm of possibilities includes sudden shifts and breakthroughs.*

- *You have to start saying that you can. You have to start thinking that it will work out. Your mind will start to build a habit that supports positive outcomes instead of sabotaging yourself.*
- *All is possible, and bringing greatness to life means that you remember your natural powers of inner freedom, empowerment, and owning your truth.*
- *You are free to be who you want to be and ask for anything you want.*
- *Our birthright is the freedom to use our will the way we wish.*
- *You are now walking in gratitude, and this will naturally become your state of being. You will only be associated with miracles. This is the beginning of something so grand.*
- *When you allow things to unfold for you, you are placing your trust in yourself like you have never done before.*
- *When you trust yourself, things begin to happen more quickly. You clear out doubt, limitations, and ideas of what can't happen from your energy field. You become so empowered that the space around you begins to alter in ways that show you what can happen.*
- *You are giving up the false illusions that have kept you away from your dreams for so long. Fear is coming to an end.*
- *It is now time to start owning the fact that anything goes for you. You are the one from whom everything stems.*
- *When you feel worthy, valuable, strong, and blessed, you send out a different kind of energy into the universe. You show confidence in your own inner power, and that reflects your faith that anything is possible for you.*

17

SPIRITUAL REALIZATION PHASE

Now that you are in a state where you have realized so much about yourself and your potential, you might be experiencing a new high like never before. This shift into a new dimension causes some people to feel inner clearance and changes that create a new feeling. The past is getting cleared out with every new realization. Be very patient with yourself. You might experience moments when you just need to rest to integrate all the inner activation that is taking place within. The more you spend time nourishing yourself, the more growth you will discover. Some people automatically begin to feel an instant change and inspiration like never before. Some people feel a deep transformation that frees them from past thoughts, and this might require some personal space for you to allow it to flow through. It is all very different for everyone. The point is to never feel guilty, never judge yourself, and never overthink whether you're doing something right or not. So much growth gets hindered when you overthink why you're not feeling positive in one moment when all that is happening is an energetic upgrade. All you need to do is love yourself in all your phases of growth, appreciate what is leaving, and welcome what is arriving.

I am physically, mentally, and emotionally ready to enter a new phase in my life. I'm ready to grow and get better. I want to be the best me.

You are evolving at high speed. What took years before is now happening in days, weeks, or months. In this period, you are realizing so much that once seemed difficult to comprehend. It all feels so natural now, and you are moving more boldly toward what has always been within you. All of these inner changes will require you to learn the power of allowing and intending greater things. Don't for one second overanalyze or worry about why you feel the way you do as you are stepping it up. You are shedding past thoughts. You are overcoming years of habits. You are starting to see more clearly and love who you are. You are recognizing that your value starts with you, and this allows you to feel new things. You are going back to your true state of dreaming, imagining, trusting, and allowing. Get out of tiptoeing around your gifts, and start moving like you were chosen for this. Allow yourself the space to step into it, and be very patient with yourself.

You are being prepared for what you have asked for. You might not understand why something is happening a certain way right now, but soon, everything will make sense. One day, you'll look back and be thankful that you decided to step it up, let go, and enter a new phase of your life.

Never wonder if you're doing it right. Understand that your experience and the way things unfold for you is very unique to you. If you overthink the timing or whether or not it's perfect, then you slow down your process. Just allow yourself to receive the messages, and let the feelings that come up spark new thoughts. Allow things to clear out. If you spend time wondering if you're doing something right, you create an energy block and self-judgment. The Inner Glimpse is a divine gift of reassurance that you're on the right path. When you get these signs from within, follow through with them. Don't question your intuition or your gut. Most of the insights we receive literally never make sense unless we look back at them and understand how much purpose they have served. This is why you have to trust yourself and how perfectly things are happening for you. Don't look around and wonder what others are creating, or what their ideas look like. Their timing is their timing. There's so much more to every single individual. There's a complex inner world of creation taking place at every second for each person. If you only look at the outside results, you'll remain in an illusion. Things happen easily for you when you invest energy in believing in who you are.

Don't overthink it. It will happen as it should. Invest your mental energy in believing in yourself and the possibility of things just working out for you.

Everyone is doing the inner work. This inner growth is so personal, and the timing is so precious to every person. We are all evolving at our own rate, and the more we are loving and patient with ourselves, the more we can flow through all experiences with faith, determination, and unwavering vision. You were chosen to be who you are. You have been given the genetic code to activate within you the power that has been within you this whole time. Every single moment, you are remembering what is possible for you. You become activated in a way that can't be put into words. So many times, I have been asked when something would happen, or why someone was still going through something when they had asked for better. Remember, asking for better also means clearing out what is currently stagnant in your life. This energy-clearing and updating of your mental world means that you are going through a change. When your spirit is ready, the change happens so instantly, you won't even recognize your past self. We are always upgrading. Moment by moment, you keep getting better.

Inner Glimpse: Fully Activated

There will come a point when you will repeatedly get signs from within that push you to fully follow your dreams. This will start to feel different, because now, you'll find yourself actually ready to step it up in ways you never thought possible. Being fully activated by your Inner Glimpse gets you to the point when you are spiritually ready for the change you have been seeking. There might have been times when you wanted to actually make alterations in your life, but found yourself back where you started. The difference between then and now is that you are fully activated on a spiritual level. Something within you has awakened to accept the new direction in which you are heading. It will feel like things are suddenly moving with ease, but at the same time, there is this motivation within you to finally go forward and make it happen. Being activated on a spiritual level allows your movement to be different from before. This isn't forceful, and it doesn't come from a place of fear. There's an understanding, clarity, and drive that provides insight into all that is possible for you. In that second, you fully experience what could happen if you followed your heart and trusted your inner guidance. This is what activates you. This is the new movement. Change won't seem like a struggle anymore. It will be something that is done, and you will find yourself moving through all your experiences with faith and a deep self-belief that you can make it through.

The glimpse you get of your full potential and what is possible for you is your spirit showing you a preview of who you can become. That glimmer of hope and flash of living your dreams is all within you for a reason. Allow yourself to be activated. Allow yourself to receive.

You are activated right now. So much is awakening within you, and you feel stronger and more motivated. Just reading this has already started the activation of own your inner powers so you can live out your dreams. You feel completely unstoppable and ready to get out of any mind-sets, habits, or cycles that have kept you away from your own truth. You are a walking powerhouse that needed a reminder. Once you realize who you really are and what you are truly capable of, you become a beam of light that radiates high energy. You start to see things from a greater perspective, and you exit all energy of stagnation. All that once kept you low is removed. All that has tried to stop you comes to an end now. You are activated with great power, and from this moment on, you will begin to experience true guidance from your spirit. Be ready for all that is unfolding within you.

Mental, Physical, and Spiritual Upgrades

You are entering a great time like never before. Everything you have been through, learned, and experienced has brought you to the place where you can finally see your mental, physical, and spiritual upgrades. This is where you are no longer held back energetically by past experiences, pain, or any shortcomings that have been present. You have now fully upgraded and integrated into your spiritual truth. Any past thoughts that hindered you are leaving your energy field and mental space. You will experience an emotional cleansing. You will feel reborn, renewed, and rejuvenated. These upgrades have always been there, waiting for you to awaken and take ownership of the fact that you are free to be who you want to be. This thought alone, and every single word in this book, is meant to activate the upgrade within you so you can finally be free of mental limitations, which are illusions that you lived by and accepted because you had no idea that you could access higher thoughts and views on life.

You can always do better. You can always upgrade. We have unlimited potential to improve, but it is up to us to decide when we are ready to step it up. No more excuses. No more complaining. It is now all about progress, evolution, and higher callings.

You are now activated on the cellular level, and your spirit is starting to shine brighter in your day-to-day life. All that seemed hard and heavy will give you a new outlook. Things you had to fight to overcome will now come to you with ease. You will feel a new energy entering your life from within that somehow takes the edge off how things appear. You are a spiritual genius. Everything within your body and mind is radiating with a higher light that takes your thinking and actions to the next level. You will seem supernatural, but the truth is, this is your natural state. You are accepting your upgrade and feeling energized to know that there is so much more to who you are. All of the dreams that have lived within you will now begin to flourish and come to life. Your spiritual upgrade also means that your mind, body, and spirit will gain more clarity about your purpose, your power, and your will to make a difference in your life.

You can't stay stagnant anymore. You're being guided to step it up and break free of past habits and repetitive cycles. It's time to soar higher and enter new dimensions within yourself. You are now ready.

Something will seem so different about this upgrade. In the past, it felt like a battle. It felt like you had to convince yourself that you needed to do better. Too many times, you found yourself returning to past habits, not knowing when you'd be truly free from those cycles. You probably wanted to make changes because you saw some kind of inspiration from the outside that you could get better and do better. The external inspiration only lasted momentarily, but this upgrade is a whole new ball game. This is a power that comes from within you. You are purely activated from within. Your inspiration is driven by your spirit. Your motivation is in your DNA. Your thoughts suddenly seem healthier. You notice that you don't need to put as much effort into your change anymore. This happens naturally, because it is now coming from within you. You are receiving your spiritual gifts and unlocking your true potential. Everything will propel forward, and you will experience increase in all areas of your life.

When Things Seem Unpredictable

What comes next is what you decide to believe in. Why be in fear of all the blessings that wait for you in the unknown? All you know at this point is what has happened in the past. To experience something greater, you have to be willing to thrive in uncertain situations and overcome the fear of things being unpredictable. You have tried to limit yourself way too many times, staying comfortable by using what you already know. When you are operating using your Inner Glimpse, you start to look at life from another perspective beyond the physical. Think of the most incredible luck or the greatest chance encounter you've ever had. How would you have set that up directly? It seems unimaginable when you're trying to see what comes next. You have to respect and appreciate the unpredictable way the universe operates. It is pure genius, responding to you based upon your desired outcomes. You're meant to simply put out your vision, speak your power, and imagine greatness in your life. The how and when will be taken care of. It will always happen when you least expect it. It always has happened that way.

Nothing and nobody can stop what's destined for you. Own your power. Claim your gift. Move forward, and move boldly.

Too many times, you have failed to take a leap of faith because you weren't so sure about what was next. Why stand still and remain stagnant? Why be limited? You have your entire life to experience so many variations, so much beauty, and the outcomes you want. Why hide away, just because you can't fully predict the step-by-step way it will play out? Time and time again, you have heard about living in the end result and already believing that your vision has manifested. This is a tactic to get your mind to stop overthinking the way it *should* happen, and get you into an energy state that it is happening for you.

A moment of doubt shouldn't stop you from making your vision come to life. You have big dreams for a reason. Move forward faithfully in all situations.

Don't be afraid of the unpredictable things that happen. Ask yourself: *What can I imagine besides what is happening?* How can you see greater? That is your power in moments of uncertainty—to smile and say *I believe in myself and where I am headed.* This powers you up so you can look at obstacles directly and banish their existence with your faith. You are a supernatural human, and highly gifted. Stop playing the small time game of *oh, I am scared* or *I am not sure.* You're not supposed to know every little detail of how things are going to happen for you. You're just supposed to believe in yourself and allow the unfolding to be so great that you rejoice in the feeling and the blessings it brings. There's nothing to fear. Only blessings are associated with your name and existence. This is starting to become more apparent to you.

Nothing Will Feel the Same

All of these spiritual realizations will bring you into deeper connection with who you are. All that you thought in the past will now change, because you are now treating yourself better and owning your power. You might have been unsure of yourself before, or even clueless about all you are capable of. You can no longer be timid. The time of doubt is over. You are stepping into true spiritual power, and it can never be taken from you. Every single thing you do will have more color and beauty, just because of the energy you bring to it. The fears you had of life before and trying so hard to keep everything together are clearing out. You are now moving in the highest state of trust in yourself, the universe, and the source of all creation. You will start to feel more alive, connected, and inspired. You will inspire many people, and share the gifts of inner freedom so many wish to have. Everyone has access. They just need to be reminded that they, too, can be at peace and live their wildest dreams.

You can always recreate yourself. You're free from the past. Never be a victim. Never give up. Never surrender your will to do better and greater. You can choose a different path today. The possibilities are endless.

In this phase of change happening on the spiritual level, you will see things in your life also changing. Your habits will change, your conversations will be different, and your interests will evolve. You'll find yourself sharing more laughter, happiness, and love with others. You're no longer forcing relationships or trying so hard to be accepted by others. You are freely thriving in your own vortex of joy, sharing it with the world. There's something so magical taking place within you. This is the beginning of being fully yourself and celebrating that daily. Every experience will bring you closer to yourself so you can understand who you are. You deeply connect with others in a way you have never done before. You go from fearing connection or trying to control how you are perceived to being yourself and enjoying sharing memories. You will also attract different people and different experiences based upon your current state of awareness. You will heal from the past much more easily, because you know that you are renewed every second. Something within you will automatically just feel free of any draining thoughts of what anyone has done to you or said. You are now a more empowered individual who is conserving your life force for what matters the most to you.

You can feel a strong, undeniable energy that your life is changing for the better.

In the past, you gave away your mental and emotional energy way too easily. You overthought situations that were meant to end for a reason. The new you knows better. You know the value of your time, your mental health, and your emotional wellness. You feel worthy of being you. You no longer need approval to be your authentic self. You no longer have to mold yourself to fit into someone's ideas of who they want you to be. You are now thriving in a healthy way and accepting yourself. You will feel so renewed that nothing will feel the same as in the past. You'll almost laugh, thinking about the way you used to live. There's no regret in your heart because you are free to be who you want to be today. This is a new moment for a new life as a healthier you.

Breaking Free from Habitual States for Spiritual Liberation

What habits are currently holding you back from living your dreams? There's always that one thing…you know if you just gave it up or stopped doing it, you could enter a whole new state. To be spiritually liberated means to break free from anything that limits your creative expression. You're here to experience the best you can be and enjoy creating your dreams. When you aren't expressing your creative energy and doing what you're passionate about, things feel heavy and hard. You're now being liberated on a spiritual level, shattering all habits that have tried to bind you into a cycle. You'll notice that it is easier for you to quit what doesn't support your evolution. You'll feel a strong rejection of habits that don't allow your spirit to thrive as it should. Something is clicking and finally making sense. Your cells and your mind are in unison with the change. A deep activation is taking place within your energy, and you no longer have any interest in cycles and habits that do not serve your spiritual evolution.

You're breaking free from past habits that don't serve you. You're entering a new state of mind that is propelling you forward.

These changes will be automatic. You'll notice a sudden shift toward a better life. You'll stop waiting around and overthinking habits. If it doesn't work, it is removed from your mind, body, spirit, and energy field. You're spiritually liberated from all things that try to keep your down. Things that take you to the next level of your evolution will now surround you. You will find that it is easier to let go of years old habits that seemed like they would take a miracle to stop. This *is* the miracle. The fact that you've even discovered this book is a sign that you are ready to take your power back and reach new heights within yourself.

No Explanation Needed...JUST FAITH

The way things are about to happen for you cannot be put into words or understood. There will just be great results. There will be something very magical and miraculous. If you keep your mind open to possibilities, all things can shift for you in this moment. I have seen many

306

great miracles happen in unexpected ways for others and myself. I have seen the impossible become possible. I have seen people get good news in an instant about something they have been waiting years for, just because they switched their mindset and energy state from resistance to complete faith. One thing I love is not trying to understand everything or having all the answers. Most of what I am sharing comes from the experience of what happened to me (and for me) once I stopped trying to use my mind to explain my reality. I moved with faith, and got rid of any thought of doing things all by myself. I connected to the Source that provides to all through faith, prayer, action, and determination. I discovered the power of my words and surrender. I got into pure faith and complete trust, knowing how well my life was being sustained. What are you really doing? Every aspect of your existence and environment shows that there's a great force working through you and with you. You will get a vision greater than anything you can see right now. There's so much we don't understand. We don't need to worry about knowing every single detail of *how*. Life is magical and very precious.

If you have faith, you never worry. You believe that it will work out as it should. You walk in gratitude, knowing that is it already yours.

When you stop attaching so many negative words and ideas to your outcomes, you free yourself from the concept of limitation. You stop living in resistance. You don't need to know it all. You don't need to have all the answers. What you *can* do is play, discover, set your intentions, speak power over your life, be hopeful, have faith, and dream big. When you move in this energy state, you create new paths that take you to where you're meant to go. Your mindset changes first. Shift from within. I would prefer for you to believe in yourself so deeply that people can feel your energy and power just by being in your presence. Faith moves everything. When you have faith, you will have a vision only you can see, no matter what the external is showing. We need to be carried by something much greater, and sometimes, that is the hope that lives within us when we choose to see beyond obstacles, pain, and struggle. We can be renewed and revived. Even if you have nothing right now or just want peace of mind, anything can be experienced. No state is final, and all moments have the life force and energy for a better and brighter future now.

Your greatest power is believing in yourself. Nothing and nobody can stop someone with vision and strong faith.

You are free from it all in this moment if you truly understand that nothing is attached to your spirit. You are fluid, able to change at any second. You can tell a new story, and you can change it at any time. Nothing is ever over. Too often, you have told stories about yourself that didn't match your true spirit. You might have limited yourself or settled out of fear. There's nothing to be scared of. What if you just went for it and took that leap of faith? What could really go wrong? Free yourself from the mental and emotional states that try to make you think it's crazy to dream big. If you see beyond what surrounds you, you'll feel the subtle energy of life. It is pulsating with so much potential. You might have gotten so accustomed to physical reality that you forgot your spiritual gift. You are a very special being who has vast potential of expression. You can have peace now. You can be successful doing what you love. You can have a great relationship and loving friendships. You can also be at peace with the things that don't make sense and the timing of how things unfold. Your only state of mind should be that you can, that you trust, and that you will keep going no matter what is happening. The rest will work itself out as you start to fully receive from within.

It's all about mind over matter, vision over circumstances, and faith over fear.

Start trusting yourself and loving who you are. Start accepting your power. Start walking in faith. Be the example of hope, and always speak words of encouragement to yourself and others. You will feel a complete shift in mindset right now, and you will believe in yourself like never before. There will be a great passion for life and making a difference. You will own the fact that you are doing what you love. No matter how big or small things may seem, everything is great in your world because it comes from your spirit. If you look at every moment as a gift, you will feel more alive and connected. The spiritual realization phase is meant for you to remember that all is okay, and you have it within you in this moment to access unlimited insight. Be very patient with yourself and allow yourself to receive abundantly, as you are now in a vortex of great change and blessings!

Key Points

- *Be very patient with yourself. You might experience moments when you just need to rest to integrate all the inner activation that is taking place.*
- *You are evolving at high speed. What used to take years is happening in days, weeks, or months. This is a period when you are understanding so much that once seemed difficult to comprehend.*

- *You are shedding past thoughts. You are overcoming years of habits. You are starting to see more clearly, and you love who you are.*
- *The Inner Glimpse is a divine gift of reassurance that you're on the right path. When you get these signs from within, follow through on them. Don't question your intuition or your gut.*
- *Everyone is doing inner work. Inner growth is so personal, and its timing is so precious to every person. We are all evolving at our own rate, and the more we remain loving and patient with ourselves, the more we can flow through all experiences with faith, determination, and unwavering vision.*
- *Things you used to have to fight to overcome will now come to you with ease. You will feel a new energy entering your life from within that somehow takes the edge off of how things appear. You are a spiritual genius.*
- *You are now entering a time like never before. Everything you have been through, learned, and experienced has brought you to this place, and you finally see your mental, physical, and spiritual upgrades.*
- *You are activated right now. So much is awakening within you, and you feel stronger and more motivated.*
- *You can have peace now.*
- *Start trusting yourself and loving who you are. Start accepting your power. Start walking in faith.*

18

END OF GAMES

You can enter a new state in which you accept who you are and discover that you are connected to an unlimited supply of love that flows through you so you can feel, experience, and share unconditionally. If we remove all concepts of how things should be in terms of our relationships with others, we end up with the most basic human understanding of love and connection. It is our natural state to understand and be understood. When the layers, misconceptions, pain, and learned blocks are removed, you start to see, feel, and understand that it is not a battle, but rather self-acceptance that transcends the need to judge, change, or overthink someone else. Yes, there exists a space where games are played, and too many people feel depleted in this state. The plotting, the scenarios, and the constant fear of something going wrong create a lot of restriction in the mind and body. Your spirit wants to flow and share what is naturally overflowing. You already understand this. You don't have to worry if someone else will do the same. The greatest secret that will automatically liberate you is knowing that every experience and detail is felt and known only by you. Everyone outside of you only knows bits and pieces of who you really are. This will help you to accept that you don't need to feel so misunderstood. We are very complex beings, and as much as we share who we are and open up, we still see reality from our own perspective. You can be free from needing to think that someone must think like you or be the way you want him or her to be.

Your power is knowing that you experience the wholeness of reality from within yourself. Everyone around you is experiencing reality from a whole different state. Someone might be feeling a certain way within, and they can seem to be in a mood that appears unpleasant on the outside. You might just see the appearance of the mood, and not understand the core of the feeling that created it for them. They might never even share why. So much misunderstanding can happen if we don't start to believe that everyone is experiencing reality in ways that are not physically apparent. People are afraid to express themselves out of fear of being judged or feeling like they don't want to share their weaknesses. This is why you have to always remember that how people are acting, what they are doing, and what they choose to do has nothing to do with you. It is never personal. Never, ever blame yourself for other people's actions and behaviors.

When you know how to manage your own inner state and wellness while understanding why something might trigger you or make you feel a certain way, you get better at knowing how to overcome it. Imagine all of what goes on within you, and all that you're constantly learning. Everyone else is also having this experience in their own unique way. The point here is that you need to begin to recognize how whole you already are. You never, ever need to force anything, or try so hard to be understood. Accepting yourself in your own unique way allows an inner flow to take place. You feel free from being so controlling of every little detail, wondering if you're good enough or doing things right.

You're too great to doubt yourself. Don't let fear play games with you. You are valuable, special, unique, and different. You can accomplish, create, and design the reality you want. Feel good about yourself, and let the universe know that you are ready to receive.

You can be in whatever state you want. People only respond to what you stay true to. You might have given your own inner power away, thinking that maybe you could change someone. Maybe you thought you could be all they wanted you to be, and then things would be perfect. It's not about trying so hard to impress, or being accepted or admired. You have to discover this within yourself and radiate it out. If someone doesn't recognize the state you magnify, they won't even enter your sphere. People in your life are only teaching you to love yourself more, accept who you are, and remember your own inner power of wholeness, completeness, and connection. When something comes up that you don't agree with, you automatically might start to think, *I deserve better than this situation.* The goal is that feeling: I am worthy of treating myself better and getting the best out of life. You then go into a state of self-improvement, and this shows you an Inner Glimpse of everything that has always been there. No heartbreak or endings stop your evolution. Every experience is meant to enrich you, even the disagreements you have with others. Each moment brings you back to this: *I am good enough to be loved. I love myself wholly, fully, and unconditionally.* What you start to create within yourself becomes an inspiration to those around you.

A great sign of growth and maturity is no longer feeding into people's drama, games, and negativity. Sometimes, you just have to know how to evolve past what doesn't lift you higher. When you step away from it, you take your power back. Use your energy to get better and do better.

You are the one who can get into a new state through choice and awareness. Take care of the inner you first. Take some time for that, and know that no matter what is happening, it is not the end of the world. There are always better days and greater experiences ahead if we decide to embrace what is so that we can turn it into what we want. Look at everything from a state of learning and evolution. You'll never have to feel like a victim or think you have overextended yourself by being all that someone else wants you to be. It is only in your mind that you think you have to do anything extra or try so hard to prove a point. Never do anything out of desperation or neediness. You will find yourself in a place where you might get someone back to talk to you, but you might not feel too good about yourself. It goes back to a state of push and pull in order to feel worthy of appreciation. You have to begin to enter a new state of mind within yourself first. Being happy within yourself by simply being you is the start of creating a healthy connection with others.

We tend to close our hearts to protect them, but this blocks you from receiving and expressing yourself. It's all about remaining open right now. Keeping yourself open shows that you trust that something greater can happen, but at the same time, you are free from the past. This will help you transcend from fear to bliss, from games to freedom.

Things will change as you evolve and get better at fully accepting and loving who you are. You will discover the importance of sharing what is naturally abundant, which is love, patience, and understanding. Every situation is unique, and every person's experience plays out in a different way. Some people start evolving and have to end old connections, and some people are able to help others in their lives see greater in themselves, thereby creating stronger bonds. How things unfold for you is based upon an increase in self-love, self-awareness, and self-acceptance, and this will be unique to your experience. Maybe it will bring ease into your heart and mind so that you no longer have to resist the greatness that's trying to enter your life. Maybe it will bring great healing and a sense of trust to share your heart with someone again. Maybe you'll discover that you need to get to know yourself better before you dive into a relationship. At the end of the day, no matter where you are on the spectrum of evolving and loving who you are, the results will always produce the best outcome for you. The only changes you can make right now are in your thinking, how you talk to and about yourself, and how you manage your expectations. The instant you alter your mindset, it influences the environment around you. You'll start to see in others what you radiate, and that energy will naturally rub off on them without you even trying.

Break the Cycle of Fear, Loneliness, Neediness, and Desperation

How many times has the fear of not being loved enough affected your relationship? How many times have ideas you held about someone fail to match what the person ended up showing you? Fear creates a lot of unnecessary problems, and this stems from the mind believing that you are not worthy. What you think has more of an influence than what you say. If you feel you aren't good enough, you attract experiences and people that validate that point. If you think something has to always go wrong in relationships in order for you to feel reassured or validated, then that will continue to happen. What beliefs are you holding right now about your relationship, or relationships in general? What are you constantly focused upon when it comes to experiencing or sharing unconditional love? You never have to play games or pull stunts to prove a point. Behaviors like these might give you a feeling of "power" initially, but soon, you'll realize that this wears off, and another stunt has to be pulled. This is literally a loop and cycle—a power game. Wanting to be in control and doing all types of tricks can perpetuate the fear that you can't be accepted, appreciated, and loved for simply being you. If you feel like you need to protect yourself, you also create an energy barrier so someone won't hurt you. This blocks real love from coming in.

Don't lower your energy to play games and become part of a toxic cycle. Revenge depletes your energy and steals from you. Move forward. What you remove your attention from will cease to exist. Get better. Attract better. You are too great to entertain such energies.

I will repeat this as much as possible: Your mental state and what you think are constantly attracting your physical experiences. You are sending mental signals out to have the experiences you truly believe in. You can say you want something, but most of the time, it is what you *don't* want and what you want to avoid that's sending signals out. What do you really want out of your experience? Don't complicate it. Your true power is getting your mental state and point of attraction in order. You have to start to own who you are and not be afraid of what you can truly manifest. Don't think of how long something might take. This is also an illusion that makes many people settle out of fear. They wonder if they might not find the love of their life, or accomplish a certain thing by a certain time. This kind of thinking creates neediness and a sense of rush, which shows lack of trust. You're better off taking some time to get yourself together instead of trying so hard to force things. Let what comes up come up as you begin to give focus and attention back to you. You have to be very patient with yourself. If you discover through your own evolution that you deserve better, then something greater will manifest for you. If you discover that all you have to do is love yourself in order for your current relationship to flourish, then that will happen, too. Like I said, the outcome of this will be very unique to you.

You will also discover that the fear of being alone will disappear as you realize that you are truly experiencing the world from within yourself. Many people have told me that they could be surrounded by so many people, but still feel alone. The point of this is finding comfort in who you are first. Find that peace in loving yourself. Being alone doesn't mean loneliness. Sometimes, what you think you're silently going through can be happening to the next person. Often, we don't share this side so we won't appear a certain way, or we do it to avoid judgment. You're never alone within yourself, because you know you are experiencing life in its entirety from within.

Don't be afraid of being with yourself. Allow yourself the time to explore who you are. Sharing space and energy with others is a great way to create greater experiences when you feel like you are fully present in the moment. Don't force connections out of the fear that you might be lonely or won't find what is meant for you. Like I said, you never want to have those kinds of thoughts. Anything you are entertaining mentally that pertains to yourself and the connections you can form with others starts with your repetitive, dominant thoughts. What we share with others is a glimpse of everything we are from within...and that goes for everyone. Knowing this, be your true self and enjoy the company you have. Be comfortable in yourself and by yourself. The more you thrive within, the more you will realize how everything on the outside can alter. Something that appeared to be a disconnection has the ability to transform into the greatest experience you've ever had. Don't hide away from feeling, living, experiencing, and enjoying all moments of your life. Sometimes, this can mean getting out of your head and not overthinking things.

Don't let negativity consume you. You can get tempted to play games, but you should always remember to switch up your focus. How you respond is more important than what is happening. Stay lifted. Stay positive. Stay centered. You can decide right now to switch things up.

Inner Glimpse is about listening to your own inner voice. It is about trusting your gut feelings and intuition. Advice is secondary to everything you already know. The complexities and details are viewed, experienced, and known only by you. When you ask your inner self for guidance, the answers will be revealed to you in ways that capture the entire scope of your being. You know yourself the best. Start practicing asking your inner self the questions you really need answers to. Start saying *show me the way, give me the guidance, I am ready for a sign now.* You'll develop your own inner communication, and this will build your faith in yourself and help you trust who you are. If you constantly seek external answers, it won't cover the full picture. Internal guidance is meant to ignite within you a state of remembering who you are and what you're truly capable of. This will bring you back to tapping in.

Freedom from Games

Games end when you decide to stop playing out mental scenarios that don't support your vision out of fear, holding on, or trying to force things. You also become free from overacting or being a button that people can easily push to get you all emotional and overthinking. This always puts you in a state that is not natural to you. You could feel threatened and need to protect your self-image. This is also an illusion, because there's nothing you need to protect yourself from. It is all just an act that occupies your energy and steals from you, when really, your true power lies in realizing that you can end it now and think new thoughts of what you want, not what you need to manipulate in your favor. Why not use that same energy to manifest greater and experience something you truly deserve? Don't play in the field of the past. Even old thoughts need to perish. This is what freedom from games truly means. You mentally exit the realm of limitations, struggle, and battle. You choose to think better, feel greater, and attract what you want with grace, dignity, and honor for your own self. If you can manifest whatever you want, why manifest in the same old energy field? Why try hard to hold onto something that's worth letting go? Why manipulate certain experiences just to control them? All of these things are momentary, and will require you to keep investing your energy to keep it up.

The best thing you can do is find a point within yourself where you are comfortable with who you are, and start thinking, imagining, and manifesting the experiences you deserve. You can watch it all happen for you effortlessly. It will feel so magical to know that all you needed to do was get clear, get connected, and love who you are while trusting that someone who understands this will manifest into your world. Even if you are in a partnership, it can get way better simply by treating your own self better and being kind to your own mind and inner world. The better you feel, the better and greater the energy you put out. It literally all starts within. You can choose whatever works for you, and focus your mental energy on seeing that outcome happening for you right now.

Anyone who tries to break you down is only afraid of who you are, what you can become, and what you can attract. Instead of falling into their games and tactics, stay focused on what matters. You're moving on. You're getting into something bigger and better. More blessings and brighter days are coming your way.

Never, ever play the game of trying to prove to someone that you are doing better without them. This keeps you connected to them because you're doing things to show them that you are valuable, when in reality, you might be giving them too much power over you. If you have moved on from a relationship, let it go. Don't play social media games or try to capture their attention or get them to recognize you. This is old energy, and a sign that you don't trust that there is better and greater in store for you. Understand that the world is filled with possibilities. You can attract a partnership right now that might once have seemed unimaginable. Why? Because there is someone perfect for everyone in their own way. Once we enter a new mindset free of games, we enter the realm of possibilities. Magical things can happen for you quickly. Why tie yourself to an experience that has ended? Why play in that field when you have already outgrown it? You need to know that there is nothing to be afraid of. Literally anything can happen for you. There are billions of people and billions of different types of outcomes. Why remain in an energy that has ended? Why go back to what you have evolved from? We naturally enjoy connections because they are a part of our nature, but we have to stop putting the past on a pedestal and embrace the unknown of the greatness that can happen. Embrace yourself. This is what being free of games means.

You know your power. You know that you can manifest something better. You even know that you can have a better connection in your current relationship simply by switching up any negative, repetitive thoughts that don't support your connection. Bring that energy back within yourself and start to flourish. I want you to radiate beautifully and magnificently. There's no sign of desperation in your energy field. There's no need to force anything. There's no need to try so hard. You are in natural alignment with greatness. What is meant for you is going to be pulled into your world. You will have better connections, partnerships, and friendships simply by believing that all of this is true right now. You have to be the one who fully loves yourself first, no matter what. You are naturally great at having a healthy relationship because you already feel worthy on the inside. You will manifest exactly what you want; you are a believer in attracting what you think and feel. You are stronger than ever in mind, body, and spirit, and that makes you really attractive. You love yourself, and that expands your energy field. You are kind, open, and enjoying every single moment of your life. You have been released from grudges, fears, and past disappointments. This is a new beginning for you—a new day to think new thoughts and feel your own self coming alive. So much is happening for you, and loving yourself is where it all starts.

Key Points

- *You can enter a new state in which you accept who you are and discover that you have an unlimited supply of love that flows through you so you can feel, experience, and share unconditionally.*
- *When the layers, misconceptions, pain, and learned blocks are removed, you start to see, feel, and understand that this is not a battle, but rather self-acceptance that transcends the need to judge, change, or overthink someone else.*
- *Accepting yourself in your own unique way allows an inner flow to take place. You feel free from controlling every little detail or wondering if you're good enough and doing things right.*

- *You are the one who can get into a new state through choice and awareness. Take care of the inner you first. Take some time for this, and know that no matter what is happening, it is not the end of the world.*
- *There are always better days and greater experiences ahead if we decide to embrace what is so we can turn it into what we want. Look at everything from a state of learning and evolving.*
- *Things will change as you evolve and get better at fully accepting and loving who you are.*
- *The instant you alter your mindset, it influences the environment around you. You'll start to see in others what you radiate, and that energy will rub off on them naturally without you even trying.*
- *You never have to play games or pull stunts to prove a point.*
- *Don't be afraid of being with yourself. Allow that time to explore who you are.*
- *Don't force connections out of fear that you might be lonely or that you won't find what is meant for you.*
- *The more you thrive within yourself, the more you realize how everything on the outside can transform from disconnection into the greatest experience you've ever had. Don't hide away from feeling, living, experiencing, and enjoying all the moments of your life.*
- *The best thing you can do is find a point within where you are comfortable with yourself, you start thinking, imagining, and manifesting the experiences you deserve. Watch it all happen for you so effortlessly.*
- *You will manifest exactly what you want.*

19

LIVING INTUITIVELY

Living intuitively is returning back to your inner self for answers and guidance. There's so much you already know and understand naturally. This is a part of the Inner Glimpse. You probably have experienced many situations in which you received signs and gut feelings that turned out to be accurate. Sometimes, we follow these inner signs; at other times, we wish we had. That's okay, though. This chapter is meant to help bring clarity about living intuitively and trusting yourself so you can be divinely guided.

Trusting your inner guidance is connecting with your intuition. Your body has the ability to detect and read energy on levels beyond the physical. Feel it, and know how real it is.

To live intuitively, you must first learn to trust yourself. This is the first step toward understanding how to listen to your inner guidance. Trusting yourself is knowing that there is so much more to who you are. Your essence and spirit are beyond the physical. There are things your mind and body naturally pick up on a subtle level that allow you to receive insight. The interesting thing about building this inner trust is learning to understand that it doesn't initially operate in a way that seems to make sense.

We live in a state that leads us to want control over all the outcomes and how things are going to happen. We want to know the details, the steps, and the answers in a way that seems predictable to our minds. However, your intuition doesn't really work that way. It can seem so irrational at first. You may even start to question why you thought or felt a certain way about something—but when you trust it, you find yourself being led and guided to naturally receive the answers you need.

Let yourself be intuitively and spiritually guided. The answers you need can be found within you right now. Remembering your inner compass and spiritual nature restores you. It makes life feel lighter. It gives you hope and lifts you higher. It opens you up to endless possibilities.

You cannot rely on past experiences alone to receive divine intervention. You must accept that the way things will happen is completely unimaginable at this moment. All you have is a vision. The way things work out will always seem magical and unexplainable. This is why faith has played a big role in humanity. You must believe in the unseen, energy, possibilities, and visions of something greater. That small amount of faith and reconnection to your inner guidance will reveal to you everything you need to know.

Too often, you have silenced the inner voice that has always been here to guide you. You have received so many signs and nudges from within about what to do next, how to move, and what kind of action to take. You have given too much of your power to external information, and not enough to your inner voice, which is meant to be heard. The insights you have access to arrive because you remember that all is within you in this moment. Imagine that all ancient wisdom and future creation lives within you. Things on the outside should trigger a reminder of what is within, not make you forget your power or make you dependent on what appears to be promising. If you are activated through remembering your own gifts, you won't need to attach yourself to anything, and you will see life from a greater perspective. You will trust your own inner guidance. The answers from within are perfectly made for you. Just as you are unique in every aspect of your thinking, being, and creation, you also receive directly from your spirit exactly what is meant for you. Living intuitively is tuning back in and accessing pure clarity of direction. You always know better. Every single time you have silenced that inner guidance, you have reverted back and said, *I wish I had listened to my gut.*

Sometimes, your spirit is trying to convey a message to you through a sign, a gut feeling, or a synchronized experience. Don't use logic to make sense out of it. Allow yourself to flow. Allow yourself to trust. Allow yourself to be guided. Great blessings are being revealed to you.

Nobody can give you better insight and wisdom about any situation than your own inner self. When you are not listening, you go on a search, and that search becomes secondary to the clarity that's naturally flowing within you. All information you receive from the outside should only bring you back to yourself. Anything that makes you dependent takes away from your inner truth. You should be free to live without any outside concepts or ideas about what flourishes from within you. The more you start listening to your spirit, the more you'll receive insight perfectly made for you. Imagine the details of your thoughts and all the inner aspects of who you truly are. Only you know yourself better than anyone else. If someone is trying to tell you something but only looking at one aspect of your life, they will miss the connective energy that makes up who you really are. This is why prayer, meditation, and talking directly to God return your access to what's been there all along. We have always done this, and those who ask for guidance have always received it. Nobody can see the vision of where you are headed but yourself, and it is a very spiritual thing to be able to directly connect with your own inner guidance. When you understand this and really know it, you feel the warmth of reassurance that everything will always be okay.

Follow the signs. Trust that gut feeling. The universe is constantly speaking to you. Listen to it. Pay attention to the synchronicities and how everything you think is connected to everything you experience.

You will also always have a connection to tune back into. You are always connected, and you honestly have the highest connection to pure insights, which are crafted and designed for you. On the outside, there might be people who are meant to guide you back to your own self so you can be powered up from within. You don't need to do anything special or extra to be connected or have access to your inner truth. You just know, because you are it, right now. You have always had it. Everything is just a reminder of what you already know. Even my books—this one and *Manifest Now*—are just reminders of your own power. You're supposed to read this and feel like you can conquer the world. You are supposed to feel energized and believe that anything is possible for you. This is what the Inner Glimpse is all about: a realization of all that can be. When people say they are awakening, it's another way of saying that they are remembering who they really are and all the potential they have always had within them. We were born with all the codes and blessings. We have it all right now. There's no difference between you and someone else when we are talking about accessing your own gifts and bringing them to life. Some people remember that they can, and others are working on getting to that point through divine sparks that keep coming up from within. The more they become frustrated by external information, the more they start trusting their own insights. Information is meant to help things click when it is time for that realization to happen. That, too, is just a reminder to awaken in you the memory that has always been there. That is what an *aha* moment feels like: when something just clicks, and you feel like it all finally makes sense.

You Know Better

You have the greatest connection right now. You are already it. Take that in for a moment. Sometimes, you may forget who and what you really are. Take in the life force that flows through you. Think of the stream of thoughts that flow through your mind, and how that changes as you evolve. I'm sure you're not in the same state of mind as you have been in the past. Even ideas from last year can look very unfamiliar to you today. You are constantly growing, evolving, and expanding from within. You have to take in just how miraculous you are. You have always gotten better somehow. Even the hardest times gave birth to new ideas about yourself that showed you just how strong you are and how much you can overcome. All of these lessons activated different codes within your mind and body, showing you firsthand how resilient you are. Deep down, you know just how much it took, and all the emotions you felt in order to reveal to yourself that the renewed you can only be fully understood by yourself. There are so many aspects to who you are that made you the best you can be, even if you're still growing right now. You truly have to acknowledge that you know yourself better than anyone else.

You're becoming more powerful every day. You're starting to feel and see who you really are. You're realizing what you deserve. Your inner light is starting to illuminate. You are getting a glimpse of your own intuition, and it's giving you back your divine power.

Everything it took to make up who you are comes as a reminder of what is within you. You've stood tall and processed many emotions that took you to different levels within yourself. You saw that things aren't as scary as they seem. Your mind and body have always integrated in the direction of change, even when it seemed like you couldn't. The point is, I want you to remember that you know better. Don't take things outside of yourself too literally, to the point that you forget the access, wisdom, and insight you have. Sometimes, we can get so consumed with what is happening that we forget we already have the tools for dealing with anything that might come up, no matter what it is. You're constantly being refined, but the truth is, you're only realizing more of who you are and how multifaceted and inter-dimensional your being is.

Asking for Guidance from Within

Something incredible happens when you deeply mediate or pray about something. Even if you don't do anything but feel a strong urgency that you need a quick solution, a spiritual intervention happens. Being in an urgent state activates quick solutions. Urgency in the moment turns into a command, but what I think is happening is that your emotions are the highest, and you're automatically surrendering to a greater inner guidance. So many people have told me how quickly things have turned around when they needed it the most. What took time was preparing to receive. Imagine waking up in the pure state you want to manifest. You would probably be so shocked. Sometimes, you make the process happen because you mature into your manifestations, or you give it time to come together based upon alignments being created and opportunities being put into place. Asking for inner guidance gives you the key to a bigger vision than what you can see right now. If your focus is on what is happening, you don't allow your mind to go beyond it. Asking is another way of allowing yourself to surrender. It is like your mind becomes comfortable with letting it go, and this activates access to a greater vision.

All illusions that were keeping you away from seeing your greatness are now perishing. You are becoming more alive and awakened. This is the beginning of your inner revelation.

If you use only what you see to build a new vision, you can only grow so much. However, if you allow yourself to start trusting that you have the greatest inner connection that provides you with guidance, answers, solutions, ideas, and insights that allow you to maneuver this reality, then you do things differently. Nothing can break you. Nothing can stop you. You will always learn, grow, and thrive, because you know that all is working out in your favor. The more you access your own inner guidance to lead you, the more magical your life becomes. All of the areas that seemed difficult suddenly look so different. Things start to beam with more life and potential, and begin to resemble what you want them to be. You no longer allow what is happening to weaken your mind, body, and spirit. You are not controlled by circumstances. You are not the past stories of what has happened to you. You are so much greater than any of that, and this is what will carry you through life, no matter what happens. You are prepared by the awareness that you can always create better, and always have access to ask for guidance from within.

All the answers you need are within you. Pray if you have to, or ask until you receive it. Never abandon the inner wisdom you carry.

Asking doesn't require some special ritual or anything extra. Your inner self already knows exactly what you want. You just have to use your inner voice, speaking it to yourself with all the emotion you are feeling. Just ask as if you were asking someone who had all the answers you need. Be bold and direct. Don't for one second overthink whether or not you will receive, or wonder too much if you're doing it right. Too many people spend so much energy wondering if they are doing things properly. There is no proper way. There is no one way of doing it. Just stop overthinking it and ask. Ask away, and ask like you're talking to an inner friend who gives the best advice, guidance, and secrets to you.

Ask to be guided, and you will never have to worry again. Speak powerfully in your prayers, meditations, and time alone for answers, clarity, wisdom, and freedom from all burdens. Feel yourself getting stronger. Remember your spiritual essence. You can ask for anything, and you can receive everything.

Don't complicate things. Just be yourself, and do it effortlessly. Just the thought of asking is already bringing you results. Too many times, you may have asked, but then started overthinking it by asking others or looking around to find it some other way. You put your inner guidance second as you went on a search outside yourself. This created a lot of work on your end. Anything that feels like you're trying too hard creates blocks or a lack of trust. You don't have to force anything. You don't have to feel like you need to do it a million times to get your request answered. The simplest way is to just ask, feel it, and let it go. Allow what comes in, and do what comes up from inside. I want you to start trusting yourself more instead of searching for everything. Search from within. The more you become familiar with asking and trusting yourself, the more you will recognize your own flow. This will be such an incredible time, and you will know that you are always okay.

What Works for You

Remember, no two people are alike. How you see things is very unique to you. Your own inner world and experience are your private space that affects how you see the world around you. The most unimaginable thing could happen for you right now, and you really wouldn't be able to explain it. It will, however, transform you forever. You have to start getting used to the idea that everything doesn't need words. Sometimes, you can't even put things into words, because they were meant to be experienced and felt by you. Words won't even do your divine experience justice. Don't worry about trying to convince anyone about what is taking place in your life. I have seen some people lose their inner fire by trying hard to find reassurance by convincing others of what is possible for them. Remember, what has awakened in you is what has awakened in you. Your revelations, insights, wisdom, and understanding came to you when you really needed them the most. You see the miracles around you because you are able to tap into a new vision that gives you a broader outlook. You can only inspire others through your personal results, the energy you radiate, and the way you live your life. We are always inspired by seeing tangible results of the inner ideas people have. Focus your energy on being the example of your own inner flow. Be the best you, and live out your thoughts.

From Information Overload to Simply Tuning In

Access to information is incredible, and you can learn so much—but too much information with too many opinions causes you to lose the clarity to listen to your own insights and the ability to think things through. You have to be able to think for yourself. You have to use discernment and see what resonates with you. If you are always overwhelmed with so much information and people telling you how to think, what to eat, what to wear, how to live your life, and so much more, you forget to recognize your own authentic self. What is for you is for you. Your body and mind are very unique. Allow yourself to listen to your own intuition to see what information makes sense. Sometimes, the information your mind attracts is what you have recently become aware of. You'll see data and information that match what you are already looking for. This is the interesting thing about the mind. Whatever you believe in is your truth, and that can always change when you switch your focus. Information on the outside is always changing. The inner insight you have has always been with you. To get clear access, tune in. If you look around, you're only using filtered ideas of your own clarity through other people's minds.

If the placebo effect is powerful enough to create an outcome that makes it seem as if something external has caused an internal response based upon belief, imagine what you're doing all day. Your mind and what you believe—from the inside out—come before what is real or the truth. You are the one who decides that. If you start tuning in and believing in your own concepts and truths, you will never again need to try so hard to seek. There will be something supernatural that awakens within you, radiating a sense of calm and trust in your inner source. You don't need millions of voices telling you what to do and how to do it. You need to go within and create your world exactly the way you want it to be. Listen to your body when it comes to what you need to eat and how you want to think. What works for you might not work for someone else. There is no one way of doing anything. Most of the time, you naturally know what works for you, but we have created so much misinformation about the concepts of good and bad that we attach our mental energy to physical things, and we create a placebo in our body. The impossible is possible. The unimaginable is imaginable. It is about freeing yourself from ideas you have attached your mind to.

The unimaginable will happen for you, and this will remind you how connected and destined for greatness you truly are.

Think about how sure you would be of yourself if you were not so dependent on ever-changing external information, but instead flowed with the wisdom that streams out of you. You would be even better at integrating external data to use in a way that supports what you are already creating. People are often indecisive about their path and what they want to do, because they have too much information and not enough inner inspiration or drive to see things actually happen for them. You have to know yourself in order to be able to fully integrate information. This will allow you to check back within yourself and see if things are actually lifting you higher or hindering you. If you're using what someone else thinks and you haven't yet decided to think for yourself, you are creating limitation and confusion. External information should add inspiration to what is already within you. Your inner world should be your space to make choices, connect with greater thoughts and ideas, and create what you want. You're meant to be inspired to reach new heights, not be limited or constrained by the placebo effects of a reality created by someone else.

Trust Yourself Even More

When you feel like doubting yourself, trust yourself even more. Just tell yourself that you've got this, and it will work out. This energy shift alone causes you to live more intuitively, because you get out of the habit or self-doubt.

The biggest illusion is the mental game you play with yourself. You constantly make up what won't work out. This requires the same amount of energy as actually believing in yourself. You have to start living by faith. You have to be so sure of yourself that it manifests right away for you. You are the one who is creating the external shifts through your own inner shift. If you don't believe in yourself, you'll get results that represent a lack of faith. If you do, you get the opposite. How big you dream depends upon how much you trust yourself and the universe. Some people don't care about obstacles, while others think so much about them that they'll sit down where there is a hurdle and stare at it all day. They'll discuss the hurdle and overthink it. All they really needed to do was just jump and go. Why prolong everything and drain your energy? You can move into your own divine gift by moving along in this reality with faith in how things play out. Trust yourself, and that will free you from the illusion that anything is too hard or too difficult. Just walk in faith that all is possible for you.

Miracles Are Normal

Anything can happen for you. Take that thought in for a moment. Any feeling of negativity that comes up when you think that anything can happen for you is a lie. Possibilities surround us if we are ready to see, feel, and claim them as our truth. Miracles are normal; anything we can't explain is always called miraculous. You should live your life believing that everything is a miracle. This creates a great feeling within you that connects you back to the freedom of your spirit. Living intuitively is knowing that everything that's already happening for you is a miracle unfolding. Your existence is an unexplainable miracle. Everything flows so naturally. Think about how many thoughts are taking place at one time, and how everyone is doing what he or she wants. You can join the wave of receiving the gifts that are your natural birthright by claiming miracles in every area of your life.

Key Points

- *To live intuitively, you must first learn to trust yourself. This is the first step toward understanding how to listen to your inner guidance.*
- *Trusting yourself is knowing that there is so much more to who you are. Your essence and spirit are beyond the physical.*
- *Trust your own inner guidance. The answers you have within you are perfectly made for you.*
- *You are supposed to feel energized and believe that anything is possible for you.*
- *Be the best you, and live out your thoughts.*
- *You're constantly being refined, but the truth is, you're only realizing more of who you are and how multifaceted and inter-dimensional you are as a being.*
- *If the placebo effect is powerful enough to create an outcome that makes it seem as if something external has caused an internal response based solely upon negative beliefs, imagine what you're doing all day.*
- *You see the miracles around you because you are able to tap into a new vision that gives you a greater outlook.*
- *Your inner world should be your space to make choices, connect with greater thoughts and ideas, and create what you want. You're meant to be inspired to reach new heights, not be limited or constrained by the placebo effects of reality.*
- *Miracles are normal. Anything can happen for you.*

20

Agreements

Everything that you personally do and experience (and, as a result, everything you are surrounded by) stems from some kind of agreement you have with what is happening or occurring. Agreements can stem from what you find yourself consenting to: what is allowed to occupy your mind, your space, and your environment. Agreements start with what you think of yourself, what you think you deserve, and what you are willing to accept. Every single item in your personal space came from a thought you once had or something you agreed to which now surrounds you. You may find yourself having repetitive thoughts, and every day, you assume they are just there; but every time you allow them, you are actually agreeing to them. The point of this chapter is to show you that nothing is random or a coincidence in terms of what you think and attract in your life. The main point I want you to take from this chapter is the knowledge that nothing is final. You can create new agreements with yourself that completely alter your reality for the better.

Keep your energy high by remaining hopeful about what can happen for you instead of being discouraged by what is happening to you. One small hope that things can get better automatically starts to create a shift in your life that will help you get out of your current circumstances.

People can hoard thoughts just as they hoard things, assuming that they can never change them. You can completely decide right now that you want to switch things up. No thought is final, and no experience is tying you to the past but your own lack of awareness or care to change it. This world is all about being passionate and wanting to see your desires, hopes, and dreams come to life. The possibilities are endless. If the physical aspects of your past thoughts keep you stuck, then you are on replay. Each moment is brand new. You can either continue to carry on with what you have created or you can say, *I want to do bigger and better. I want to be the best that I can be.* This isn't some concept of being unfulfilled, or an absence of contentment. This is the life force of expression, creation, and living out what you want to see come to life. You are pure potential in any given state. More life force comes to those who use the level of energy that is needed. There is no lack, and you should never think you are overexerting yourself. The only time I have noticed things feeling heavy or tiring is when I have been doing things I am not passionate about. Every single action should be supported and powered by your visions. If you have a vision, you have direction, and the path to get there will not seem hard for you since you are being carried by your imagination and driven by your faith.

What Are You Currently Agreeing to?

Take a moment to think of everything that surrounds you in your personal space. Every little item, no matter what it is, came into your life through a thought of yours. This can be something you went and bought for yourself, or something someone gave to you as a gift. It all stems from your mental world, and it came into your life due to some kind of interest. Nothing in your personal space is random. It all came from a choice or interest of yours. Now you can remove anything you want and bring in something else. Your new attractions and interests come from new thoughts. If you notice, it all comes in the mind first. There has to be a mental awareness of everything you agree to before you have it in your physical space. Understand this power you have. Sometimes, we can get so comfortable with everything in our lives that we forget that it has all resulted from thoughts that turned into physical objects. Your mental space is populated by thoughts you agree to and keep on repeat. When you want to do better in any area of your life, the first thing that always changes is your mindset. You can learn something new and invite a new outlook that alters your life for the better. What surrounds you stems from your mind, and your power is to know that you can either continue to agree to the reality you're in or say that you want something greater.

Imagine a better life for yourself, and affirm that it is yours. Believe in it until it happens for you. Whatever you create in your mental world will manifest into your life.

Anything is possible for you. What you are aware of continues to create the reality around you. You will literally only see more of what you want or expect to see.

341

People don't realize this, and sometimes, they assume they are trapped by negativity or problems. The only trap is the mental loop you continue to agree to day to day. If you talk down to yourself, you are agreeing to lower treatment from your outer reality. Lower treatment simply means how people talk to you, what you attract, and what comes into your life. If you feel good about who you are and constantly agree to thoughts that build you up and support you, then you will experience a reality that agrees to the same. Nothing we experience is a coincidence. Don't wait for people to change the way they treat you. You are the one who has to decide on the energy you want to put out. Do you currently agree with the thoughts you're having? Do you agree to the lifestyle you are currently living? Do you feel like the people in your life represent your new way of thinking? Sometimes, the person who needs to change is you. Too often, people blame the outside world, the environment, and other people, and this keeps them in a trap.

Blaming is the same energy as agreeing to what is happening. If you complain, point fingers, and constantly see what is wrong with others or the world around you, you'll see more of that. Your mind can only show you what you are looking for. It's not good or bad; it's just saying, *I want to see more of this,* or *please show me this, since I spend all day thinking and talking about it.* That is a strong agreement. Your words form a bond that agrees to show you the outcome you speak into the universe. You will start feeling a different kind of freedom as you read this book. The empowerment you find in every sentence will turn on that Inner Glimpse and remind you how powerful you are. There is absolutely no judgment in what you have attracted up to this point. This is another major realization I always feel like I want everyone to understand. Your past shouldn't keep you trapped through feelings of guilt. The only person who keeps repeating your past is yourself—through your thoughts, conversations, and agreements. It has nothing to do with who knows about your past. Nothing attaches you to what was.

You can create what you want for yourself through positive thoughts, consistent action, and healthy habits. You have the power to change and get better right now.

What has happened is now gone. Just as you can change up what surrounds your personal space, you can also change up your thoughts about how you feel about yourself and who you are. Get into a new energy of redefining your life the way you want. Think about this: You came here all by yourself, and you will leave here all by yourself. The experiences we share shouldn't make us feel low or unable to enjoy this life. Something is totally wrong when you aren't living up to your true potential. You have life force within you for a reason. You can be all you want to be. You can do great things. I want you to get right mentally. Simply understanding new information related to self-awareness and self-empowerment will unlock your superpower to finally see that you were born to do great things. Your dreams are valid. You can have anything if you truly want it. Stop agreeing to thoughts that keep you away from living your dreams, just because someone told you to be humble or content with what used to be. Contentment comes from knowing that you are already whole. You're not looking to things or people to define you. We are much more than trying to explain why we should be content or why we should express our creative energy. It is so important to always remind yourself that you are whole, complete, and much more than the physical. When you forget this, you are prone to go on searches outside yourself, feel unfulfilled, and/or overwork yourself and feel like you need a break from everything. The point is to know that everything is here for us to create and learn from. It all expresses our highest and greatest, even if that takes some unfolding.

New energy is entering your life. New opportunities. New paths. You are being renewed on a deep cellular level. You are shifting energetically and spiritually. Things are clearing up for you. Be ready to receive, and be open to great changes. This is truly your time to shine.

The concept of overworking and constantly pushing yourself can also put you into a place where you start to see things as a burden. Everything should be done in a state of faith, ease, and understanding that time is on your side. You don't have to agree to concepts that cause you to feel depleted just because you're constantly on the go. Your highest creativity and expression come from feeling good about yourself and accessing the Inner Glimpse that you have great potential. When you follow your spirit, you will move differently. No external concepts can limit you. You will see inspiration even in the most challenging moments, because your spirit will give you a vision of hope. Most of the time, solutions fly higher out of difficulties. If everything is an agreement, why would you agree to anything less than the highest and greatest thoughts about yourself and your reality? Why not chart the world with the vision that everything is possible instead of the opposite? Why not give your energy and focus to thoughts that build you up? Every second, you have a choice that can completely turn things around in your favor. Make the choice, and agree to your own personal greatness.

You are being lifted out of all negative situations right now and entering a new state of possibility, hope, miracles, and unstoppable life force that propels you forward. You will dream bigger and feel better about yourself. It is all activating within you right now.

Nobody can write your life story for you but yourself. Too many people give up their power and allow others to tell them how to live by putting a cap on how far any one individual can go. They listen to external voices that say what is and isn't possible, when in reality, their own spirit is unbounded by space and time. You can never suppress a spirit with a mission. Even if a person deals with hardship or difficulties for some time, they still have that moment when they awaken to their true power. All that they have been through, refined, and prepared for potentiates the greatness that is to come. This is the most powerful message I want you to take away from this chapter. I want you to know that you can be in any stage of your life or in any situation, but your spirit cannot be stopped once it realizes its true potential on the conscious level. Previously, you might have felt this here and there, but now, you will be fully activated, ready to live out what is divinely yours. You will start telling the story you want. You will understand how powerful your mind is, and that nothing can stop you. No amount of fear, doubt, judgment, or criticism can get in the way of your mission. This is your life. This is your story. You can do anything you want. Don't let yourself live out other people's thoughts of who they want you to be. You're the one who feels so deeply everything that goes on in your inner world. Declare your own state of mind and the direction you want to go. Your mental dimension belongs to you, and nobody will be able to fully comprehend, understand, or decipher your internal identity but you. Own your truth without needing to explain yourself or be understood all the time. Some things are a mystery, and unexplainable for a reason. Stay true to your own inner empowerment so that you can stand strong no matter what happens.

You have the power to think greater and harness the energy to lift yourself higher. Anything that puts a cap on how far you can go is an illusion. I truly think that even now, humanity is barely reaching an understanding of our full capabilities in mind, body, and spirit. Slowly, we are realizing that we can create our reality, and that seems fun and exciting. Sometimes, it trips people out to even think that they can attract what they want or create their own reality. This lack of awareness has made them forget that they are beyond the physical. What is so exciting now is that more and more people are owning their inner truth and feeling empowered. Nothing can constrain you. Your imagination opens up a link between the present and what can be. It is all possible, and you will discover this as you continue to love who you are and accept the Inner Glimpse that your spirit is constantly showing you.

Alter What You Agree to

Remember, nothing is holding you to any one state but the fact that you have agreed to whatever that one situation is. You can explain it off or make excuses for why you need to continue to agree to it, but know that you have the choice to alter what you agree to and enter a new state that supports the direction of your growth and evolution.

Nothing ties you to anything but your own will to accept it. Give yourself more inner power by agreeing to thoughts that support your mental health and inner well-being. You can choose to agree to new relationships, connections, and opportunities right now. You can agree to accept inner peace as your natural state and welcome new energy every single moment. Don't harden your reality with so many structures that you end up feeling trapped. Keep an open mind, and always think creatively by being adventurous in terms of what is possible for you. Make each moment memorable, and give life to what you want to see multiply.

Every time you're positive and hopeful about your vision, you add momentum to it. It starts to multiply for you. It starts to open new paths. It starts to create greater opportunities. Everything starts with you consistently staying positive, no matter what the situation.

If you've had ideas about relationships that you feel are limiting you, then alter those agreements. Who said you have to live your life unhappy? Who said that you need to stay stuck in a cycle you have outgrown? You don't owe it to anyone to remain in situations that drain your energy or dim your inner light. If you find yourself thinking that you deserve better in a relationship, then you do. That is just your spirit reminding you that you can evolve now, and not to be afraid of what's next. Don't be scared to express yourself. Love unapologetically. Another thing I have realized is that some people hold back the flow of love that is trying to come through them just so they won't appear desperate. Maybe they are afraid of how someone else will respond. If this is you, alter that lack in your thinking. If you feel like you need to express yourself, be open and genuine. You'll live your life knowing that you acted on your feelings instead of wondering how things could have been different if you had just expressed your truth. Be you unapologetically. If you feel like pouring love out, then do it. Living according to your personal agreements and remain true to your highest self. This allows you to express the things you might have been afraid to say before. It is your time to start shining. It's your time to stop holding back what you think and feel. Communicate, and allow yourself to express who you are. No matter what your direction, go boldly!

You're about to step it up in ways you have never imagined before. Any setbacks you have experienced can no longer hold you down. You're moving upward now. This is a time for great change. Don't be afraid to move boldly.

The more you express your truth and do what you feel, the more your energy increases and ascends. You'll feel your best knowing that you can be yourself. We all want to be understood, but we have to accept ourselves so we can share the true energy of love, companionship, and understanding. You don't need to tiptoe around anyone, scared to be who you are. You don't need to hold back just because you are afraid of getting hurt. Don't miss out on living just because you have agreed to some idea of who you are instead of who you *really* are. This is the time for true inner freedom, expression, and openness. We need to move out of past fears that have closed us off from building authentic connections out of fear of being hurt. What could ever happen to you if you already know that all is momentary, and you're only visiting this space for a moment in time? You don't have to be so serious about every little thing. Even the idea of being hurt creates blocks. Avoid forming around you an energy that repels natural, healthy connections. Everything is about learning and evolving, not avoiding or hiding away. If you trust your inner guidance, you will always be good. Don't take how things appear so seriously that they hinder what could be. There's great potential in you, and there are great possibilities surrounding you. Be ready, and be open.

You Always Have a Choice

Just think about the fact that you could make a decision right now that could completely alter the path of your life. You literally have choices, and what you choose creates new outcomes. I have been noticing my outcomes and how they result from the choices I make on a daily basis. I am realizing that each choice creates the next experience. It's like building up a world around yourself that agrees with the vision you have. Each choice produces an expected outcome. That is a powerful statement. You know that if you made a better choice right now, you could alter any area of your life. Every single day, it all adds up for you. It's all about making the choice and having the vision. Choices are influenced by vision. Day by day, you create habits that support the direction you're headed. A week, a month, or even a year later, you'll look back and be totally surprised at how far you have come. All of this comes from momentary choices that add up. Imagine what you could do right now if you made a new choice about something!

We always have to remember how quickly things can change for the better. Nothing is final. Your current emotions or situation might seem so real, but they are only momentary. It will pass. It always does. Everything will get very clear for you. Stay mentally and spiritually strong. Brighter days are coming!

Don't stop, even if you've had a moment that made you feel like giving up. Okay, so you had a lapse and fell back into old habits. Why judge yourself for it? Get out of that space, and get back in the wave of being your greatest self. You don't have to stay stuck or overthink it. Reorganize this, and get back to your vision and your purpose. The better you get at moving forward from things that seem like failures, the more you can make better choices to bounce back stronger and greater than ever before. You always have a choice, and that should give you peace of mind, even in the darkest moments. Anything is possible for you, and you will start to see your evolution and inner growth reaching new heights. You will start to see that you don't have to accept or agree to ideas that do not resonate with your vision. You will no longer be hindered by any state. You will feel free, creative, and open to live out your dreams. You're about to be so successful, so blessed, and so at peace with yourself that it will almost seem unreal that all of this is actually possible. Welcome to a new state of being, feeling, and seeing the world around you. You are going to thrive like never before, and you will impact others by being an example that allows them to remember who they truly are.

I will thrive in all ways, in all situations.

Start agreeing to greatness. Start agreeing to things as possible, even if you can't fully explain how it will all happen. Start living life using your imagination and balancing it out with action. Start agreeing that dreams can turn into reality by believing they can, and being living proof of it. Start agreeing to your mental health, inner wellness, and peace as a natural state. Start agreeing that success, abundance, and financial freedom represent a natural state that you can have. Start normalizing material things instead of putting objects as greater than yourself. Start agreeing to healthy relationships, friendships, and connections. Start agreeing to your resilient energy to bounce back from anything and reach new heights out of the ashes. Start agreeing to how unstoppable you are. Your vision can and will manifest. Start agreeing to trust your inner guidance. Listen to your own spirit. Start agreeing to what you want to see more of instead of talking about what you don't want to see. You make the agreements, and you decide what surrounds you and stays in your life. You can choose to do things differently, and you can get the outcomes you want. It is all literally right here and right now. Make it your greatest experience, and enjoy the process as it unfolds for you.

Key Points

- *You can create new agreements with yourself that completely alter your reality for the better.*
- *This world is all about being passionate and wanting to see your desire, hopes, and dreams come to life. The possibilities are endless.*
- *Each moment is brand new. You can either continue to carry on with what you have created already, or you can say, "I want to do bigger and better. I want to be the best that I can be."*
- *Every single action should be supported and powered by your vision. If you have a vision, you have direction, and the path to get there will not seem hard for you since you are being carried by your imagination and driven by your faith.*

- *Anything is possible for you.*
- *If you feel good about who you are and constantly agree to thoughts that build you up and support you, then you will experience a reality that agrees to the same.*
- *Blaming is the same energy as agreeing to what is happening. If you complain, point fingers, and constantly see things that are wrong with others or the world around you, you'll see more of that. Your mind can only show you what you are looking for.*
- *The only person who keeps repeating your past is yourself—through your thoughts, conversations, and agreements. It has nothing to do with who knows about your past. Nothing attaches you to what was.*
- *Stop agreeing to thoughts that keep you away from living your dreams because someone told you to be humble or content with what used to be.*
- *You can do anything you want. Don't let yourself live out other people's thoughts of who they want you to be when you're unhappy with it.*
- *You're the one who feels so deeply all that goes on in your inner world.*
- *Don't stop, even when you have a moment when you feel like giving up.*
- *Anything is possible for you, and you will start to see your evolution and inner growth reach new heights. You will start to see that you don't have to accept or agree to ideas that do not resonate with your vision. You will no longer be hindered by any external state.*
- *Start agreeing to greatness. Start agreeing to things as possible, even if you can't fully explain how it will all happen.*

21

CELEBRATE YOUR LIFE

Get into the state of mind of celebrating who you are, no matter what. The more you acknowledge the greatness of life by simply thinking of your aliveness, inner power, energy, and spirit, the more you will attract a new outlook. Things don't have to constantly remain in a thought pattern that doesn't resonate with your highest ideals. Too often, we assume that we have to be realistic in one state, and constantly talk about this as reality. Actually, you always have the choice to change your mindset, how you feel, and how you see the world around you. You can start to create a new narrative that surrounds your energy field with the best life has to offer. If you feel like you need to keep yourself in specific thought patterns because you believe they comprise your identity, that will be what continues to play out for you. We only see what we believe is true until something gives us the greater vision that more is possible. You can be lifted to new heights and experiences simply by experiencing a mental shift. This is something I understand and feel so passionate about that I wrote this book to share the message of inner empowerment...so you can claim what has always been yours. The lovely thing about the universe is that it constantly gives, even when what we ask for comes from thoughts that aren't refined according to our greatest vision.

You think your value will increase when that one thing happens for you, but what you don't realize is how worthy you already are right now. Don't wait around for the day that one thing happens for you. Choose yourself today. Celebrate your life. Love who you are now, and value yourself.

We keep getting better as we evolve. The moments we were tested have allowed us to learn that everything happens in order for us to grow, reflect, and express our greatest self. This brings a different kind of ease. Celebrating your life isn't waiting around for that one thing to happen for you. It is a state of mind and a state of being that alters what you expect, look for, and attract. Don't fear anything. Claim everything boldly. So what if something goes wrong in the midst of your self-discovery? How else would you be refined if you didn't learn the layers of who you are and the unlimited strength and potential that is within you? Too often, you can judge moments that were only meant to take you to the next level, simply because you overthink why something is happening the way it is. If you really stood back and took it all in, you would be celebrating the new direction your life is headed. You have no idea how much is unfolding for you at every second. I want you to start seeing it that way, so your mental state can align with all the blessings that are taking place within you and all around you.

What you focus on is a choice. You can look at every situation as it is, or how you want it to be. When you start getting into the mindset of celebrating your life, you enter a reality that empowers you on a deeper level, because you know that every single thing is momentary. All of your conversations, relationships, and experiences are moments produced, experienced, and created by you. Why not celebrate them? Why not cherish them? Why not see the best in everything, no matter how it appears? You can completely turn things around right now. You can speak a different kind of power over your life that impacts your energy field and what you radiate out into the world. If you hold thoughts of living fully and truly in the moment, you activate new connections and opportunities. You can even create better relationships. Your thoughts change because the mental energy you put out is different.

Understand that your inner world of thought reflects in your skin, your posture, your style, how you talk, how you treat others, and what you create. Your thoughts are literally an energy field that surrounds you, and the more you repeat certain thoughts, the more you create an identity that will continue to represent you until you make some kind of inner shift. This is why the change always starts within. You can't alter other people, or try to ask yourself why certain things are happening in your life. The minute you declare a new energy state in your mind, everything shifts. What doesn't belong in your life literally scatters and disappears. You get renewed energetically. This is why you attract better when you get better. It is like a signal within you that alters the experiences you are having, simply because you feel better about who you are while cherishing yourself spiritually.

It's time for new beginnings. So much is clearing out of your life. New energy is entering. You might be experiencing a lot of mental, physical, and spiritual transformations that are unlocking new levels within you. Be patient, and prioritize self-care and self-love right now.

355

The new you will look at your past, and things will seem unrecognizable. You can even think of moments right now from your past that seem so unfamiliar, you might even laugh at yourself for once having thought the way you did. You might have been through heartbreak, pain, or the end of something, only to realize that it made you discover your own self. It was all a lesson to arrive at that moment when you realized you were okay, you could get better, and you could get back to your natural state of wholeness. That one situation turned you into a greater you, and a situation happening right now will reveal something so unimaginable that you will be grateful it happened and you overcame it. We are always learning. The more you start to recognize the patterns of your own personal evolution, the more you'll see that things aren't as bad as they seem.

Every moment serves a greater outcome, and every moment takes you to the next level. Your mindset of celebrating your life starts with gratitude for who you really are. You are beyond the physical, and you came here for a moment in time to express, create, learn, and be yourself. You're living it all out right now. The past, present, and future are all in this moment. The more you take the pressure and overwhelm off yourself so you can breathe and take things one moment at a time, the more efficiently you'll operate. Things will become clearer for you. Make the best of all moments, and amplify the mindset of celebrating life, existence, and simply being as you evolve through it all.

Celebration State

The celebration state is a mindset and energy field that exists right now. You can enter it and welcome it in. Start celebrating what you want to attract or experience. If you're waiting for some news about something, celebrate it now. The celebration state is a very high-frequency because it activates gratitude for the outcome of what you want or already have. The more you celebrate something, the more is grows in your life. Imagine the kinds of words you speak and think when you're celebrating. They are the highest and greatest. Even the people with whom you celebrate all share the same frequency of joy, and this creates a beautiful state for everyone. Understand that you can access thoughts, feelings, and a new state of being in this moment, not just in the distant future. Too often, we wait to rejoice, and count our blessings when we have received something instead of feeling blessed, as if it were happening right now.

There's something so powerful about declaring a celebration over anything you intend to manifest or create. This has been something that I have personally done in so many moments of my life, and each time, I felt uplifted, energized, and a deep gratitude that shifted everything. I noticed that my results were more instant, but what I loved the most was the feeling of not worrying or overthinking the process. I didn't mind celebrating something that I wanted to receive before it even arrived. Don't live in an energy state that is the opposite of the direction you're headed. Create a powerful vortex around yourself on a mental and emotional level that energizes you to feel your own success. No matter what you're intending to experience in this moment, optimize yourself by being grateful for your health, wellness, peace, financial success, and healthy relationships.

Celebrate your personal victories, because no one else will understand the depth and complexity of what it took for you to accomplish them.

Being in the celebration state will initially feel different from what you're used to. We think of our physical experiences as if they are happening in timelines, when really, our mind, imagination, and spirit go beyond the physical. If you have spent most of your life waiting for things to happen in order to be happy, you'll feel like you're pretending, when in reality, you're not. Your mind and body believe in what is real according to how you choose to feel and think about the world around you right now. I am sure this will be a powerful breakthrough in your awareness as you start to create your world and experiences as if they have already happened. You'll feel like it is all a movie as you walk your path, just as if you have already lived it in your mind and emotions. This is also very powerful for your mental peace. Too often, we wait around for things to happen in order to be happy or at peace. Even when those moments do come, we celebrate, then find ourselves back on the chase. Happiness and peace aren't far from you. You can feel any emotion you want right now based upon how you respond to the world around you. So many great things will happen in your lifetime, and there might also be moments you can't fully understand; but somehow, they bring greater strength, growth, and awareness than ever before. Don't judge or be afraid of the things that happen in life. Just be prepared to decide how you want to feel about what is happening, and make sure that you know you can decide at any moment the direction you want to take.

Being Magnetic

We all have felt a connection with someone we can't fully explain. There's something magnetic about their spirit and how they think. The way they brighten others or light up a room has a lot to do with the energy going on within them. Being magnetic is very attractive, because it is an inner energy state that naturally communicates with your spirit. It is not really about what we have or how we appear. It is the aura, vortex, and energy that exude from within us. Being magnetic starts with how you feel about yourself and the world around you. If you don't energize yourself from within with powerful thoughts of self-love and deep gratitude and appreciation for life, you will feel low about yourself and wait for outside reality to give you something that isn't sustainable. Your magnetism starts with your mindset. This is what makes you successful and great at what you do. You attract the mindset, beliefs, and ideas you hold within. Start being magnetic to what you want to attract, and surround yourself only with things that match it. You will notice yourself elevating in ways you never could have imagined. You'll find that things will begin to have a natural flow, because you know you are magnetic to what you want.

Imagine yourself as a magnetic person who always attracts great experiences, unlimited opportunities, and good news. Believe that you're naturally blessed all the time.

You will start to see all around you that which you hold within yourself. This has happened before, but it will seem different this time. The speed of how it happens changes, and your awareness of your own inner power is shown to you. I am sure you've had moments you might describe as coincidence or random, but now, you're more aware, more connected, and more conscious of your own thinking and how you feel. You will start to see more of your inner thoughts, beliefs, and ideas surrounding you, and this will upgrade every aspect of your life. You will start to make better choices with your time and energy. Live in the mindset that you are a magnet for good luck, blessings, miracles, opportunities, and great success. Feel like you are a magnet to the best life has to offer. Stop thinking less of yourself and your life. That sort of thinking requires the same amount of energy from you as thinking you are positive, abundant, and highly blessed. You are the miracle, and that is the truth. All illusions will fall from your mind and awareness. Anything up to this point that tried to make you forget your power will perish out of your mind, body, and spirit. You will be renewed, reenergized, and revived in ways you never thought possible. You will no longer be in a cycle, loop, or state of mind of doubt, fear, or uncertainty. You are very powerful, and you must start realizing this.

You were already validated when you were created. You have been given life for a reason. You don't need anything extra. Just accept yourself, and feel the love from within. Your heart will expand and your aura will naturally be magnetic, just by being you.

You cannot waste another second of your life acting against yourself. You are a walking genius. Your mind, body, and overall being are so special and unique. Everything is automatically in this state, but your mind has experienced some forgetfulness. This feeds into outer illusions that constantly try to dictate your worth, value, what you need to do, how you need to do it, and the expectations you have to live by. For so long, your true power has been silenced—not by outside forces, but by forgetting to give yourself the power to claim your divine gifts. All it takes is remembering, and suddenly, you activate the energy to awaken. You find yourself thinking newer and greater thoughts. You find yourself actually spending more time feeding thoughts that enhance and expand you. You'll notice so many changes all around you. You have now become activated to reclaim the gifts and seeds that have always been within you.

Imagine yourself as a healthy, positive, vibrant, energetic, magnetic, loving being. Let your mind be filled with strong, positive visions of yourself. You are greatness. You are strong. You are whole and complete already. Accept it, and allow yourself to welcome this new mindset.

Being magnetic is being in your divine truth and living from an inner-powered state. Nobody can define your value. Nobody can take your worth. It really doesn't matter what has happened or how you have been treated. Nobody has power over you, and you are now free—mentally, emotionally, and spiritually—from any lower thoughts. Your empowerment completely banishes any thought that doesn't belong in your mental sphere. Your whole energy field is clear and renewed. Your activation started when you accepted your own greatness. Just that thought alone got rid of past thinking, habits, and energy that kept you in a loop. You will notice brightness in your life and the world around you. Too many people want to implant thoughts to make you think of the outer world as doom and gloom. How can we have solutions when the focus remains exclusively on what is happening externally? We need to be able to dream bigger and imagine the possibilities for humanity, then integrate them with action. If every single person reclaimed their inner power and discovered that ideas from the past (and beliefs that are no longer of service) don't belong to them or identify them, they would start to move differently. Your magnetic energy already makes you impactful, and you are an example of great possibilities, change, and hope for us all. Your life matters in ways I can't summarize in words, but I know you feel every single moment of it. This is a new beginning for you, and you will make a difference in your life as well as in the lives of those around you.

Every Day Is Another Chance

Think of every moment as something that is leading to a greater discovery. Don't allow yourself to be held back by current situations, assuming that they will last forever. Let the emotions clear through. Allow yourself to drop all resistance and flow with what you feel in the moment. The more you give yourself time to integrate all the changes taking place within you, the more you can overcome, even in the most difficult circumstances. There is nothing that can hold you back from the gifts of rebirth, recreation, and being reenergized. You have vital energy flowing through you. You can choose what to do with your time, your mindset, and how you feel. Things happen sometimes that seem so unpredictable, and those moments test our growth and the extent to which we have evolved intellectually, emotionally, and spiritually. Once you remember that this is another moment to apply your spiritual wisdom and faith, you will see that things aren't as bad as they seem. Too often, people are controlled by what is happening, and forget all the spiritual tools and insights they already have within them. In this moment, no matter how old you are or where you're from, you have had many revelations and experiences that have taught you how to overcome. When you get caught up emotionally in the moment, become reactive, or overthink what appears to be happening, you forget the wisdom that is within you.

It's a new day for you. Stop replaying the past in your mind. It's gone. Use your mental energy to manifest and attract something new. Don't waste your precious life force stuck on what didn't work out, or what you could've done. Do something new today. Each moment is another chance to create.

I want you to start remembering in every situation the power you have to get better, do better, and create the best, no matter what is happening. I want you to know that right now, you have another chance—and you always will. There is no judgment, and there are no mistakes that can stop your growth. You know your abilities. You know that you can make a choice right now that shifts your mindset and helps you see what you can recreate. It doesn't matter what your past has been. It doesn't stop who you are right now and who you can be. It starts with you making the choice that in this moment, you can. You can actually do it. Take back your mental energy from identities of the past that try to limit your spirit. Remember, your spirit is free to be and do anything. We are the ones who create identities and hold onto them, even when they don't resonate with the direction we are headed. It's okay to rethink, recreate, and revamp what doesn't resonate. You are free to make that choice. Take your mental power back from the past, and appreciate your true potential and unlimited possibilities. You can have another chance right now.

You are not your past. You can completely change your mindset, lifestyle, and how you see things right now.

Much of what has already happened in our lives has perished into memory. Every single moment continues on, and we take what we learn so we can build a better understanding of who we are. Start altering the way you see things. What happens externally can no longer control you, but you can take it in and look for the best in the moment instead of thinking it is final. Don't let yourself become overwhelmed or weighed down by emotions that are meant to be released. How many more times can you play that one story over and over again? How many more times can you fantasize about it? You are precious, and the world is grand, with so many different potential outcomes. You don't have to tie yourself down and accept what doesn't elevate you or open your heart. You will start to understand who you are more and more. This will help you discover just how much power you have instead of feeling hopeless. You have no idea just how much your entire life can shift for the better. So many times, I have seen people regain strength, overcome bad breakups, go from struggling to discovering their true abundance, and most of all, be at peace with themselves after years of battling for self-acceptance. All is possible for you. We are superhuman, and we have the power to shape-shift. We have been given the ability to adapt, regenerate, and recreate ourselves. This is the true success story: discovering our innate ability to change and create a more loving space within ourselves to thrive. It is so incredible how we are designed, and the unlimited opportunities we have when we make choices about what we want to do and how we choose to experience our lives moment to moment.

Be Open to New Experiences

Do something different. Learn something new. Get out of your routine, and allow yourself to have new experiences. You become hardened by life when you stick to the same environments and close your mind off to dreaming. This whole planet is for exploring and discovering. You can do it in your own city, or you can travel the world. It doesn't always have to happen the same way. It can start with trying new foods or even visiting new places you haven't yet seen. There's something magical about how alert we become when we are exploring new things. Your senses start to awaken, and you feel more alive. It's hard to put into words, but I am sure you have had that feeling before.

New experiences awaken your curiosity. We are supposed to be curious and open to newness. Allow yourself to see from a different perspective, and keep an open mind. What memories do you want to take with you? Share joy as much as you can, and the warmth of love as you overcome hardships. Understand others, and be open to meeting new people. It doesn't always have to be so deep. It can be a moment of laughter or kind words. Make the Earth your playground, and direct your movie. Celebrating your life will give you a completely new outlook that will take you on an adventure of new blessings and opportunities. Start being grateful, and start looking for what is going right. This new mindset will become your point of attraction as you release and let go of all the past ideas that once seemed so heavy. You're now stepping into your true power and unraveling all that is within you.

Key Points

- *Celebrating your life isn't waiting around for that one thing to happen. It is a state of mind and a state of being to alter what you expect, look for, and attract. Don't fear anything. Claim everything boldly.*
- *When you start getting into the mindset of celebrating your life, you enter a reality that empowers you on a deeper level because you know that every single thing is momentary.*

- *The minute you declare a new energy state in your mind, everything shifts. What doesn't belong in your life literally scatters and disappears. You are renewed energetically. This is why you attract better when you get better.*
- *So many great things will happen in your lifetime, and there also might be moments you can't fully understand. Somehow, they will bring about strength, growth, and awareness like never before.*
- *Being magnetic starts with how you feel about yourself and the world around you.*
- *You cannot waste another second of your life acting against yourself. You are a walking genius. Your mind, body, and overall being are so special and unique.*
- *Your magnetic energy already makes you impactful, and you are an example of great possibilities, change, and hope for us all.*
- *Think of every moment as something that leads to greater discovery. Don't allow yourself to be held back by current situations, assuming that they will last forever. Let the emotions clear through. Allow yourself to drop all resistance and flow with what you feel in the moment.*
- *Take back your mental energy from identities of the past that try to limit your spirit. Remember, your spirit is free to be and do anything.*
- *New experiences awaken your curiosity.*
- *We are superhuman, and we have the power to shape-shift. We have been given the ability to adapt, regenerate, and recreate ourselves. This is the true success story: discovering our innate ability to change and create a more loving space within ourselves to thrive.*

22

INNER GLIMPSE AFFIRMATIONS

The next 100 affirmations are meant to support you in igniting your Inner Glimpse. The words written here will awaken insights, guidance, and reassurance as you speak power over every area of your life. Affirming means so much to me. I have seen magical things happen in my life when I have boldly and passionately spoken power over every moment. No matter what the situation, you can tap into the energy behind every single word I affirm here and create a boost in any situation, state, or circumstance. These 100 affirmations are meant to support you through the process of reading this book. These words are tools you can use anytime to amp your own energy and feel the connection within. I wrote every single word from a special place. I have felt how much things can shift in a new and positive direction when you know what to say at the right time.

Every single day, we use our words to define ourselves, create our reality, and connect with others. Everything we say has meaning and purpose. When you forget the power of your words, you start to allow in negative words, when really, that's not your truth. No matter what the situation or how things appear, you can use words that change your outcome to how you want it to be. Stop accepting words that do not define you. Stop spreading false words about yourself to others when you speak about what is going wrong in your life or the issues you think you are having in the moment.

Everything is energy being spoken into existence. Every single word you speak is something you are making the choice to define yourself as. It can always change for the better as you discover your own inner powers. You'll realize that you no longer think the way you used to, and that limiting words no longer define you. The point of this section is for you to be so energized, so connected, and so inspired that every single word you affirm and speak into your life will carry great power. You will no longer just say random things about yourself; you will be conscious, aware, and open to great miracles.

Inner Glimpse affirmations will take you to another level. Every single word will activate within you what has always been there: pure greatness. Your light will start to shine more brightly, and you will be more confident in everything you do because you know what to say to yourself, no matter what is going on. This is a different kind of movement, and it starts from within. You are the one activating yourself with every single word. I'm just here to help you remember. Your experience of everything in this book will show you exactly why you are fearless, unstoppable, magical, and highly blessed. It will go from thoughts to words to tangible experiences. You will remember exactly what has always been there within you, and you will reach great depths and heights unlike ever before. Cherish each affirmation, and take the time to fully allow yourself to connect with the words. Allow what comes up, and feel through it.

Each affirmation section will support previous chapters in the book. When you are working on your self-mastery, you can get into affirmations about self-liberation, greater perspective, and igniting your intuition. Every time you speak these affirmations, say them with so much passion and energy. Add feeling to them. You can super-charge every single word. You are the one who is saying them and using your energy to speak them over your life. You can see miracles start to take place simply by reading the words and feeling them. The great thing about these affirmations is that they belong to you, even as I write them. They are meant for you to repeat and speak as often as you like. Begin to feel that you are already in your desired state. Feel how blessed you are. Feel powerful, strong, and energized. Get yourself into the mindset that every single word you read is meant to create a vortex of energy around you that pulls in everything you are saying. Be bold with your words. Believe in them, since every single thing you speak immediately comes alive. Let yourself see what can happen when you begin affirming power over every area of your life.

Inner Glimpse Affirmations

These sets of affirmations are meant to activate within you the Inner Glimpse of seeing your true inner power and potential. Everything this book stands for is the inner experience we have all felt at one point in our lives when we felt we could do anything. This is what these affirmations are meant to remind you of—that you can do it, and you have it within you to be all you can be. There is nothing stopping the power that's constantly pouring into you. Imagine that this whole time, you have always had unlimited energy flowing as a life force: creative energy, health, wellness, and abundance, and everything that expands you. This flow has always been there, and it will always be there. The difference is that you're now aware of it. Before, you might have assumed that you had to do x, y, and z to feel it, but now, you're just going to accept that it is there. Knowing that you have unlimited energy right now to do what you want, what would you be doing?

Inner Glimpse is meant to remind you and help you get activated on your adventure so you can stop chasing the things that are already right inside of you. All you need to do is start remembering, claiming it, dreaming bigger, and imagining what you want. When you start to feel worthy and valuable while understanding your inner connection, you can make an impact in your own unique and special way. You can take the action you need to, do what you love, and share your gifts with those around you and all over the world. Inner Glimpse affirmations will make you feel like you can dream again, and that you can finally get out of illusion and reclaim your reality. You can do anything. You can start in this moment. You can make a difference in your life. Let's get started, so you can be on your way to speaking your desired reality into existence.

1. My Power Is Awakening within Me

I am feeling ACTIVATED. My thoughts are clearer now. I see the vision of where I am headed, and it is a strong feeling that anything is possible for me. I am getting reminders from within that expose the amount of potential I have. I am finally feeling the power awakening within me, and I feel excited about life.

2. I Follow My Inner Glimpse

I follow the signs I am getting. I trust that the Inner Glimpse is showing me all that I am capable of. Every thought of inspiration I receive comes from my spirit. Every thought of healing, love, and motivation is from my spirit. I will start to trust the inner empowerment I am getting, and follow through with it.

3. I Am Highly Connected

I am connected, and that means the unimaginable can happen for me. My connection to the source of all of creation and life is strong. My connection reminds me that life is beyond the physical, and energy is the moving force of the universe. I am made of energy, and my spirit is vibrant. I am a miracle, and I am always connected to the miracles life has to offer. It is a natural state that I am accepting right now.

4. My Power Comes from My Inner Empowerment

My inner empowerment is increasing every second. I notice that I am feeling more energized and more determined daily. I am feeling more self-love and self-awareness now. Something within me has shifted. I am free from what was, and I am entering what is and what can be. I have the choice right now to start following my own inner empowerment.

5. I Have Access to Unlimited Resources and Ideas

Unlimited resources surround me. There are so many ideas, innovations, and inventions right now that are still untapped. The possibilities are endless, and I am connected to this powerful energy. I have access to unlimited resources. I welcome all ideas that allow me to create, express, and share with the world the blessings that they, too, have within them. I am an example of unlimited resources.

6. I Am a Creative Genius

I only see abundance. I only see solutions. I only see a bright future and a great now. I choose to be a creative genius because this way of being is my natural state. All thoughts that support my creative expression will multiply in my reality. I will start having more optimistic thoughts and seeing the world from a place where things can change and get better. My outlook has officially shifted.

7. I Have More Energy

I have more energy to do what I love. I am passionate about my life and what I feel is next for me. The universe provides me with more and more energy every single day to live out my purpose. The more energy I have, the more I can accomplish. I will now begin to feel a surge of power that moves me forward in the right direction.

8. I Am Highly Blessed

I will start recognizing how blessed I already am. This thought of being highly blessed is my new energy signature. I walk, talk, and think like a highly blessed person, because I am. This is what allows me to start seeing the miracles the universe has put all around me. This helps me to see beyond how things appear, and connect to the subtle power of a state of gratitude. I am highly blessed!

9. I Choose to Imagine the Best

I will start imagining the best for myself. I will imagine the best in all situations. Every second, I know that I am choosing to imagine something. From this moment on, I will imagine the outcomes I desire. I will imagine them already working out. I will imagine them actually happening. I will imagine the breakthrough. I will imagine the miracle. I will imagine my manifestations coming to life. It all starts with my imagination.

10. I Trust My Inner Voice

I trust my inner guidance. I trust my intuition. I trust my gut feelings and inner guidance that continue to tell me to follow through with my purpose and support my vision to get clearer.

11. I Amplify All Thoughts That Lift Me Up

I will amplify and magnify every single thought that comes to mind that supports my positive self-image, my ability to accomplish all my goals, and my positive outlook on life. All thoughts I attract right now build me up and create a magnetic energy for more positive thoughts.

12. My Mental Energy Is Strong

My mindset is healthy and strong. I only seem to attract thoughts of optimism, hope, peace, love, and prosperity. I have unlocked higher access within my mind that allows me to have a strong mental attitude and energy. I only build from this space, and it feels so good knowing this.

13. I Am the Connection

Everything I need is within me already. I have to actually start seeing things from this perspective. I am the connection. I have the access. It is all here inside of me right now. The minute I decide that I want something, the entire universe begins to shift in that direction. Automatic connections are made. Instant alignments are formed. Paths are cleared. I am navigating from within, and I am narrating my story. I have the connection, and I am the connection. If I want it, the shift to obtain it now begins to happen.

14. I Choose How I See Myself

I am the one who sees the world from within looking out. I am the one who chooses how I see myself and how I feel about myself. I am the one who chooses what I speak over my life, what I attract, and what I choose to continue to entertain. It all begins with my own self-image, self-love, self-acceptance, and self-awareness.

15. My Spirit Is Strong and Resilient

I can feel my own inner power. I can feel how strong I am. I am taking in how alive I am right now. My life is precious, and I am going to recognize my own breath as a gift. The more I see the abundance in chances and overcoming what was, the more I unlock how resilient, powerful, and strong my spirit is. I can do this, and I can do so much more.

16. I Am Activated

This is a new beginning for me. I am telling a better story about my life and myself. I am rewriting and recreating exactly how I want things to be. I am activated now, and I can feel the power that has always been here with me. I am aware of it, and I am choosing to move forward boldly, confidently, passionately, and purposefully.

17. I Trust Myself

I trust who I am. I trust my gift. I trust what is being revealed to me. I will walk through all uncertainty with the greatest faith, allowing myself to surrender to the unknown. The mystery of life unfolds as I flow, and my faith in myself allows me to experience how magical life truly is.

18. I Have Superpowers

I have the ability to imagine. I have the ability to dream. I can learn new things and experience so much of what life has to offer. My superpower is that I have the will to make greatness come to life. The treasure is within me, and my mind can show me the way. I can see it all before it happens. I can imagine it into existence, and I feel it to be true. My world is brighter knowing this.

19. I Can Multiply Greatness in All Aspects of My Life

I believe in abundance in all ways. Abundance is a flow that's constant and consistent in my life. I am connected to this great resource and provider of life. Everything I do that creates a positive impact in my life and the lives of others multiplies and grows at high speed.

20. I Bend Space and Time

I can step into any state I want right now. I bless what I want to experience, and believe that it has already happened. My mind and body enter a state in which I feel deep gratitude for all I have received. All things in the mental world are instant, and as I start to trust myself more and more, I begin to discover that I can instantly manifest in the physical, as well. Things are beginning to happen for me in ways that once seemed unimaginable. My inner connection is stronger than ever. I trust myself, and I know that I can alter my reality and create what I want intentionally and immediately.

Divine Guidance/Divine Timing Affirmations

Divine Guidance and Divine Timing Affirmations are meant to remind you just how perfect things are, even if you don't fully understand what is happening. So many times in life, you've probably had moments when you've looked back and understood that things ended up working out for you in ways you could not have predicted at the time of your predicament. One thing I know is that everything always ends up working out. You always end up making it through and coming out on top. You might get pushed out of things you want in the moment, but you move toward something far greater that you truly needed. This is what divine guidance is all about. The moment we decide to surrender and trust that things will be okay, they become okay. There is nothing to fear about the unknown. The next affirmations are meant to help you ease up so you can begin to trust the natural alignment and guidance of the source. This is where big things begin to happen for you. When you repeat these affirmations, you will discover yourself experiencing things you can't fully put into words. Everything around you will start to work in your favor. You will feel a strong trust within yourself, and an even greater trust in everything grand about life and the universe around you.

Divine timing is just as important as trusting guidance from within. Things are happening for you right now. You have already begun the changes if you've made it this far. A lot of what we can do, as far as action goes, begins with strong inner self-belief and trust that is unwavering. If you believe in yourself and trust in divine timing, you become unstoppable. Worry takes so much energy from people because they think of great ideas, then spend the hours that follow worrying about when and how. Remember, when you think of what's next, your mind only uses what it already knows. When you can't fully access or imagine what is possible for you through faith, you limit your own potential by overthinking what didn't work before. Past data and information can only take you so far. Faith is what gives you a vision of the unseen and the trust to know that you can make it through. You have to see beyond ideas and thoughts that are limiting, even when they are being told to you repeatedly. If you believe in something, the way will be made for you. What is in your mind is in your mind. Nothing and nobody has the right to tell you that something is not possible. Nobody has authority over human potential. Greatness is born through those who trust divine guidance, imagine the best, and envision a new world, even when people aren't ready for it.

What you will do here and what you share in your own unique way will all depend on how much you allow yourself to trust and believe. The more you see what you want clearly and allow yourself to be guided from within, the more you will see miracles happening all around you. Don't wait for approval or validation. You already have it all, simply by being you. Now you are going to claim what is divinely yours. Anything is possible for you, so dream big and believe in it until you start to see it all come to life. This is your time to shake off all ideas, thoughts, and beliefs that don't lift you higher, and begin affirming your divine connection and divine timing. This is where you really start to live by faith.

21. I Am Divinely Being Guided and Provided For

I am choosing to recognize how my existence is sustained. I am provided for in every single breath. My body is being taken care of in ways I can't even try to comprehend. So much is happening for me, and this shows I am being divinely guided and provided for. I have to start noticing the subtle miracles in order to actually recognize how grand my blessings can be. If I see beyond how things appear, I connect to the possibilities of what can be. This is my playground to enjoy, thrive, grow, and allow.

22. My Timing Is Perfect

Things happen for me right on time. I always notice that breakthroughs are in my favor, and this shows me how much the universe supports me. I look back and see that time after time, every single thing I have intended came together, even if it was greater than what I was asking for. I am going to live my life knowing that MY TIMING IS PERFECT!

23. I Receive Insights

Inner guidance comes to me with ease. There's a greater purpose and vision for my existence, and each time I receive insight, it is shown to me. The way is being made for me, and I am receiving answers, guidance, and wisdom from within. I can make it through.

24. My Vision Is Complete

Every single time I have ideas, I get so much energy from within to execute them. It feels like I am succeeding at finishing what I have started. This is the new way I am being moved, and I feel myself taking back my power and actually finishing my goals. It is all here right now, and I can do something about it. I am victorious.

25. Answers Come Right On Time

The answers I need come right when I need them the most. I am starting to see that my inner voice is most powerful when I actually listen to my own intuition. The more I tune in and follow my inner guidance, the more I notice that I am getting great results and access to insight I had no idea was here. This is the beginning of great success for me. I know it!

26. The Blueprint Is Within My Mind

Everything I need to access is already in my mind. The blueprint, the experience, the outcome, and the process are all there. Now, I am being led to each positive experience in the physical. I am seeing more of what I think, feel, and talk about happening all around me. The entire universe continues to respond to what I choose to entertain, believe in, and accept as my truth. I will begin to trust myself and think the greatest thoughts. I feel the state I want to be in. I will activate the codes within me and access a greater reality. All is possible for me. I can do it.

27. My Timing Is Magical

My timing is always perfect. Every single thing I intend and speak always happens, and sometimes, it is even greater than what I have imagined. Every action I take is building up what I will soon experience physically as my reality. I just have to be consistent in faith, and continue to know that all is going accordingly.

28. I Know That I Can

All possibilities exist within me right now. There is a world of newness that surrounds me. I can choose to enter a space where it all has happened for me, and I can actually begin to feel that truth. This is a new moment for me. It is time for me to tell a greater story about my life. It is time for me to write what I want. I know that I can. I accept this new beginning, and I know that I can create even better.

29. I Can See Myself Already There

I can see myself already living my dreams. I can see myself with so much energy, health, abundance, wellness, and happiness all around me. I can see how I am being guided in that direction because it is my natural state. I keep getting reminders from within that I am powerful, strong, and can do great things. My inner thoughts are starting to lift me higher. I feel a change, and I can't explain it, but I know that it is exposing my true worth and potential to me. It all feels so surreal. I am so glad to have discovered my own inner guidance. I trust myself!

30. I Am Noticing Positive Patterns

Every single thing has always worked out in some way. I have either learned something from it or have been put into better situations. It seems like there is a positive pattern to my life when I look back. No matter how things once seemed, I am now in a much better place. This can happen again. No current circumstances are final. I am living a positive pattern, and am surrounded by the energy of miracles. Things are always getting better and better for me. I am destined for greatness.

31. I Am Allowing Myself to Receive Divine Guidance

I am open to receive in all ways from the Most High. I am ready to accept my blessings and recognize the miracles that surround me. My vision is changing to hope and optimism. The more I follow my own inner guidance, the more I gain access to greater vision. I have automatic trust now, and it seems to be growing every single day. I am so grateful to finally allow myself to receive in a major way.

32. I Am Aligned

The more I follow my heart and intuition, the more things seem to align. It is effortless now. I am aligned, and have always been. I am aware of it, and it is causing a positive shift in my life. I am receiving at a higher rate. My blessings keep multiplying the more I trust myself and let go of trying to force things. I feel a natural flow building up within me. I feel a state of calm and trust that all is happening in divine timing.

33. I Will Follow Through with Action

The signs have shown up for me now. My inner guidance is leading me on a journey that is unfolding so beautifully. I will step into that state now by being what I want to experience in this moment. My actions reflect my thoughts, desires, and dreams. I am showing myself that I am a living proof of consistency and self-trust in my own inner voice. The more I follow through with action, the more I continue to see great progress unfold for me. This is all very exciting and reassuring to me.

34. I Am Surrounded by Powerful, Subtle Energy

Everything is connected. I am connected. My access and connection are pure and alive. Every breath I take is a reminder of all the possibilities within me. I will start to see the patterns, connections, and subtle energy that show me that everything is always working out. I will live by faith, be carried by vision, and walk with great trust. There is so much more to life, and I will align with everything that reflects my true potential. Each experience is teaching me how to tap into my own greatness, and I am finally seeing things for what they really are. I feel a new sense of clarity and a boost of energy to live my life consciously.

35. I Acknowledge My Own Divine Guidance

Every single day, I feel a strong energy of gratitude for the Source of all life. I am grateful that I am being guided, protected, and loved. The more I acknowledge that everything comes from within me, the more I am shown the way in all that surrounds me.

36. I Can Tap in Anytime I Want

I am surrounded by warmth, love, care, health, abundance, and great revelations. I am always going to remember that I am okay and connected. I will always feel support from within. I will tune in and ask for guidance anytime I need it. My inner relationship is getting stronger daily. I love who I am more and more, and I am spreading hope by just being me.

37. There's Always Hope in All Situations

I have faith in humanity. I have faith in myself. I have faith in the future and all that is happening right now. When I am fearless, I show that I trust in something far greater. I dissolve all illusions when I have faith. This is what takes me to the next level. I know that I am being guided, and that life is a very magical and a miraculous experience. Everything will be okay, and the way will be made for things to work out. There is nothing that is too grand for the universe to bring back into equilibrium. I trust the power that sustains me. All is well.

38. Things Are as I Think, Feel, and See Them to Be

My reactions and attention belong to me. What I choose to respond to is what I give my energy to. I will start to focus on what I want to see more of. The universe is always responding to what I want to see through my thoughts, feelings, and beliefs. I will be responsible for my experience and make my dreams a reality.

39. It Is Normal and Natural to Live a Miraculous Life

I am living a miraculous life. Miracles are normal in my world. Blessings are constant in my world. All I see around me is pure possibility and great potential. My inner vision is showing me the greatness of life, shattering illusions all at once. I feel revived, reenergized, and ready to constantly receive. I am the starting point and the end according to my thinking and outlook. There's so much happening around me, and I am being guided to see the way. Things are getting very clear for me.

40. I Am Receiving Guidance on a Daily Basis

I am always receiving. I can ask for guidance anytime. I can ask for a sign when I want. My flow is constant, and the universe is open for me to explore. I have to start recognizing the flow that is taking place within me.

Self-Mastery/Self-Liberation Affirmations

You have the power to free yourself from any negative thinking from the past. You can get out of any habit you think doesn't serve your greatest purpose and growth. You have the choice right now to make a difference in your life in terms of how you speak, think, and feel about yourself. Every single action you take after listening to these self-mastery and self-liberation affirmations is meant for you to take back your own personal power and know it all starts within you. Self-mastery affirmations are meant to help you remember that you have choices right now. You are not a victim who continues to be defined by what was. There's great potential in your spirit to mold yourself and your reality into exactly what you want. Any energy of lack, laziness, or low productivity is cleared from your space. You will start to follow your heart and know how to tap into what has always been there. You'll finally step out of the loops and cycles that no longer serve you. You will break free from connections you have outgrown. You will feel liberated, and it will all come from within you.

I want you to remember who you were before all of this happened. Remember what a carefree spirit you were? The openness in your ideas and thoughts? Remember when you did what you wanted, and felt the passion for life? You still have that spirit within you. There's so much to who you are. You may have collected lessons and learned so much, but that doesn't mean you're defined by what used to be. Lessons are tools, not identities. You are a new you today, with so much more wisdom. You're discovering how to love who you are and how much this empowers every aspect of your life. You understand that all situations are momentary, even if you find yourself getting caught up in it sometimes. This is all just a reminder not to judge yourself. Whatever happens in life, you can make a choice today to do way better than you have ever done. You always have a chance. Please never forget that. Your story is never over. Trust your own process. Your growth is natural to you, and very unique to your experience. How things happen for one person is going to be completely different for someone else. This is why you have to be very patient, loving, and consistent with yourself. These self-mastery and self-liberation affirmations I am going to share with you are meant to unlock within you what has always been there. You will feel truly uplifted. You will see everything in your life changing for the better. You will realize that nothing is random, and that you are okay no matter how things appear.

These affirmations support your self-mastery and self-liberation of choice and forward movement. Your greatness will shine through. You will feel unstoppable. You will notice that it is easier for you to make changes toward what expands your spirit. You will start following your heart and seeing life from a whole new perspective. This is just the beginning for you, because you are reclaiming yourself. You are free to be who you want to be. You can live out your dreams exactly how you want. Any illusions, thoughts that don't serve you, or ideas of limitation that others may have shared will come to an end at this moment. Your mental state is being cleared out with every single word. You will feel a true freedom, and it will begin in your mindset— the most important space for cultivating true peace, wellness, success, and the things you want to experience in life. Actions always follow a mental declaration. This is why this next set of affirmations will ignite more energy within you to master yourself and get to know everything you're truly capable of.

41. I Am Creating Habits That Support My Vision

My habits are aligned with my vision. I master the art of being bold in my direction and choices, and I am great at creating healthy habits that support where I am headed. I am making the choice right now to do better and greater in all ways. It is a new beginning for me today.

42. I Master My Thoughts

I am directing my thoughts and mental energy toward the outcome I want. I choose the thoughts that stay in my mind. I choose what I give my mental energy to. I feed ideas and thoughts that support my healthy, strong mindset. I am a master at redirecting all thoughts and transforming them into the ones I want to see multiply. I keep getting better at building my own mental state of wellness, knowing that I can choose which thoughts I feed.

43. I Master Myself

I am mastering myself every day. I am getting to know my true potential, and all is being revealed to me right now. I am accessing my true abilities. At every moment, things just click for me. I am learning that my thoughts and emotions move me into new dimensions of possibility. I have so much hope now...more than ever before. I feel myself transforming into the vision I have always had. It is truly a miracle to discover what has always been inside me.

44. My Mental World Guides My Physical Reality

I am building the most magnificent mental world that aligns everything for me in the physical. I am getting better at visualizing and seeing the results of what I want to experience as already complete. My surroundings instantly show me what I want to see more of, which allows me to think thoughts that support me in my discovery of all I can do. In my mental world, I create all that I want to see in my physical surroundings. I believe in myself, and I know that everything will start to show up. I automatically trust myself because life is already a mystery, filled with possibilities for me to explore.

45. I Recognize the Patterns

I am getting better at recognizing the patterns of my life, which show me that all is momentary and I am constantly evolving. I am learning from everything, and this empowers me in ways that give me the peace and clarity to know that I will always prevail. I can make it through, no matter how things appear. I have overcome what was, and I can power through what is and what will be. One thing I know is that patterns always turn out in my favor. This is why I will always be grateful. I am living a miraculous life, and I am conscious of the signs that connect the dots.

46. I Am the Miracle I am Looking to See

I am starting to see and feel how powerful I am. I am starting to recognize that I am already living a miracle. The more I notice the subtle energy of my own existence and my will to do whatever I want, the more I feel empowered. Miracles multiply in my life every second that I breathe. I am seeing things more clearly now. I am listening to my own inner voice. The path is unlocked. I am now in it, and I can feel that I have always been supported. This is truly changing all that I can do and will do. I feel so alive!

47. I Accomplish All That I Put My Mind to

I am constantly getting things done. I am so productive, and it shows. I am noticing great results in my projects and ideas. It seems like I suddenly have a natural boost of energy that is nonstop. My creativity and expression have doubled, and they seem to be growing by the second. I am living my purpose now. I am moving forward into action, and I am seeing things happen. I feel like I have entered the most powerful vortex that produces abundance and great success. I am starting to really win on all levels, and it feels so good to know that I can be balanced as I move through my experiences.

48. I Can Concentrate My Energy

I have discovered the power of focusing, and I use it on a daily basis. Every idea that comes to my mind is there for a reason. I focus on what I want to see happen for me, and I focus on what I want to accomplish. I get things done!

49. It Feels So Good to Be Free

I am free to be who I want to be. I choose to master myself and be liberated from the past and activated in the present. My future is so bright. I am unstoppable and fierce. I am connected and loved. I am supported and aligned. My life keeps getting better, and I keep expanding in unimaginable ways. I have entered a magical world of constant wins, no matter what is happening. I know that I can do what I want, and that all things are just learning experiences that give me power to move through life with the energy of *all is well*.

50. I Am Worthy and Deserving of the Best

I am a highly valuable person. I am worthy of the best. I am deserving of the greatest. How I feel about myself is what I attract. The way I think is the example I silently project out into the world. It is now all about the energy I send out, not how things appear. I love myself more and more. I accept myself more and more. I am the representation of my inner world, which is what I want to see in my physical world. I am living out my inner truth. My energy speaks for itself, and I am illuminating, radiating, and magnifying all that I want to see. It all starts within me. This is my secret to being great!

51. I Am a Highly Functioning Individual

I tap into the Source of unlimited energy. I have a flow that is constant and consistent. I am naturally receiving more and more energy to accomplish my goals. I feel determined, motivated, and accomplished.

52. I Have Strong Willpower

Whatever I put my mind to, I accomplish. My willpower is very strong. Once I make the declaration or set the intention, it gets done. I am very dedicated, and this activates my willpower even more. I am moving boldly, and I see constant success in all I do.

53. I Am Seeing My Thoughts All Around Me

I am starting to really see how my thoughts are manifesting all around me. Everything in my life was an idea first. Everything others create comes from their minds. This awareness allows me to see more of the thoughts I consistently entertain. I am visualizing my outcome. I feel like I have already entered the state of living it. I feel so successful. I am getting the results I want.

54. I Experience Constant Synchronicities

I am officially in the mindset of knowing that nothing is a coincidence. I am experiencing what I think and feel, and it is showing up more quickly. I am now in a new mindset of recognizing and acknowledging synchronicities and signs as a natural state. I am open to greater breakthroughs and understandings of life. I welcome signs and synchronicities now. I want to see the alignments and experience my own inner power. I am already uplifted, just by knowing that this is all happening in the moment!

55. I Am Well

I am healthy. I am whole. I am love. I am okay. I am good enough. I am blessed. I already am all that I want to be. I see things as complete. My mindset is healthier. My emotions are balanced. My outlook is clear. I am feeling an overall wellness and deep acceptance of who I am.

56. Everything Turns in My Favor

I am a master at turning any situation or circumstance in my favor. I am the one who decides how I react or respond. I choose to fly higher and think greater. I choose what stays in my life and what I allow to continue on. I know my own power, and I will exercise my will to stay focused on positivity. My life is great, and I choose to keep it that way.

57. I Am Unlocking Great Possibilities

What surrounds me isn't just what I can see. There is so much more to life, and I choose to be curious, adventurous, and open to questioning everything. The more I think for myself, the more I can unlock great possibilities within me. I am feeling open, free, and expanded.

58. Everything Is Right Here Where I Am

Everything is right here, right now. No matter where I go, I am within myself, and the way I think is where it all begins. I see a great vision for myself no matter how things appear. I am entering my mental world where I engineer and design my reality. I am getting better at visualizing and executing. My surroundings will alter completely the more I alter my mindset. Things are changing so fast for me. I feel so connected and supported. I am so glad I have discovered my inner guidance.

59. I Am a Magnet for All Things Great

I am a magnet for all blessings, abundance, prosperity, love, happiness, clarity, wisdom, and insight. I attract great experiences and wonderful people into my life. I put out good energy and receive it back. Everything is flowing for me. I am a magnetic, radiant spirit.

60. I Am Already Complete

I am a spirit filled with possibilities. All wisdom is already within me. I choose to receive and be open to all the greatness that is coming into my life. Every second, I am starting to remember who I am, and things are getting exciting for me. It feels so good to know that I am already whole. Every part of who I am is already complete.

THE GREATER VISION
AND THE GREATER POSSIBILITIES:
AFFIRMATIONS

This next set of affirmations will take your mind out of any lack, limitations, problems, or shortcomings. You will gain a new perspective and a greater vision that anything is truly possible for you. The words you'll find here will give you a new outlook and realignment with your true potential. Greater vision means that you will see things not only as they appear, but also in the context of the end goal you desire. You will start to imagine the world you want, and shift your own thinking to see what has always been there. You now have a new way of thinking and seeing things. What changes is what's inside of you. The environment responds to your inner world. The goal here is to start speaking possibilities over your life. You can choose new thoughts and words every single second. Why hold yourself to past thoughts of what used to be? Why use words that don't represent your greatest vision? This is the time to change things up. This is the time to take back your own personal power and navigate your reality.

Every moment is beaming with so much life. How will you use your next second? What will your day represent? What are you building up from within? So much is possible for you, and I want you to start to remember this. I want you to feel unstoppable and full of energy. I want you to live your dreams and love who you are. Greater vision affirmations are all about seeing outside of how things appear, and molding, orchestrating, and creating what you want. Too many people become limited by seeing one situation as final. The end of one thing is the beginning of something even greater. You don't have to stand still, fantasizing about what used to be when you are so alive and full of adventure right now. There is so much for you to experience, and new people for you to meet. There's so much to see and do. You are a big part of this world, and you have the chance to make it all memorable. Don't allow yourself to become stagnant. Let yourself be open, free, and curious. Allow yourself to explore, feel, and live fully. There's nothing to be afraid of. These next affirmations will empower you to imagine bigger and better things, and see the greatest vision for yourself. The words I share here will guide you to be lifted higher and give you a vision of true possibility. Every word you read and repeat will clear your path, amplify your potential, and open you up to receive all that you're currently intending and praying for. You will start to feel a great power of hope and a mental reassurance that you can make it happen.

61. I See Beyond How Things Appear

I see beyond what is happening. I see the end already. My mind shows me that nothing is final. I am constantly winning. I change my mindset first, and watch things around me get better. I am strong in mind and powerful in my vision. I feel myself already living, celebrating, and sharing good news.

62. The Greatest Vision

I imagine the best for myself. I see myself thriving, shining, and loving what I do. Every moment, I lift myself higher and higher to see that my greatest vision already exists right now. If I can see it in my mind, and I can experience it in my reality. All is possible for me right now.

63. Possibilities Surround Me

I can be whatever I want to be. I can dream, imagine, and create what I want. The possibilities are endless. I am starting to see that I have the choice to make a difference in my life. The universe has always supported me. It is up to me to make a decision right now to believe in myself, move forward, and ride the wave of constant blessings. I am already successful. I was born a winner. I feel so alive and full of life.

64. I Believe in the Unseen and the Unimaginable

The unseen is busy at work for me. All of the thoughts I have been putting out are coming together for me to show me a new world. I had no idea they even existed. My own potential is being amplified. I feel creative, and more energized than ever before. I feel a magnetic pull of success, breakthroughs, and blessings coming toward me. I find myself in the right place at the right time. My life is starting to feel magical. I can't explain how it is all happening, but I trust that I am connected to the greatest Source that constantly provides.

65. I Am Lifted

I choose to enter a new state of mind. No circumstance or challenge is final. Things are always evolving and changing. I am always evolving. I will only see the bigger picture in every situation so I can remain open to new solutions that lift me higher.

66. I Am Dreaming Bigger Today

I have an imagination for a reason. I have the power to think something far greater than ever before. I will use every single moment to dream bigger and believe in myself. I have the power to change the direction I am going right now.

67. I See It Before It Happens

I see the outcome right now as a complete vision. I am already where I want to be in this moment. My mind arrives at the destination, and my physical being follows. I change my thinking and see that my outcome changes, too. I am noticing a pattern of mental shifts that create a physical shift. I have powerful thoughts that create what I want. I am a great visionary and believer in wonderful possibilities.

68. Each Moment Is Filled with Vast Potential

This moment has great potential. I can make a different choice right now that will change where I am headed. It is all about my choices, my focus, and my vision. I am the one who decides what I want to experience. There is great power in this moment, and vast power in my mind. I choose to see opportunities, blessings, miracles, and success all around me. My vision pulls toward me all that I choose to experience in my life.

69. The Possibilities Are Endless for Me

I can step out of what is and into what I want. Nothing is final, and this is what I must always remember every single moment. I can make new experiences come to life. I can command greater. I can take action to get what I want.

There's so much power within me, and this moment is filled with great choices. Today, I choose to accept my gift, live out my dreams, and be bold in all that I do.

70. I Am Always Learning and Getting Better

I keep getting better and better. I keep learning from every single situation, and that only lifts me to greater heights. My wisdom comes from within. My spirit is guiding me, and I am receiving answers through my faith and believing in myself. I see results because I already accept them as truth. All circumstances allow me to evolve and learn something new. Everything continues to teach me and bring me back to my own inner awareness that all is just. Everything always works out. I am so grateful for all of my experiences. I have learned so much, and I just keep getting better.

71. I See Hope in the World

The bigger picture is that everything always ends up working out. I know the power is in having hope and believing in what I want to see transpire. The more I believe in the success of the planet, the more I will see solutions coming up in how I can make a contribution. My thoughts alone are the change the world needs. If I send out hope and project that things can get better, I can add to the collective state of wellness, evolution, and solutions.

72. I Will Make an Impact

I will be a part of the solution by being myself and loving who I am. The better I feel about myself, the more I can put out good energy and bring value to the world. The more I take care of myself, the more joy I share with others. I have to make sure that I am good first in order to make an impact. The energy I radiate represents the state I am in. I choose to shine brighter at every single moment. I choose to do something great for my family, my friends, my community, my nation, the universe, and myself. The impact I make is just being loving to who I am and enjoying the experience of sharing wonderful moments.

73. Things Are Naturally Revealed to Me

I always receive great insight that shows me the bigger picture. I see beyond the illusions and break free from all cycles of limitation. I am lifted higher every single moment. The answers I need come naturally, and they come with great speed.

74. I Get Things Done Swiftly

My energy has multiplied. My creativity has doubled. I am getting things done right away. I feel a surge of energy, and my productivity is at its highest point. I am constantly and consistently fueled by the unlimited source within me.

75. I Am Talented and Gifted

I have great talents within me. I was born a creative genius. My imagination is now fully activated, and I will do what I am passionate about. I will express myself more. I will bring to life what is brewing inside of me. The universe supports my vision and allows me to see it through to completion.

76. I Am the Example of My Inner World

Everything that surrounds me starts in my mind. The way I treat myself represents how I think and feel about myself. I am the example of my inner world. The more I believe in myself, the more I attract wonderful things. Everything is possible for me. I have to begin to remember right now that I am projecting what I want to experience. My inner conversation will be healthy and loving. My vision will be clear and direct. My expression will be open. My mindset will be strong. I will radiate from the inside out all that I want to experience. My outer world is the representation of my inner world. I will nurture myself from the inside out and live unapologetically!

77. I Will Imagine Greater in All Ways

My mind is now in solution-oriented mode. I naturally think of solutions in the most complex situations. I always seem to have a breakthrough. I am naturally successful at figuring things out. My brain is wired to see the bigger picture, and to always move upward and forward in life. No matter what is happening, I always know I can make it through. Something within me continuously shows me the way. I trust myself, and feel so good about my state of being.

78. I Am Renewed Every Second

I am in a new state at every second. I can think something new. I can imagine something greater. I can choose to feel better. The possibilities are endless for me. All I have to do is remember that I have choices. I am free from all illusions and limitations. I see the life force in this second, and I see the possibilities within me. I am great. I can live a beautiful life no matter what. I am so grateful for this new chance!

79. I Alter What I See, and Imagine a Greater Perspective

I only accept greatness in every moment. I choose to alter what I see because my perspective is what continues to create for me. The outcome will always change when I focus on the greater perspective. I will look at every situation as a learning experience, and move on to bigger and better things. I will always fly higher and dream bigger. I will always have hope. I will always imagine the best. I am naturally good at getting over things and focusing on a new vision. I am the best at altering my reality to create what I want. The bigger picture is that things always get better, and everything always ends up working out. I am so grateful to be free from the past, and to know that I can choose to think differently right now!

80. I Am in a New State

I am healthy in mind, body, and spirit. I am at peace with myself and successful at everything I do. I define my reality. I enter a new state every single moment to take a quantum leap in a new direction. The universe supports me in all ways. My thoughts are healthy and vibrant.

Self-Love/Intuition/Patience Affirmations

It is now time for you to enter self-love affirmations. A big part of energizing yourself is accepting who you are and knowing that you are already great. All the self-judgment and noise is an illusion picked up from the outside world: what others think of you, or what you have allowed yourself to be defined by. If you've made it this far in the book, then you have already been activated on a whole new level in the way you think, feel, and see the world. You feel more powerful about who you are, and you probably even have a new drive and determination to make better choices every single second. You are so free and so great that you can no longer deny it or hide from it. There are no excuses. The power of your existence is so apparent. It is obvious that you are a walking genius put together in such a magical way that words alone cannot define the greatness that is within you. I want you to start loving who you are, not for any particular reason, but simply for being you. There is nothing extra you have to do to get to this point; you just have to accept it now, and remember what has always been. Understand that what is happening within you is experienced by you. If you think people are judging you or something is stopping you, then that is what you will feel in that moment. Whatever is constantly taking place within you is what you will constantly say to yourself about yourself. This is your private world. Why see yourself as anything less than great?

It is now time to build yourself up from the inside out. It is now time for you to end this battle against yourself. You will now start to speak powerful words about yourself. You will now see yourself as good enough. You will know that you can do it. You will follow all of your dreams. You will feel worthy and valuable. Your mental space will be supportive. Your inner world will be filled with loving thoughts. You will remember that you have always been good enough. From this moment on, you will have a train of thought that constantly builds you up. The affirmations I write here will shatter past thoughts of limitation and lack, and open you up to a new vision. You can actually be in a space of peace and love toward yourself. You will begin to feel clarity like never before. You will be filled with so much gratitude and energy of pure love that you will feel revived and refreshed simply from your own thoughts. These affirmations will open you up to a stream of remembering your greatness and unlocking your true inner powers. What comes up within you is for you to discover, explore, and enjoy. You will feel expanded and connected like never before. Enjoy the gifts of loving who you are, being at peace with yourself, and being open to the magical world within you.

This set of affirmations on intuition is meant to help you start looking at the world around you as a reflection of your inner world. There's always a sign for you to follow. I want you to start trusting your inner voice. The more you listen, the more things will start to happen for you. The chase and the search will come to an end when you realize that you have always had it. Every moment was meant to bring you back to yourself so you can listen, understand, and receive. Your life is an adventure. You are meant to be curious and explore, enjoy, and discover. You are the one who chooses if you want to be passionate about life. There's nothing wrong with what you choose and how you live it out. Every single person is navigating their own universe and getting the outcome they want based upon what they think, feel, do, and believe. The more you follow your own heart and listen to your own spirit, the more things will clarify themselves. Nobody knows you better than your own self. You are the one having your own private inner experience. The complexities of your inner world will almost feel like you are living in a parallel universe when you compare thoughts and discover just how differently everyone sees the world around them. You are unique. You are you, and nothing and nobody can live out your life better than you can. What comes up within you is for you to receive, decipher, and create from. You have to start trusting yourself more. Everything will bring you back to how powerful you are. You are the one who is supposed to remember that you harness incredible energy.

The more you tune in, the more you receive. External motivation is only meant to bring you back to you, so you can see your own potential. We are all examples of what is possible. When someone else is succeeding and doing something grand, that is meant to help you see that anything can happen for you, too. What happens for everyone will be unique to his or her own experience, but we are all motivating each other according to how we decide to paint our own pictures. Discoveries in science, business, personal development, and creative expression demonstrate human potential. The more we all see how far we can go, the more your inner power is ignited to believe that you, too, can do this and more. You have access right now to tap in and follow your heart. What is your contribution? What do you want to share? How do you want to ignite the message in others that all is possible? The affirmations I share with you in this section will allow you to remember to listen to your own voice and empower you to ride the wave that is beaming out of you.

This set of affirmations on patience is all about allowing things to unfold through trust, and learning the momentum you are building daily as you dedicate yourself to passion and purpose. These affirmations are meant to support you during this period when things are coming together for you. You can repeat these words to yourself and know that you are building great energy on the mental and spiritual level that will change the world around you. So much is happening for you at every single moment. You must now live your life from a place where you automatically trust that what you have visualized, prayed for, intended, and worked toward is coming together so perfectly. Patience isn't supposed to be wondering when it will happen. It is a time when you know that you have already planted your seed, and it will flourish for you. You are now in a new mental word where you don't even bother to concern yourself with the how or the when. You have become so trusting of yourself that you already know it will happen. You even speak in a new way about your vision. You have an *it is already done* mentality. There's something so incredible about the way you see life now that just makes you feel the flow of favor.

Self-Love Affirmations

81. Loving Myself Multiplies My Blessings

The more I love myself, the more I notice everyone around me treating me better. I am finally seeing that people respond to how I treat myself and what I allow. I've noticed that I have even started to attract better, and I have seen all my blessings multiply. I am now in a vortex of self-love, and it amplifies my energy field of potential.

82. I Am Stronger Than Ever Before

I feel so much stronger, and I know that I can accept who I am right now. Loving myself has opened up a whole new world for me. I am accepting that it starts within me, and I am radiating self-love and self-care simply by being me.

83. I Am Kind to Myself

I use empowering words to build myself up. I have thoughts that support my mental wellness and self-love. Every single positive thought I have multiplies and attracts thousands of other positive thoughts. Uplifting energy surrounds me, and I feel it.

84. I Love My Body

I am designed so beautifully. My body supports me and takes care of me. I am kind and loving to myself. I love my body. I love all that my body does. I treat myself well. I am good enough, and I know that my thoughts influence my cells. Every single thought I send out creates within me the state that I perceive. I choose to be more loving to myself and gentler with my words. I am now shifting my whole state of being—mentally, physically, spiritually, and molecularly—to be filled with self-love.

85. I Am Valuable

I am officially free from the past. I am free of all past thinking. I walk around knowing that I am valuable. I know that I am worthy. I feel so deserving of greatness, and I claim it now. I am great. My life is grand. My thinking has changed, and my life now reflects that. Everyone I meet sees my value, and they recognize my worth without a single word. My energy speaks for itself, and it speaks of pure greatness.

86. I Define Myself

It all starts with me. I am the one who defines who I am and who I want to be. I am the one who chooses what I think and feel. I am the one who allows what stays in my life and what continues on. I have the power to make a change now that switches things up. I am the one who is narrating my story. I get to say when I edit, cut, and start over as I choose. I am the director and the main actor. This is my story, and I get to write it exactly how I want. I get to make changes when I want. The power is in my hands, and I feel so free to be able to make my own choices. This is a new moment for me, and it all begins with remembering the true freedom I have over my life.

87. My Words Build Me up

I use great words to describe myself. I only speak positive words to myself. I encourage myself all the time. I continue to build myself up every single day. I am starting to see the benefits of my positive self-talk. The most important conversation is the one I have with myself. I am going to be a representative of what positive self-talk can do in your life when you apply it.

Intuition Affirmations

88. I Have Strong Intuition

I already know it before it even happens. My intuition is very strong and powerful. I feel inner guidance taking place, and I keep following the signs I get.

89. I Follow Through with My Intuition

When my intuition shows me a sign, I actually follow through with it. When I get a gut feeling, I trust it. The more I trust what is being shown to me, the more I start to connect the dots.

90. I Trust All the Signs

Things always add up for me. I always make sense out of the codes I am receiving. The signs I get are very clear and direct. I am noticing that every moment has something to give me, and I am finally open to receive it.

91. I Am Good at Decoding My Intuition

I automatically know what my intuition is sharing with me. What is coming in allows me to get solutions for the questions I have asked. When the answers I need come in, I act swiftly and with faith. The more I show that I trust myself, the more guidance I receive. Every moment is in my favor, and I am the one who now accepts my blessing to see past the way things appear and trust what I can't fully understand. I am thriving in this mysterious world and using my inner faith to navigate my adventure.

92. I Trust Myself

I am now moving forward in all ways. I am taking bold action. I am the walking power of true faith. I trust all that I am receiving from within. My inner guidance and intuition are so strong. I am giving myself more credit and allowing the best to finally happen for me. I am officially winning in every way. I am already there!

93. I Live in a Secret World of Possibilities

I am now aware that I am fully connected. My inner world is so powerful and strong. The signs I am getting are so evident. I finally feel like myself. I am so grateful to discover what can happen for me when I trust myself. This is only the beginning of the wonderful things I will do and experience in my lifetime.

94. All Is Revealed to Me

Every time I ask a question or need answers, my intuition always responds. I always feel supported.

Patience Affirmations

95. I Already Believe It

I believe that what I have spoken into existence is already done. I have patience because I believe in myself. The energy has already been put out there. The momentum has already been created. The seed has already been planted.

96. I Am Allowing

I am in a state of allowing. I have done my part. Once I have visualized something or desired it, the energy comes together. I already know that things always happen in my favor. Now, I will begin to see the physical results of my energy work. All that I have done, thought, and prayed for is now going to present itself to me. I am a believer!

97. Patience Is Trust

When I am patient with myself, I am showing that I trust the Source that provides all of life. The more I trust, the more I see miracles happen in my life.

98. I Create a Catalyst When I Am Patient

Energy moves faster when I plant it and let go of it. I already know the universe is doing great work in the unseen for me. Every single thing I plant comes to fruition.

99. I Am Unfolding Daily

My blessings are unfolding on a daily basis. I see the things that I have been patient about happening for me. I see that what I have planted comes to life. I am living in such a magical time. My entire life has taken a turn for the better. My trust and faith have multiplied more than I could ever have imagined.

100. Patience Brings Me Great Success

My timing is perfect. Every single thing happens for me when it should. I know that when I am patient, I get better results. I automatically receive better than I could imagine when I surrender and allow. The universe is so powerful in the way it aligns me with the right people at the right time. The best opportunities show up when I trust myself and know that I only attract greatness.

You now have access to 100 powerful affirmations to constantly use as needed. You will expand and empower yourself like never before. This is your time to switch things up and speak greatness over your life. It is time for you believe like you never have believed before, and access all that is within you. The more you speak these affirmations, the more you will unlock your own inner potential. You will start to think more clearly and actually start seeing things beyond the physical. You will naturally be good at visualizing and feeling any state before it happens. Allow yourself to feel every single word you read here, and connect with your own insight about what comes up. The point is to build strong self-trust so you can allow yourself to remember that you have always been gifted.

The more empowered you become, the more you can actually discover your purpose and passion while living out your dreams. You will do more of what you want, and it will feel good to know that you can finally settle into yourself and allow things to flow through. These affirmations are like a companion on your adventure, and will constantly speak power into you. When you read these words, you will easily enter the state of your true potential. There is nothing standing in your way. You are living in a limitless world waiting for you to discover. Your imagination is now activated!

23

Inner Glimpse Daily Thoughts

The 30 thoughts provided in this chapter are meant for you to use as tools of activation to recharge your energy and become inspired instantly. You can read these 30 thoughts daily, and refer back to them when you need them most. As you are starting to discover your inner powers, you will also realize the importance of these words and how much they will impact you. You will feel supported along your adventure, and find comfort in knowing that you have access to read this as often as you like. The energy behind the Inner Glimpse Thoughts is meant to lift you higher and give you not only hope, but true reassurance that you can be, do, and have what you wish. The goal isn't only to create what you want; it is also to recognize your own inner potential and the vast possibilities that surround you. The more you realize who you really are, the more things will start to make sense. You will continue to avoid control by the outside world, and you will discover that everything stems from what you give your energy to, what you decide to focus on, and the direction you choose to go. I want you to read these Inner Glimpse Thoughts over and over until you feel stronger and more connected to your own guidance.

Being empowered is a state of mind and an outlook. The choice is always in your hands. These Inner Glimpse Thoughts will put you in a state of mind where you feel like anything can happen for you. This is your personal world of possibilities. You have the key to access it already. As you start to build up your own momentum of self-belief, self-awareness, and self-acceptance, you will find yourself attracting more thoughts aligned with the positive love shared here. Your mental space always sends the signal out for the thoughts you want to attract. If you feel powerful within your mind and constantly speak and think thoughts that allow you to evolve, you will notice that this state becomes habitual for you. The change begins in what you constantly think and repeat to yourself. Every thought has its own energy pattern. You will notice that the more you think great things can happen for you, the more you will begin to attract other thoughts that show you the way. It's fascinating what you can remember when you create thought patterns that support the direction and vision of your purpose.

The 30 Inner Glimpse Thoughts shared below will constantly give back to you so you can remember that you actually *can* do it. You will feel so motivated and determined that things around you will instantly begin to change for the better. I want you to remember that your mindset is what changes first. The outside world starts to follow through with great success when you cultivate the mental energy that all is possible. Start now, and repeat these words to yourself on a daily basis. Feel every single word, and allow yourself to accept the changes. You will only get better and better. You will rise up and claim what has always been within you. It's time to think greater, live it up, and make wonderful and magnificent things happen.

1. I have so much potential.

New thoughts can completely alter the direction of your life. Something within you will awaken and take you to the next level, simply because you have shifted from within. Your destiny is so grand. Stop playing it small and thinking this is it for you. It's not. It is up to you to dream bigger, see greater, and believe in all that is possible for you. The universe is filled with potential. Enter the higher dimension of thinking and living. Your potential is activated!

Repeat Daily:

I am now activated.

I can see my value. I can see my potential.

I feel the change that is taking place right now.

I feel a surge of new energy that shows me that my shift in thinking has already created a shift in everything around me.

You have so much potential. Every single thing you've experienced has served a great purpose, and this continues in the present. Trust the process and the unfoldment. You might be getting a recurring thought or feeling that you are worthy of so much more. You might even be receiving signs that it's time to finally do something about it. It's time to finally take your power back by deciding to choose how you want to live your life. You can't be afraid anymore. Fear has kept you stuck for way too long. Now more than ever, your potential keeps popping up in your mind. You keep getting that feeling that there's more to who you are, what you can do, and all that you can have. This Inner Glimpse is your spirit communicating with you, reminding you that you have unlimited potential. I know it feels good to see and feel that you can do anything in the moment you receive a thought. Now let's move that state into action. Let's not be afraid of uncertainty or the unknown. What comes next is what will transform, change, and alter your life completely.

On the other side of where you are now lies all that you can be, but you must declare today that you are ready to step it up and step into your highest potential. Be okay with letting go of what's familiar and no longer works. Embrace all that is possible to enrich your life. You know all of this deep down within you. This is just a reminder to you, and a confirmation to move forward. Go right ahead into it. The answers, guidance, and clarity will show up as we take the risk of venturing off into unfamiliar territory. Your spirit will guide you. This is a world of great possibility. You can renew yourself. You can renew your mindset. You can change what you do. Decide to listen to your spirit.

2. It is my time to start receiving.

You have to start seeing what you desire as something that is natural and normal for you to have. Don't put things on a pedestal or make yourself feel small. You are the powerhouse here. You are the one with the mind, the life force, the energy, and the center to create it. You can receive what you want, because it is normal for you to have anything. There is nothing greater than understanding that everything is just an experience. You create the ideas, and you are the one who chooses what to give meaning to. Take your power back. Value yourself first, and watch the golden rush of blessings enter your life.

Repeat Daily:

I allow myself to receive.

I am open to receiving.

It is natural for me to be successful and happy.

My timing is perfect, and I am so grateful for it.

This is your time! I hope it finally all happens for you: a spiritual breakthrough, a financial breakthrough, a high-energy breakthrough, a healing breakthrough, a love breakthrough, a healthy living breakthrough, a mental health breakthrough, an emotional health breakthrough. It is time for you to finally receive. You deserve some kind of breakthrough that gives you a sign to restore your hope and make you 100x more of a believer because you have finally seen a miracle happen. This is your time. It is now. You are ready. Get your mind and emotions in order. Get yourself together. Celebrations are arriving in a major way. The inner breakthroughs are so important...the *aha* moments that life is starting to make sense, the trust you're starting to have, the self-love you're starting to feel just by being you. This is the beginning of it all. This is your reminder.

I hope these words resonate with your heart as you begin to make your dreams a reality. You are living the most unexplainable life, beaming with mystery and possibility. All you can do is trust, right? All you can do is believe. It's all so fascinating—why not imagine your wildest dreams, while you're at it? Loosen up a bit. Play more. Relax. Don't be too serious. Don't get all caught up. Laugh at yourself and your situation. Lighten things up so your spirit can thrive. You are okay, and you are doing your best. Step out of your own way and let your inner light shine. This is your time!

3. I am rising up out of all situations.

Move upward from that one situation. It has served its purpose. You don't need to let it live on within you. You are now renewed to recreate and experience new adventures. Your life is rich. You still have so much life within you, which means you can make anything happen. You will now begin to rise up out of the ashes of the past and go higher than you have ever gone before.

Repeat Daily:

I choose to go higher.

I choose to think greater.

I am experiencing new blessings.

I am entering a new state of being.

My world has completely transformed for the better.

You might be experiencing changes on a mental, physical, and spiritual level now more than ever. This is all new energy, but truly, it is all familiar energy. Something you already are is revealing itself to you so that you can step into your purpose and reclaim your divine power. All that seems like chaos and uncertainty is actually a reshuffle for you to loosen the grips on controlling everything and remaining the same. This is a time to start trusting more instead of trying to hold everything together so you can be in a familiar place. It almost feels like a rebirth; in all ways, and in all parts of your life. This is completely normal. You are okay, even if you feel symptoms you can't explain. There's so much happening on a cellular atomic level that sometimes, we might not have all the words to explain it.

This is a reminder to welcome new energy. Welcome change. Welcome what doesn't make sense. Don't fantasize about "that one time when everything felt so good." It is all good right now, and it is all going to be greater. It's a space of authentic reflection, acceptance, and evolution within your own self. You are always okay. In change, we always try to find what can hold us together, but you are held together right now by the greatest source of power. You can breathe as you flow. You can continue on as you discover. There isn't this or that. It all just is, and the more you trust yourself and trust that it's okay, the more you'll accept your peace. Accept your new blessings. There's so much being revealed to you. You are so powerful and precious. You are safe and okay. You are loved. This is what you must constantly remember. In the darkest hour or the most trying time, it's all just new energy entering. A greater clarity is emerging. A new beginning is rising up within you. Be very patient right now, and trust more of what you can't explain.

4. I give myself credit for making it through.

Acknowledge yourself. You're doing your best. It's not about rushing or getting to a goal instantly. You are unraveling, maturing, learning, and growing through it all. Every little thing that has happened was only teaching you a greater lesson in order to evolve you. Be gentle with yourself. Be loving, kind, and patient with yourself.

Repeat Daily:

I am strong enough.

I can make it through in this moment.

I have an unstoppable spirit.

I am already good enough.

I am resilient, and I continue to get better.

You are doing your best. You have come so far, and sometimes, you just need to pause for a moment and acknowledge yourself. Look at what you have overcome. Look at how strong you are. Look at how much better you're doing. The end of anything is the beginning of something greater. If you spend more time acknowledging how magnificent and magical you are, you'll get out of the fears and overthinking of what's next. The next thing that will happen for you is the greatest thing that will occur. In every moment, you're evolving. Sometimes, you might experience challenges that feel like a part of you is coming to an end, but it's needed. You're evolving spiritually. You're awakening. You're realizing so much about yourself: who you really are and what you deserve. During the transformation phase, it can feel heavy or even uncomfortable. It's not about avoiding everything, but rather not being defined by anything. It is happening...what now? Smile about it. This gives you back your power. Breathe through it; it lightens things up.

Release the need to control everything. That's a safety mechanism to keep yourself the same, when in the blink of an eye, you can be living, feeling, and experiencing all that you have dreamed of. Familiarity creates repetition, and that can feel comfortable. However, change doesn't mean the end. It means new experiences are possible, new feelings await, new adventures are here, and a new thing to learn and do surrounds you. For once, feel a moment of letting go of all control. Breathe. You don't have to fully understand the why or when, the how or the timing of it all. You just need to allow and believe. Dream and imagine. Trust and pray. Be grateful for who you are. You are magnificent. Magical. Powerful. Gifted. Special. You are loved! You are whole! You are complete as you are.

Nothing can be added or taken away from you. Just realize this throughout life, and things will become more joyful. Learn to accept, love, and appreciate yourself. This expands your heart. It starts within you. Always know that you are okay, and that it is all okay. Everything will be fine. Be patient and loving to yourself. Give yourself credit, because you are truly strong. Your past shows your ability to overcome the most challenging moments. Look at you, still here, standing strong. Nothing can break you. Gather yourself up and claim your divine truth right now.

5. I am already highly blessed.

Take a moment just to be grateful for who you are and all that you love. Remember how precious your life already is. You were chosen for this, because you are strong enough and highly gifted. You are intelligent and capable of great things. You can shine through any circumstances with the power of remembering that you are already highly blessed.

Repeat Daily:

I am highly blessed.

My gratitude multiplies my blessings.

I am so grateful for my life. I have the power within me.

I feel energized knowing that greatness is unfolding for me.

No matter what's happening around you, you must always remember that you are a highly blessed person. You have always been. No situation or experience can change the fact that you have been chosen. You have no idea how much is currently working for you in places you can't see. Every thought, action, feeling, and intention is a powerful force accumulating for you and building up a world of experiences getting ready to manifest. It is law. Focus and consistency must produce. This is just how it is, and your consistency to believe in yourself, invest in yourself, and trust yourself will now start to show up. Blessings must make themselves apparent, because that is law. It is universal truth. We receive what we consistently think and do.

We are constantly making an energy investment in thought, action, and intentions. It's all going to pay off in a major way soon. It's already working for you. Don't be confined by what you see as evidence right now. Be empowered by your vision. Daily, you are building a world that will reveal itself to you through unexpected opportunities and alignments, sudden connections, and automatic shifts that might not initially make sense. You'll look back and remember you asked for that, so be willing to receive anything new. Be willing to flow in chance encounters and unexpected invitations. Be willing to be guided, but also be bold in what you ask for and what you believe will happen for you. It's time to start claiming and being consistent in all ways. Your life is about to experience a positive shift, and every blessing associated with your energy field will locate you. Be ready, and be excited! Start smiling and celebrating. Life is happening now for you! Let the affirmation *I am a highly blessed person* be your daily state of mind.

6. My mental energy is at work.

Your mental energy is producing great results for you. Direct it, claim it, see it, and access it. Everything is in motion to turn into a physical, tangible experience for you. A new state has opened up for you. This is a vortex of healing, blessings, love, and opportunities. It is unlimited and constant. It is yours, and you are connected to it. Your mind might have taken you in other directions before, and you might have forgotten how gifted and special you are, but this is a reminder to your spirit. You're feeling so alive again. You are now remembering. You are activated to reclaim what has always been there. Start knowing that your mental energy is at work, ready to produce the physical experiences you desire. It is all possible, and it is here with you right now.

Repeat Daily:

Things instantly begin to happen for me.

I see my thoughts quickly manifest.

I feel so powerful, so alive, and so connected.

The universe continues to reflect my mental state.

I feel empowered, knowing that I can alter my reality.

Your energy is at work right now! The results are showing up. It doesn't matter how or when. It is all right now. It is all happening, and it is all working itself out. You could be experiencing new things and rapid changes in your life because you have decided to stop living in regret and start claiming greatness. Things could seem very uncertain, because you are now charting the unknown. This is the best place to be; this is where your spirit comes alive. You might not know what's next, and being in that space can sometimes feel very uncomfortable. We want to be so in control with every step and the way it happens.

The magic and beauty of life can be found in speaking, thinking, and feeling what we want, allowing the guidance of our innermost self to lead us to what works best for our evolution and growth even when it initially doesn't make sense. One day, you'll look back and say, "Wow, I'm so glad that happened for me!" Live in the space where you surrender the need to control every moment, and allow some magical experiences and sudden miracles to manifest in your life. Relax after you do your part. Be consistent in your positivity, and keep believing until you see it all happening for you. The clarity in this message will lift you higher and bring ease to your mind and heart. You'll find yourself trusting. You'll feel a sense of joy and inner bliss that all is well. No matter what, you are always okay, and that is such a beautiful feeling.

7. Things are starting to get very clear for me.

You're starting to see things you're thinking and feeling pop into your reality faster now. This can be a big sign that reminds you of your true ability to think things into existence. You're starting to gain more clarity. Pay attention and recognize the connections. You're going to gain a lot of momentum by seeing the patterns. Things are now becoming more obvious.

Repeat Daily:

I follow the signs I keep getting.

I constantly attract good news.

My world is starting to feel magical.

I feel great clarity and peace like never before.

May you receive an answer, sign, message, good news, or some kind of blessing. You no longer have to overthink about it. Let it go. You did your part. You prayed about it. You visualized. You took action. You did everything on your end. Now, you can relax and breathe. Things are moving toward you. They have already happened for you. The minute you thought it, it aligned to manifest in your reality. Now is the best time for patience and celebration. See it as a complete vision. How would you feel if you received good news? Put yourself into that expectant state. There's no separation between your intentions and their manifestation. Right now, it is already done. It's happening.

This is a message to bring you ease and comfort so you can have reassurance that you've got this. On the spiritual level, your creation is complete. The realm of thought is our space for creation. Whatever we think, we also see, hear, and experience on the outside. You have already created what you're about to receive. Now enjoy yourself. Have a great time, with yourself or loved ones and friends. Do what makes you happy instead of sitting around overthinking or worrying about how and when. Miracles happen when we are just living. Expected blessings come suddenly when we are celebrating. Lift your mood and believe as you live and experience the best of what you want. Breathe for a moment, and lift your mind higher. Good news and sudden breakthroughs can happen for you even before the manifesting thought has ended. Be ready for it!

8. I imagine it into existence.

Create a mental image in which you see your vision clearly. Your mental world is a powerful space where you build and create what you want. Your mind is just as real as things in the physical. Feel it already happening. In your mind, lift out of your current situation by becoming the new state you want to enter. You are unstoppable once you realize just how much things can start to shift when you change your mindset.

Repeat Daily:

Everything I visualize happens for me.

I build the best mental world, and I see it happen.

I can turn any situation to my favor.

I have power over any circumstance.

I only give my energy to what I want to see multiply in my life.

You have a powerful mind! Your intended vision is already yours. The second you thought of it and believed in it, it had already been claimed by you. It's making its way to you now. Our minds operate on the mental plane, where we visualize, imagine, and create our next experience. This mental plane is as real as the physical one, but at first, it can't be seen except in your inner world. This is all taking place when you speak, think, and feel something into existence. This is your power. We give external experience more credit because it is tangible. Sometimes, we might even believe in it too much, and forget that the mental plane exists. There, we see what's possible and understand the true potential we bring into the physical world.

Your experience shouldn't be limited to what your physical senses are showing you. You have the power now to reimagine, recreate, and redesign your life. The only thing is, you can't worry about how or when. Just stay busy designing, celebrating, and having fun, because you know that what you want is already yours. There's nothing else to it. Fear and doubt have gotten in the way for too long, because we only trust what we see, not what we believe. Not anymore! All of this changes right now. It's time to claim your power and what is already yours. This brings automatic ease without needing, forcing, pushing, or trying too hard. Be calm about it, because your faith is stronger than what you see. Things can instantly change for you. Don't ever doubt that. Live in the space and mindset that anything great could suddenly happen. The world is filled with possibilities. Why not expect the best for yourself?

9. I am headed somewhere so incredible.

You are destined for greatness. The codes for success have always been in your DNA. Start knowing that the cards are in your favor. Walk, think, feel, and act in the state of mind that you know you were created by greatness and destined for greatness. You are the one who feels it. You came to this Earth perfectly designed, with all the tools in your mind. You have it all within you right now, and this reminder is sparking great change in your life.

Repeat Daily:

I have greatness flowing through me.

I radiate greatness automatically, simply by being me.

I am perfectly designed, and I choose to recognize it.

My mindset is the healthiest and strongest it has ever been.

You were born with the code of greatness. Think about how you can imagine, dream, and find solutions. You are made up of atoms and energy, filled with potential. Why doubt who you are? Why spend your life against yourself or living in regret? So much of your mental and emotional energy has to be reclaimed by you. You can no longer allow yourself to live in denial. If everything is energy and all is momentary, why not believe in what could happen for you (and what *is* happening for you) instead of the opposite? You have some serious codes within you. Experiences literally activate you. Lessons are there to remind you of your potential.

Every single thing that happens in your life brings you back to the feeling that you can make it through. You overcome things so you can remember how strong you are. Every moment enriches you and refines you. This learning experience is now going into the mental space, because your activation will no longer require mere obstacles or lessons. Now, you will begin to know things intuitively. You will see them before they happen. You will transcend the state of struggle and repeated cycles where you had to re-learn the same lesson over and over again. It is now time to see who you are and accept yourself. You are deserving of great things. You can finally break free of limitations and illusions. You are the one who had to personally accept that all along. Nobody can do it for you but yourself. This is a new level of empowerment, and you are now in it so deeply that nothing can make you forget it.

10. Today is the day
my life changes for the better.

Things are changing for you right now. You are receiving new energy that's lifting you back into the motion of wellness, success, and inner peace. Your happiness is right now, and you are starting to simply be it. You are realizing that there is so much free energy for you to tap into. Knowing this will change your life today. You will now start to get more energy that gets you motivated, inspired, and determined like never before. You will find yourself breaking free of habitual thoughts and emotions that no longer serve you. You will start to find yourself getting things done. You now have new energy to complete your projects, accomplish your goals, and make your dreams a reality. You have officially entered a state of being where you are optimal in all ways.

Repeat Daily:

I have access to unlimited energy within me.

I can change my thoughts and change my life.

I am optimal, strong, and determined.

Great blessings flow out of me and into the universe.

I impact everything and everyone for the better.

I excel at all that I do, and I naturally get things done.

Give power to yourself in this moment. Feel charged up, electrified, full of life, and completely trusting of what's next. Today is your turning point. You have declared power over your life, your situation, your business, your family, your dreams, and your blessings. This is where you claim all of this as your truth. We're no longer living in the distant future, hoping that one day, things might turn around. Not anymore! Today is the day. Now is the moment. Breathe in a new life. This all feels so different. Your faith is restored. Your mindset sees a whole new world: one of possibility, potential, and miracles. You are everything! You are so gifted, and so special! You can ask for it. You can instantly receive! Let's get your energy up. Trust your heart, and declare this moment to be your turning point!

11. I take my power back.

Get out of the overthinking. Stop doubting yourself. Stop fantasizing about the past. Let it go right now. Start over in this moment. You can make a new self-declaration right now, taking your power back from what you no longer agree with. You can release what was and build something even greater. You can start overusing new thoughts, instead. Why be repetitive of what doesn't evolve you? You can choose something new.

Repeat Daily:

My inner word belongs to me.

I release what no longer serves me.

I feel powerful and strong as I start over.

I feel renewed, revived, and reenergized. I own my power.

You have the choice to decide to take your power back from the past, from things that don't elevate you, and from situations you give too much of your energy to. You are too powerful to waste your life force on allowing something outside of yourself access to your precious inner world. Allow yourself to be free to change...free to decide to make a better choice every moment, so you can be lifted higher. Remember, nothing and nobody has control over you. No thoughts or emotions are more powerful than your conscious mind deciding and willing right now that you want better. You are the one who needs to boldly state that you deserve better.

No matter what the situation, you can stop allowing it. When you awaken to this thought within you, you will feel negative things exit your reality. You now know that you have the choice, and you no longer have to settle. You'll now find yourself feeling the warmth of peace and a surge of hope that all things are possible. You aren't defined by your past, a certain situation, or whatever it is that's currently happening. You are beyond all of that, and you must declare it. You must claim a new state and see how much the universe supports you. It's a new day for you. It's time to feel your aliveness and make the choice to live exactly how you want.

12. I will prevail.

Don't let the little things make you lose your focus. You are too powerful and too great to get caught up in any momentary issues. Remember who you are. Remember why you even started. Remember your gift! You will prevail and overcome so much, simply by staying persistent in moving forward and upward into your own greatness.

Repeat Daily:

I always make it through.

I always come out on top.

I am unstoppable and fearless.

Everything is momentary, and I will always prevail.

I am stronger, wiser, and more dedicated than ever before.

You will always overcome the difficult times. You have the code of resiliency. You are the greatest adapter to any and all conditions. You metamorphose and rise up like a phoenix. Illusions fall off of you like ashes as you rise. You shed all limitation and past thinking. You feel stronger than ever before. You always prevail! Your spirit is pure greatness! It's never final. It's never over. Believe in it until it happens for you. Believe in it until it manifests for you. Believe in every situation, even when you feel like the odds are against you. See everything happening in your favor. Our faith and vision carry us into the world of possibilities. You need faith, vision, and a feeling of trust. Everything is a miracle in this life, and those who have vision will recognize that. The most important thing is what you choose to see in a situation, not what or how the situation appears.

The way everything happens reveals a power at work that is beyond the physical. Don't be limited by what you see. Don't think that what's happening is all that's real and solid. We have changed many times up to this point in our lives. You have changed in so many ways: mentally, physically, spiritually, and emotionally. A lot has come into your life and left. You have learned so much, and you've evolved many times. Your patience has been tested before, but you have prevailed. You have come out strong from situations that you thought would break you. All of the power you have used in the past is still within you. Nothing is final. You clearly see this in your life. So look at your current situation in this way. What can you believe into existence today? What can you imagine happening for you? It's all possible. Why not? Breathe so deeply, and trust. You are connected. You are a miracle. You have access 24/7 for the rest of your life. The point is to stop playing tricks on yourself. Stop putting fear into circumstances, and start putting faith into the power that sustains you, the power that gives to you, and the power that continues to nourish you. It's all beyond the physical, but by being here now, you can be lifted in mind and spirit first so you can alter what you're creating. Take back your power. Believe the greatest things into existence. It doesn't matter how. It doesn't matter when. Just believe, and watch things beginning to happen for you. What you need to do now is believe until it happens. Have consistent faith until you start to see physical results.

13. I own my greatness.

Do you realize who you are? Not the thoughts that tell you otherwise, but the greatness that you really are? Look at how alive you are right now. Look at how blessed you are. You are supported in ways which you might not even realize or even see right now. It is all here in this moment. You must accept your pure energy of greatness. Nothing else has to happen but for you to simply recognize and acknowledge what has always been there.

Repeat Daily:

I feel great about myself.

I am already so blessed and so gifted.

I own the energy I want to attract right now.

*I am already in the right state of mind,
and it will come to life.*

*I am pure greatness,
and I choose to accept that and acknowledge it.*

You were born to be great. Greatness is in your DNA! You have the genetic codes within your body. You're only going up from here. You've been strong long enough. You've overcome so much. Now is your time. The shift starts in your mindset and how you feel. Claim a new reality for yourself. Claim a new state for yourself. Believe even when it doesn't seem real. What is real is what's imagined, but sometimes, our rational mind will try to convince us that what's in front of us is factual when we truly have other faculties, such as our ability to imagine and leave space and time using our minds. You are a visionary. You are the creator of your experience through free will, choice, and intentions. You can decide today to think new thoughts, forgive yourself, feel greater, and be accepting of yourself so you can redirect your life force, attention, and time toward new outcomes.

What has happened has happened. Unlimited potential is waiting for you to either decide something greater or recreate from past pain, a past mindset, or past ideas. You have a choice, and it's the best feeling to snap yourself out of a somber mood of doom and gloom and into brightness and a hopeful state of mind. You are here so that you can still change, you can still advance, and you can claim abundance for yourself, your friends, and your family. It's time to accept a turning point and welcome a great blessing. Your mindset has shifted. You are now aware. You are claiming, speaking, doing, thinking, and feeling what you want into existence. That's your superpower. Use it, and be grateful that you are able to even understand this. Your blessings are now. Your abundance is today. Feel this deeply, and just smile. Stop taking everything so seriously and making everything you're experiencing more real than it really is. What's real is what you choose, what you imagine, and what you intend to create for yourself. Be the living miracle that you are.

14. I only imagine the best for myself.

I can choose how I see myself. If my imagination creates my reality and shows me what is possible for me, then why not see the best? Why not have great hope for myself? I choose to be constructive in my imagination and create what I want intentionally. I have a choice every single second to see greater and know that it is all tangible and possible.

Repeat Daily:

I think highly of myself.

I can imagine what I want into existence.

My imagination is extremely powerful.

Everything I intentionally want to experience happens for me.

*I feel good about myself
and choose to be positive about everything.*

*I believe in myself. I have so much potential,
and I will live out my dreams.*

Consistently see yourself as your best. Imagine it. Talk positively to yourself. Your inner conversations need to be empowering. Focus on imagining what you want. Take some time to get your inner world in order. Sometimes, you might be playing a negative, repetitive thought that you don't want over and over again, and it becomes habitual. Break the cycle. Think newer, greater thoughts. Love who you are. Let go of the guilt. These are all choices you can make right now. Not "one day." Not gradually. It's a decision and declaration that you love who you are now. You can choose to release past guilt and pain. You can be free from it all right now. Once you say this to yourself, your mind, body, and spirit will ignite with the power of change. A positive shift will take place. Don't judge the process or how quickly you're supposed to feel good about yourself. It's not about speed, but rather your consistency in imagining, speaking, thinking, and feeling great about yourself right now. This will be the start of something amazing. I hope you feel a rush of empowerment, love, hope, and change all over your mind. You are a new person today. Think that way, and feel it.

15. I am free of the past.

My mental energy belongs to me. My emotional state is my choice. I choose to be free of the past. I break all cycles that once kept me down. I release people and situations that no longer belong in my life. I am so at peace with myself that it almost seems surreal. My inner wellness has sparked, and I can feel it pervading all spaces within me and around me. I have literally made it through, and it feels so good to know that I am finally free of the past.

Repeat Daily:

I choose what I think and feel.

I choose what stays in my inner world.

I choose what I let go of and what I welcome in.

I have the power of choice, and that frees me automatically.

I am making better decisions today,
and I choose the best for myself.

How are you using your mental and emotional energy? Where is your precious life force going? The past is gone. There future hasn't arrived. What is there to be scared of? You can reimagine and recreate yourself. You can let go and forgive yourself. Do it right now. See the best-case scenario in your situation. What does that feel like? What if it does all work out for you? Think about that for a moment. Imagine that. Entertain that. Start using your mental force to see something different. Be optimistic about it. I know it's easy to entertain habitual thoughts from the past, but you are no longer there. This is your moment to be liberated. Some negative habitual thoughts seem real because you have entertained them for way too long.

When you start to think positively, you might find yourself uncertain if it's real, or if it is even working. One thing you need to understand is that repetitive thoughts always become strong, and you begin to feel like a new person day by day. Start your new state of mind today. Think new thoughts. Feel new emotions. Bring yourself out of the negative, pessimistic attitude, and own your inner power to change your mindset. It all starts with switching what you think to the opposite, most powerful thought. Do this more often, and you will notice a strong momentum toward optimism, hope, and strength in being positive. Be patient always. Start now. The best will begin to happen for you because you expect it and believe it. You will begin to know deeply that all is possible for you through your own will. Results will become apparent. Be ready, and be open.

16. I move forward boldly.

You made a choice to get better, and now you must move forward. You must move boldly against any currents. You must be persistent and consistent with your change, no matter what happens. The difference between where you currently are and where you visualize yourself is in your daily choices and actions to do better and get better. Don't look back. Don't give up. Don't judge any moments that might cause you to revert back. The point is to recognize, decide, and go forward always. You have a great purpose, and it is time to live it out.

Repeat Daily:

I am good at letting go and moving forward.

I see my vision as if it has already happened.

I am so inspired by how far I have come.

It is so easy for me to release what was.

I am consistently getting better, and it feels so good.

Don't go backward. You have declared that you want better for yourself. Now is the time to show your consistency and determination that you truly mean what you say. Change starts with every little action you take. Every second is a choice that opens you up to greater possibilities or puts you back where you once were. It can seem comfortable to want to do out of habit what you used to do, but not now. Not anymore. This is a new beginning for you. Nothing should be the same. It's time to do something completely different. It's time to be fearless. You're going somewhere special. You're going to manifest your wildest dreams. You're going to shine so brightly. You will be healed, healthy, and whole. You will be very successful in all ways. Your greatness will be seen. Go into your mental world and start removing, replacing, and releasing anything that limits you. Get your mental world in order first. Once you start there, you'll see the changes externally. Be consistent, and keep making choices that help you tap into your highest potential.

17. I forgive myself for everything.

I choose to be a peace with myself. I choose to free myself from all things from the past because I know the power of this moment. I am free to be who I want to be in this moment. I am always changing and getting better. The more I forgive myself for everything, the more I open myself up to greater miracles, because there is no regret in my energy field. I am only prospering and moving onward from what was to what is.

Repeat Daily:

This is a new day for me to be greater.

I am renewed in mind, body, and spirit.

I still have a chance to switch things up and do what I love.

*I have the freedom to think greater thoughts
and choose a new direction.*

Forgive yourself right now, so you can make peace with the past and free up your mental and emotional energy to do greater things. You have a choice in this moment to decide that you are no longer going to allow the past or people who have done you wrong to steal your precious energy today. Even mistakes you've made, or things you did or didn't do, shouldn't keep you away from using your precious life force right now to create a new reality for yourself. You are forgiven, and you are loved simply for being you. Want a new start? You can have it. Nobody deserves to be judged for the past. Nobody needs to constantly hear about what used to be when today is a new day for all of us to get better. Start living your life this way and seeing hope in others...and even in yourself. Everything that has happened only gives us lessons, experience, and awareness to do better.

You shouldn't remain stagnant, playing out something mentally and emotionally that no longer exists in your life. You shouldn't be drained by the past just because you aren't consciously deciding to focus your energy upon what you want instead. Make peace with the past. Make peace with what might seem like missed opportunities or lost chances. You might not be able to go back, but you can do something new today. You still have the chance to create the life you want and live the experiences you desire. Each time you think *what if?* or *should have/could have,* you steal from this moment...when you CAN change your life. Today, I want you to forgive yourself. Today, I want you to make peace with your past. I want you to release the energy, thought patterns, and emotions you feed your attention to. Deny the past access to your current life force. Say to yourself that you'll no longer be depleted by what was. Harness that energy into new possibilities for yourself.

18. I am abundant and highly prosperous.

I now enter the state of mind where I see the abundance of life that surrounds me and dwells within me. I am naturally abundant in all ways, and I have always been a highly blessed person. I choose, in this moment, to start recognizing how prosperous the entire universe is. I will look at the world from a different perspective. I will see possibilities, solutions, opportunities, and miracles all around me. My inner shift has already created a change in my energy field in terms of what I attract.

Repeat Daily:

I only attract the best.

I constantly see what I think surrounding me.

My thoughts are magnetic to great blessings.

I am naturally prosperous and highly abundant.

When you are busy counting your blessings, you switch your energy state from lack and limitation to abundance and manifestation. *I am blessed* is a declaration and a deep feeling of trust in the universe. You are always taking your mind from the repetitive cycle of looking for what's wrong to seeing what's right in your life by celebrating your blessings now. This is a powerful way of thinking and speaking that will shift your life. It uplifts your mood, opens doors within your spirit, and takes you on a journey of bliss. Happiness is a choice. When you are busy declaring that you are blessed, you can change how you feel. You will no longer wait for circumstances to change in order to be blessed or happy. You are speaking it now. Shift your mind, and welcome what's already yours.

Your attitude and outlook are the most important things in your life, not the way things appear. Adjust your mental thoughts with calming blessings now. There's so much good happening in your life if you choose to see it. There are things you might not even notice because your mind has made you forget what's real. The truth is, you are blessed. You have always been blessed. You just choose to recognize it when "something exciting" happens! That way of living only takes away from your everyday happiness, because you're waiting for things to happen in order to feel blessed. Celebrate now. Count your blessings. Look around yourself and see the miracles. Look inside and acknowledge your greatness.

19. I am a manifesting powerhouse.

Manifesting is very natural. You have always manifested what you want, even if you don't remember it. Nothing happens in physical reality that doesn't go through someone's mind. We are always creating, co-creating, and bringing to life all that we imagine. You cannot forget this power that you have. You are a manifesting powerhouse.

Repeat Daily:

I manifest everything I want.

I always get what I want, because that's normal.

Manifesting is so easy for me.

I only attract what I want or greater.

*"Manifest Now" is my command,
and it all instantly happens for me.*

You're already living something you once dreamed of. You will soon be living something you're currently dreaming of. The point is to never give up and to never stop dreaming; to never stop manifesting and imagining greatness into your life. Believe so deeply, and do it passionately that all you do is think, feel, and manifest your visions into reality. Doubt and fear are just things that come up to test your strength and will. Your wildest dreams are valid. Your greatest vision is real and tangible. Just like that, this new feeling and new way of thinking can be your push forward to strengthen your faith today.

No adversity, challenge, pain, or obstacle can stop one who believes. We have the natural ability to imagine for a reason. We go into a mental space and see what can happen for us. It feels like a glimpse of your total potential— like, "Wow, I truly can make it happen, and that is possible for me." This is your spirit, unbounded by space and time, giving you a glimpse. A glimpse into all you can be if you decide to accept who you are today.

Lift yourself from that which weighs heavily on your heart and mind, and soar to great heights. You are powerful. You are able. You can, and you will. You are full of life. You are healed. You are complete. You are beyond space and time. You are the life force. Reclaim your divine truth. Accept and love yourself. Forgive yourself. Welcome peace into your heart and mind. Your inner freedom shifts all of your life experiences. You alter the way you respond to everything, and this gives you strength and hope that it will all work out for you.

20. I am receiving unlimited energy.

You are now remembering the free energy that surrounds you. You don't need to wait for something to happen in order to feel an energy shift. You can choose to create within yourself feelings and thoughts that recognize your access to free energy. This change in your mindset will now open you up to a world in which you feel more creative, more energized, more productive, and more at peace. The chase, desperation, and rush will come to an end right now, because there is no shortage or lack. You have a new outlook that takes you into new dimensions of seeing the world. You are now in your own state of mind and being, and that brings in free energy to optimize yourself in any way you want. The stronger you feel, the more you can do. The healthier you are, the more you can express all that is within you. May the unlimited energy of the universe constantly pour into you. May you feel it, see it, and experience its blessings.

Repeat Daily:

I have access to free energy.

My productivity has multiplied.

I make my dreams happen, and it feels so effortless.

My mindset is in the dimension of possibilities.

*My potential has increased,
and I feel energized like never before.*

You are receiving so much energy right now, and it makes you feel unstoppable. This is why you feel like you must make a change now. This is why things seem to be flowing for you. Thoughts keep showing up that remind you to step into it. Move forward boldly. You are being poured into energetically at an accelerated rate so you can access your true purpose, passion, and happiness. All is now, and all is possible today. This is your turning point. This is where you feel that switch from lack to abundance. Your productivity is up. Your ability to take action has multiplied. Your trust in yourself is now magnified. Feel the surplus of energy coming in. Breathe it in. Smile about it. All of your projects will now come to fruition. Everything you touch and do will be full of energy and the highest creativity. You came here for a reason. You deserve the best that life has to offer. Paint the world exactly how you want. You are literally on another level—mentally, physically, and spiritually. Move right into your divine state.

21. What is real is what I believe in.

My mind shows me more of what I want to see. I am surrounded by my own thoughts and how I see the world. When I choose to have a different perspective, the things I see and attract change. I am now remembering that I don't have to stay in the cycle of what is right now. I can switch up what I believe, what I look for, and what I constantly focus on. The more I alter my own outlook and believe in something greater, the more the world around me takes me to the next level. I just keep getting better and better, and I am so glad to discover that I don't have to remain in thought patterns that no longer serve me. I am evolving and discovering myself. It feels so great to know this!

Repeat Daily:

What I think changes what I attract.

I believe in something magical, and it shows up in my life.

I remain open to the miracles of the universe.

My new thoughts attract better experiences for me.

*I keep getting better mentally,
and the physical world responds to it.*

Everything you believe in comes to life. Your imagination is powerful! You are powerful! Your brain cannot tell the difference between fantasy and reality. What's real is what you choose to bring to existence through visualizing, believing, and completely trusting it as truth. Doubt and fear take the same exact amount of energy to believe in. You are the one who chooses where to invest your inner energy. You can sit there imagining worst-case scenarios or best-case scenarios. It is all up to you to imagine what you want. See yourself in a new state and a better condition, living in harmony with your inner truth. Feel yourself actually following your heart and breaking free of cycles. Your best self is emerging, and you cannot hide from your own greatness. This is what's moving you forward, out, and into your purpose. Spend time today imagining your best. See yourself doing great things. Speak power to yourself and over your life. You are stepping it up, and it's starting to show! Let your light shine, and illuminate the world simply by being you.

22. I declare a positive change over my life.

I know the power of this moment. I expect a positive change to happen for me right now. I only want to see positive changes, no matter how things appear. I command, declare, and speak into the universe right now to be lifted higher into a new state. The positive change starts right this second.

Repeat Daily:

Positive changes happen for me daily.

I have positive encounters and experiences.

I attract positive people and opportunities that make me better.

Every circumstance turns out positively for me.

Never doubt how much this moment can change your life for the better. We aren't waiting around or giving away our energy to "one day." You are making the declaration right now that there is a positive shift happening in your life. This is what your mindset should be every day when you wake up. Your brain and energy field will look for what's right, what's good, and what's exciting for you. You will naturally see solutions and opportunities. No matter what's happening, you will remain hopeful and positive, because you know there's a positive shift happening in your life. No challenge or circumstance can deter you from your mindset. You are a firm believer that a positive shift is happening for you right now. That's such a good feeling! You can choose this state at any time. Wake up every morning and decide that anything and everything happening in your life is a positive shift. May things keep working in your favor every second because of this mindset.

23. I will be patient, kind, and loving to myself.

I choose to take care of myself and be gentle with how I talk to myself. I will build myself up daily. I will be kind and loving to myself. I will cultivate an inner world that is supportive. I am already good enough, just by being me. The more I treat myself well, the more I create inner balance. I choose to accept myself no matter what is happening, and I always cheer myself on. I am my biggest supporter.

Repeat Daily:

I love myself.

I accept myself for who I am.

I am already great. I am already good enough.

I give myself credit for making it this far and continuing on.

I will take care of myself daily, and be kind to myself.

My inner conversation and self-image will be positive.

No matter what's happening, give yourself that extra love and care. You're transforming, growing, releasing, and becoming more aware. You're realizing your worth and what you deserve. You're awakening to your own mental powers and awareness that it all starts within you. This realization brings so much potential, hope, and possibility, but at the same time, it brings rebirth. You're shedding so much of your past self and coming out on top. Step by step and moment by moment, you continue to get better. It's all happening in such a divine way. Don't judge yourself for your current situation, experience, or circumstance. Learn from it. Grow from it. Evolve from it. Decide right now that you are ready to move forward into your blessings. Loving yourself is the highest frequency. Nurture your mind, body, emotions, and spirit. Take some time for yourself to get your inner world in order.

Everything that is external is something you have already created. Something new must now emerge from your inner world. It's time for new thoughts, new visions, and new goals. Old habits and things that haven't worked aren't surviving your personal growth. It's getting easier to let go of what doesn't work, because you love yourself. It is all good right now, because you're making peace with it. You are forgiving yourself, because you know better. You are forgiving every situation, because you are rising up. You are free, feeling lighter as you let the excess go. Your mind and heart are feeling lighter. You're more peaceful. You are such a gift for this planet. Your existence makes an impact on everything. Love yourself. Feel good about who you are. This is the start of your magical journey. Everything will begin to seem so wonderful and unreal, and you'll be so glad you decided to treat yourself well.

24. I am getting signs and guidance daily.

The universe is speaking to me. Now more than ever, I am getting revelations, signs, insight, wisdom, and guidance. I am seeing my path. The way is being shown to me, and I trust the process of it all. Everything is very clear and direct.

Repeat Daily:

I constantly receive signs that guide me.

I get the guidance I need right when I need it the most.

I always receive divine breakthroughs and wisdom that lead me.

My insight is all I need, and I trust my inner voice and intuition.

464

Your greatness is exposing itself to you. You feel a subtle nudge that's pulling you toward your own realization. Things are making sense daily. You're receiving revelations that give momentum to your growth, healing, self-love, and complete wellness. You feel a surge. You feel an undeniable drive and a sense of renewal. This can happen on a subtle level initially, but you're also seeing it all around you. There are synchronicities and signs that remind you of your true greatness. You feel a gentle guidance of love that supports you. This is where you begin to accept who you are and what you came here to do. Feel vibrant, and feel okay. Everything is okay. Soon, you'll see why things happened the way they did. Be grateful for all the details. Be grateful for every little thing. Focus on keeping your heart open and allowing yourself to just be. You are already complete!

25. I have the choice right now to change my life.

You always have the choice to do anything that you want. The difference between where you are and where you are going is a collection of all the small choices you make every single day that eventually add up. The power you have is the power to choose. It is always up to you to decide.

Repeat Daily:

I am choosing better habits.

I choose better thoughts.

I choose to follow my heart and trust myself.

I choose to live out my dreams and believe in myself.

It's time to make a bold move. Don't think that anything that's happening to you is final. You can choose to make a different choice today: a choice that involves some kind of risk, a choice to end procrastination, a choice to believe in possibilities, a choice in the direction of new habits that support your wellness and vision. You can choose today, but you must be bold about it. You must not be afraid to get out of your comfort zone. There's nothing to be scared of. Doing and moving forward produces great rewards.

The universe will support you and your new changes. It is all up to you to decide and watch how miraculously things begin to work in your favor. If you've been receiving signs, then this is it. It's time! Be bold in your choices and actions as you move forward. Radiate such a positive state of mind and being that the universe must correspond externally. It will match up. Let go of the details about how and when. Trust and believe instead. This is your time. No more settling and letting things just randomly happen. Be bold. Take some risk. Make better choices. Try something new that helps you step out of your routine.

26. I am healthy, vibrant, and full of life.

I radiate health. My energy is so vibrant, and I feel so alive. My body is strong. My mind is strong. My outlook is healthy, and I am attracting thoughts of wellness. I love my body. I love who I am, and I shine brightly simply by celebrating myself.

Repeat Daily:

I am getting stronger every single day.

I feel good about who I am.

Loving myself has changed my life for the better.

I am so healthy in my thinking that I transform all areas of my life.

You are already optimal, healthy, vibrant, and full of life. Your mindset is now realizing this and accepting it as your truth. You are claiming your natural, optimal state. Anything that told you otherwise is now being removed, cleared, and purged out of your field. You are remembering, and you are owning your natural state. As you return to it, you'll experience many changes and transformations that help restore you at the deepest level. Breathe! Be completely open to it, without trying to control it or overwhelming yourself by wondering what's wrong. Nothing is wrong.

Be bold and be faithful. Be patient! You are truly powerful, and very strong spiritually. Nothing can break you, not even when you feel like you are being tested. You are optimal! You are healthy! You are strong! You are able and capable! You are okay right now! Breathe, and let it be felt in every cell of your body. Let it radiate into your energy field. Let these be your dominant thoughts: I am okay! I am optimal! I am vibrant! I am strong! I am able! I am faithful! I trust myself! I trust my body! I trust the divine guiding power that sustains me! I am optimal! Repeat this to yourself and watch miracles happen right now.

27. I master what I give my energy to.

I am getting better at directing my mental and emotional energy toward what I want. My life force is so precious, and my time is very valuable. The more I remain consistent and focus on what I want, the more quickly things begin to manifest for me. I am the master of what I give my energy to.

Repeat Daily:

My mental energy belongs to me.

I choose what to focus on. I choose what I entertain.

I am highly valuable, and my time is very precious.

*I feed positive thoughts into my reality,
and they multiply in my life.*

Take back what is yours. *You* choose what to tune into and what you allow to live on within you. You can just be an observer in situations that test your patience. You might be working on yourself and evolving past dramas that once pulled you in. There are certain situations that return to test your evolution, but it's not about anyone else. It's about how much you have worked on yourself, and how it no longer affects you. When we're learning to master our inner self, we can clearly see what triggers us, and those situations are the ones that require us to grow. So be thankful when triggers come up, because you now know how to work through them instead of overreacting and overthinking. Mastering yourself is an everyday experience that helps you get better at being the best you. You'll realize that you no longer have the energy to play along or react so easily. You find yourself investing your time in what adds value to your life.

Your focus becomes about living a more enriched life, because anything less isn't worth your time. Ask yourself: *Is it even worth giving my precious life force to something that happened in the past? To someone who doesn't deserve it? To a situation I have outgrown?* Remember, your attention and focus are your power. The scenarios you overthink and constantly replay don't evolve you. Stop the self-judgment and move on. Decide now that you're going to be better at managing your energy. You're going to think, feel, and do what evolves you. You're going to make peace with what happened and what you can't change. Starting today, you're going to take your power back by consciously deciding what you feed your energy to. Don't allow anyone to thrive off of you feeling low or down about yourself. You have the power to manage your mental and inner world, and that will reflect in the way you handle everyday life. Be very patient with yourself. You're evolving and learning. Things will become better for you.

28. I will keep moving forward.

I am continuously progressing and flourishing. I am going to remain focused on the direction that allows me to be my best. Nothing can stop where I am headed, and I feel a new kind of energy that allows me to thrive in all ways.

Repeat Daily:

I will keep getting better.

I will continuously outgrow the past and keep going.

I will push myself forward, no matter what is happening.

I am in a state of consistent growth.

You have come way too far to fall back into past habits and situations you have outgrown. Things might pop back up emotionally, physically, or mentally, but you are too strong spiritually to be drawn back into that. You know better. You feel better. Your thinking has improved so much. You're not who you were, and this glimpse of how much you've grown will serve as a reminder to avoid falling back into the past. Sometimes, things return to see if you've fully evolved from them. This is actually a great way to reflect.

The point is to move forward, even when you find yourself repeating something you've outgrown. This is just a reminder to snap yourself back on track. Don't judge yourself if you've regressed a little. This reminder will help you get back into what's next for you. You're too great in every way. You are propelling forward. You are being renewed on all levels. It's all a learning experience, so be gentle and bold in your direction. It's time to move forward and see all the new things that life will unfold for you.

29. I always experience miracles.

I am a magnet for miracles. I am a miraculous person. I always attract great miracles. I am naturally blessed, and my life seems to unfold in such a magical way that everyone keeps asking me how I even do it. I have the gift of miracles within my spirit, and this reminds others that they, too, have access to the miracles of the universe.

Repeat Daily:

I see miracles everywhere I go.

I attract miracles in every situation.

I am surrounded by a vortex of miracles.

Everything I do just miraculously works out for me.

I see miracles. I expect miracles. I attract miracles. I am a miracle. Life is completely unexplainable, so why settle into believing that you can't just dream, imagine, and receive what you want? Get into a mindset of gratitude. From this moment on, see everything as a miracle and a blessing. See the universe supporting you. Feel yourself entering a state of mind, reality, and experience filled with abundance, joy, and creativity. Be grateful for everything you've experienced, because it has given you the powerful tools of wisdom, strength, and discernment to overcome just about anything. You are a powerful spirit, and you are a miracle just because you're here. Everything is only going up from here. From this day on, you are a magnet for miracles. Everything will now begin to happen in your favor. You're on the miracle frequency!

30. I have a new state of mind.

My mindset has changed. I am now in a new state of mind. I believe that anything can and will happen for me. I feel better about myself. I trust myself. I believe in myself. My mindset has literally shifted, and I am so grateful to have evolved out of what was and into what can be. I can do anything I want. I am a dreamer. I am a creator. I am imaginative. I have the ability to visualize what I want. I take daily action toward everything I want to see happen for me, and it all instantly aligns.

Repeat Daily:

My state of mind is winning and thriving.

My state of mind is healthy and positive.

My state of mind is always thinking that greatness is possible.

*My state of mind finds solutions
and attracts great opportunities.*

*My state of mind carries me out of the past
and into my vision.*

*My state of mind is very powerful,
and I get exactly what I want.*

You have just entered a new state of in mind, body, and spirit. Something has shifted for you, and you have started recognizing and accepting how great and grand you truly are. Accept this new state right now. No matter what's happening or what you're going through, it is already done. Now elevate your mindset, outlook, and attitude to a new state. Think of your current situation from a different perspective—a positive perspective. The past no longer has power over you, but you have power over it and the way you see it. You choose how you respond. Accept a new state now. Don't think that what's happening is final. You can decide right now that it's a complete vision, that you are healed, that you are okay, that it has worked out, and that it is all good right now.

Feel something new within yourself that brings you ease. It's all just a moment, and you are the shining light and guiding the way. You are on an adventure. This is just a reminder to take it easy on yourself. You're doing all you can. You have so much strength for keeping it all together and still continuing to evolve. That is admirable. You've overcome so much, and every single moment, you continue to thrive with so much life. You are beyond powerful. You are so special in so many ways, and you sometimes forget to see it. Your superpowers are your natural abilities. Feel a renewed sense of self. Your day-to-day life empowers you to love, remain open, and be clear with your words, thoughts, and feelings. Each time you find yourself getting caught up in something, always say, "I welcome a new state of mind!" This automatically lifts you up instead of going into what's happening. Solutions come through elevation of the mind and declaration of something greater.

You now have full access to the 30 powerful *Inner Glimpse Thoughts*, meant to activate you to reclaim your natural power. You are the one who is already gifted. There's nothing that is a coincidence about your life and what you came here to do. You are the one who will discover your purpose by constantly remembering the greatness within you. The more you follow your heart and listen to your inner spirit, the more will be revealed to you. The 30 Inner Glimpse Thoughts are here to support you through your own self-discovery and adventure. You can read them as often as you like. Make sure you feel every single word. You will soon look back and be grateful that you have discovered your own treasure.

24

LIVING THE INNER GLIMPSE

Living the Inner Glimpse means that you have finally decided to follow your own inner voice. You have finally decided to listen to that spark of insight you have been receiving for so long. The moment you feel like anything is possible for you is a real moment and a real feeling. The inner inspiration you receive during your most difficult times is the Inner Glimpse, telling you that you can make it through. Anything that demonstrates that you *can* is a reminder from your own spirit of the possibilities, blessings, and unlimited potential that are right within you. The world is only responding to your energy state. You are the one who needs to dream bigger, see greater, and have hope like a true believer who knows that your vision and manifestation are already complete. You are very powerful and capable of what might seem unimaginable to others. You are the one from whom all things originate. Everything around you was once a thought, so what thought will you bring to life now? This is where things begin to change for you.

Everything in your life will begin to go upward. Now that you have read this book and reached its final chapter, be ready for incredible miracles, life-changing manifestations, and the most empowering energy of self-belief, self-love, and self-awareness. Many magical things will happen for you. This book isn't just something you read once; it is a support system, a tool, and guidance for your adventure that you can refer back to when you need it the most. Every word is meant to lift you higher, out of illusions and thoughts that don't represent your greatest self. You have many gifts, and you are full of potential. I wrote *Inner Glimpse* so that you can feel empowered, motivated, and energized in trusting your own inner voice again. I want you to feel very powerful. I want you to start remembering that you can, and that you have what it takes. I want you to live out your dreams, not only to show yourself that you can do it, but to serve as a representative of what is possible. You will help others believe in themselves just by you living your dreams and loving who you are.

The Inner Glimpse is all about allowing your energy to speak for itself. This is why so much of what you do will be about staying true to your vision and being real with yourself. It will be about what you want, and allowing yourself to grow, evolve, and get better daily. The focus of power and awareness is about going back within. It is no longer about how you want to be perceived, but rather how you're truly feeling, thinking, and taking care of yourself from the inside out. Mental health and inner wellness are so important to me. I know that once you take care of yourself from the inside out, you'll unlock many opportunities, not only externally, but spiritually, as well. There's something so special about going within and asking for the way to be shown to you. Inner Glimpse is all about balancing your inner and outer life to the maximum.

All of your visions will come to life when you use the gifts shared in this book. Your Inner Glimpse will manifest. You will feel so empowered that you have now decided to follow your heart and listen to your own intuition. Every moment when you feel like you can make it through and create your vision is your own inner guidance showing you that all is possible. You will no longer deny yourself any blessings. You will no longer treat your powerful inner voice like it is something random. You will start to own your truth and walk boldly in action. You will no longer be afraid of small things going wrong or not going accordingly. You must stop being scared of life and things that happen. You have to be a strong spirit, and understand that all of this is just a moment. Don't judge things as they are; see them as you wish them to become. You are an alchemist with the ability to change energy from one state into another. You can take something negative and turn it into something positive. The point is to continue transmuting situations and turning them in your favor.

Don't be controlled by external appearances. Your spirit is beyond space and time. You have greater access than you realize. The words in this book are meant to activate you! You will find yourself changing for the better without even realizing it. The change begins the minute you read these words and feel them. What you expose your mind to can and will take you further than what you think is surrounding you. Nothing is final. God gave you the ability to imagine. You were given the ability to see visions and alter experiences in your mind, then see the changes all around you. Take your Inner Glimpse and make it a reality. It is no coincidence that you have made it this far. You are full of wisdom, and you have to stop playing it small. You can do whatever you want and bring to life to anything you wish. The external world (what you see right now) has already been created; however, there is unlimited space for new ideas, new connections, new experiences, and new blessings. You are the one who can choose to live according to what you see and create from the strength of your belief. The fun part about all of this is that you can change anything at any time.

People are sometimes scared of their own success and what they are capable of, so they prolong the process so they can ease into it. You can just accept your success right now and move into it daily. You can go from your imagined state to your desired physical state instantly, according to how ready you are. The beautiful thing is that the timing is perfect for your own needs. There's nothing wrong with something taking one week, one month, or even one year. It is all about what you are ready for, and how quickly you can accept the power of your mind. It can even be instant. I am sure there might have been moments when you manifested something you were thinking and felt kind of tripped out by it. That *whoa* moment is a natural state. It will happen more and more as you start to integrate, accept, and allow yourself to live fully in your true abilities. You will start to make a great impact just by being you, and the more you feel alive in your own body and trust your own spirit, the more miracles will become everyday occurrences.

Inner Glimpse is one of the most powerful books you will ever read because it gets to the point. It is all you. You have the power within you. You are the one with the choices. You are the one with the ability to completely alter your entire life to your liking. Nobody else can do it for you. The information found here will activate you, energize you, and remind you of your true potential. This is the nudge you may have needed to step into your greatness right now. *Inner Glimpse* is meant to banish any energy of lack, procrastination, or negativity. Illusions and limitations will be removed, not only from your energy field, but from your thinking, as well. A free mind can do more in this world. If you are your own source of inspiration and you receive divine inner guidance, you can break the barriers you thought were once in front of you. You will be stronger in all ways, and more trusting of your own self. You will know how to access the unlimited energy that is available to you through your own mental command. You will not need to go chasing, searching, or trying too hard to find some hidden secret. Sometimes, things are so easy, we enjoy complicating them just to feel like we have accomplished something. Everything wonderful is all here right now. It is within you, and you are the one thinking from that point of view. You are the one feeling from that state.

Inner Glimpse is meant to lift you higher so you can thrive in all situations. You will be much more successful, even during uncertain times, because you are seeing from a vision. You are going to love yourself more, because there are more blessings and peace in self-acceptance. You will start to trust more, because you know your timing is unique and special to you. You will know how to use the power of your words and your ability to let go to experience newness. You will realize that nothing is as scary as it seems. You will know that every moment is teaching you something that you can turn around. Nothing is ever final. All is momentary or a memory. You become more refined through experience, and you evolve consistently. In every situation, you will come out a winner. You will no longer feel drained or overwhelmed, since you have access to unlimited free energy. You can tap into yourself and clear your mind, emotions, and energy field anytime you need to let go of something. Consistently altering your own state of mind and the way you feel gives you back your own power. You are the one who makes the choice about what stays.

I want you to feel so full of life that things outside of you no longer have control over you. I want you to think, feel, and believe that anything is possible for you. I want you to live out your dreams, make an impact, and do what you love. You are always contributing to humanity, simply by being you. Your day-to-day effort matters. How you treat yourself matters. Everything about you has a purpose. I want you to bring your gift to life. I want you to dream like you have never dreamed before, knowing that your vision matters. I am so delighted to be able to share this message with you. I know deep inside the love I have put into this book, and how much it will transform you for the better. I am so happy for all the success you will receive from *Inner Glimpse*. My first book, *Manifest Now*, has changed many lives and taught many people how to manifest exactly what they want. I want this book to help you discover, reconnect, and access your own inner powers so you can take it to the next level. It's time for you to live out your Inner Glimpse. I believe in you!